Away for the WEEKEND®

MID·ATLANTIC

Away for the
WEEKEND®
MID·ATLANTIC

BY ELEANOR BERMAN

Great Getaways Within 250 Miles
of Washington, D.C., in: Delaware,
Maryland, Virginia, West Virginia,
Pennsylvania and New Jersey

REVISED AND UPDATED EDITION

Clarkson Potter/Publishers
New York

Acknowledgments

My sincere thanks to all the state and local tourism offices that supplied information and guidance during my travels for this update and revision of *Away for the Weekend*. I am also grateful to the innkeepers and readers who have taken time to write, helping me to follow who is in and out of business.

A special word of appreciation is due to my diligent researcher, Terry Klewan, as well as to my editors, Shirley Wohl and Amy Schuler.

Copyright © 1987, 1990 by Eleanor Berman

Maps copyright © 1987, 1990 by Susan Hunt Yule

Published by Clarkson N. Potter, Inc., distributed by Crown Publishers, Inc., 201 East 50th Street, New York, New York 10022. Member of the Crown Publishing Group.

Originally published as *Away for the Weekend™: Washington, D.C.* by Clarkson N. Potter, Inc., in 1987.

CLARKSON N. POTTER, POTTER and colophon are trademarks of Clarkson N. Potter, Inc.

Manufactured in the United States of America

Library of Congress Cataloging-in-Publication Data

Berman, Eleanor, 1934-
    Away for the weekend, Mid-Atlantic : great getaways within 250 miles of Washington, D.C., in: Delaware, Maryland, Virginia, West Virginia, Pennsylvania, and New Jersey / by Eleanor Berman. — Rev. and updated ed.
        p.   cm.
    Rev. ed. of: Away for the weekend, Washington, D.C. 1st ed. c1987.
    Includes index.
1. Washington Region—Description and travel—Tours. 2. Middle Atlantic States—
Description and travel—Tours. I. Berman, Eleanor, 1934- Away for the weekend, Washington, D.C. II. Title.
F192.3.B47   1990
917.504'43—dc20   90-14174
                                                                                  CIP

ISBN 0-517-57510-8

10 9 8 7 6 5 4 3 2 1

Revised Edition

Contents

Introduction

From the placid waters of Chesapeake Bay to the rugged mountains of West Virginia, from Virginia plantations to the silent battlefield at Gettysburg, the mid-Atlantic region is packed with weekending treasures. This is a guide to the best of the getaways, places offering a change of pace and a recharge of spirits for every mood and season.

The 52 weekend trips that follow will take you through six states—from small-town charm to city sophistication; from gardens and galleries to solitary woodlands; from festive celebrations to great resorts. Throughout, you will discover the rich history of the region where much of our nation's future was forged.

All of the trips are within 250 miles of Washington, D.C. They are also within easy reach of Philadelphia, Baltimore, Wilmington, Richmond, Trenton—in fact, much of the Eastern seaboard from Virginia to New York. Since Washington is at the heart of the mid-Atlantic, driving directions and mileage are given from the D.C. area, but major routes are noted to make it easy to plan a trip from any direction.

It should be noted from the start that this is a personal and selective guide. Instead of trying to include all the myriad possibilities for travel in Delaware, Maryland, New Jersey, Pennsylvania, Virginia, and West Virginia, I've selected what I feel are the cream of the weekend destinations. Nor is every single sightseeing attraction, lodging, and restaurant in each location included. I've limited the book to those I've visited myself or had recommended by knowledgeable local sources or frequent visitors to these areas—people whose opinions I respect.

Since many mid-Atlantic lodgings are very special places, the best are noted in each area, and a few even become destinations in themselves. However, this is primarily a guide to destinations and events, not a guide to inns or resorts, so where motels are the only accommodations available, the listings reflect this.

Bed-and-breakfast is another lodging option, long popular in Europe and rapidly catching on here as well. There is sometimes confusion as to what the term means, since many small inns that serve only breakfast call themselves bed-and-breakfast inns. "Bed-and-breakfast" here does not refer to these inns, but to private homes that open a few rooms to guests and serve them a homemade breakfast. These are often reasonably priced and very personal accommodations offering the chance to meet local residents and get the real flavor of living in the areas where you travel. They are also a good alternative when you make last-minute plans and inns are booked. Because the homes are far too numerous to list individually, the listings here are for registry services offering reservations in many homes in their areas. There is a roster of all the registry services at the beginning of the book, and a reference to local registries is repeated with the information for individual trips.

Since different seasons often bring different events in the same areas, you will find repeat mentions of some destinations. The trips themselves are arranged by season not only because activities change with the calendar, but to give you time to read ahead about upcoming events and to reserve rooms early. This advance notice enables you to make the most of a special show or open house, planning a relaxing and leisurely weekend of sightseeing rather than a last-minute day trip.

Don't feel bound by the calendar, however. Many of these destinations are equally appealing and less crowded when nothing special is going on, and places on the ocean or on Chesapeake Bay can be a special delight on a weekend out of season when you have them almost to yourself. The information listings at the end of each chapter are appropriate to any season you make the trip.

HOW TO USE THE BOOK

Like its predecessors for the New York area and for New England, *Away for the Weekend®: Mid-Atlantic* assumes you have a normal two-day weekend to spend, arriving on Friday night and leaving late on Sunday. Each trip suggests activities for a two-day stay, with added attractions to accommodate varying tastes and time schedules. I've included what I hope is just enough history and background to make each area more interesting without bogging you down in detail. If you become intrigued and want more detailed information, you can get it on the spot.

When there is enough to do to warrant a longer stay, a symbol at the start of each trip will tell you so. When you do have more than a weekend to spend, use these symbols as a cue, or use the maps at the back to combine nearby weekends to fill out an extended stay. Norfolk, Williamsburg, Richmond, and Charlottesville, for example, might all be combined for a mid-Virginia tour. The same is true for destinations in and around Pennsylvania Dutch Country, the Shenandoah Valley, and Chesapeake Bay.

Symbols also indicate trips that seem appropriate for children, though you are the best judge of what your own family might enjoy.

A final symbol marks a few trips that can be done entirely via public transportation. There are many other destinations where excursion airfares make it possible to extend your weekending range and to cut down on winter driving, and others where easy Amtrak connections can save you the hassle of driving out of the city in Friday night traffic.

The symbols that indicate these various categories are as follows:

C = recommended for children

T = accessible at least in part via public transportation

L = recommended for long weekends

Dollar signs with lodging indicate the price range for a double room; dining listings show the prices per person of main courses rather than complete dinners, since not everyone chooses to order a three-course dinner.

For accommodations:

$ = under $60

$$ = $60 to $85

$$$ = $85 to $125

$$$$ = over $125

When meals are included in the rates, the following symbols are used:

CP = continental plan (breakfast only)

MAP = modified American plan (breakfast and dinner)

AP = American plan (all three meals)

For meals the symbols are as follows:

$ = most entrées under $10 per person

$$ = most entrées between $10 and $15

$$$ = most entrées between $15 and $25

$$$$ = most entrées over $25

When prices bridge two categories, you will find two symbols.

Rates frequently increase yearly, often before a book makes it from typewriter to bookstore. The price ranges for food and lodging also tend to go up as months go by.

The rates and price ranges here are as accurate as could be deter mined at the time of publication and are included as a general in-dication of what to expect. Please use them just that way, as a general guide *only*, and *always* use the telephone numbers included to check for current prices when you plan your trip. It is well to verify current hours and holiday closings as well.

When it comes to restaurants and lodgings, remember that a new owner can make a big difference, and changes and closings cannot always be predicted. Again, use this as a general guide, and, I hope, a reasonably accurate one.

If you find that any information here has become seriously inaccurate or that a place has closed or gone downhill, I hope that you will let me know in care of Clarkson N. Potter, Inc., 201 East 50th Street, New York, NY 10022, so that the entry can be corrected. If you discover newly opened places or some appealing ones that I have missed, I hope you will let me know about them as well.

The maps in this book are simplified to highlight locations of suggested destinations. They are not necessarily reliable as road maps. One way to get excellent free maps of each state included is to write to the travel or tourism office of that state. These offices offer many excellent free guides to their state attractions as well. Names and addresses are included at the end of this section. In most cases, addresses for additional information for individual destinations are also included at the end of each chapter. Use these addresses to get advance information that can make your trip more enjoyable.

One last tip: Reserve well ahead if you want to stay in small country inns or visit beach or ski resorts in high season. Most lodgings offer refunds on deposits if you cancel with reasonable notice, so write ahead and take your nick instead of settling for leftovers. Three or four months ahead is none too soon to book.

For this New Yorker, the past year of travel in the mid-Atlantic states to research this book has been a wonderfully rewarding experience. Pennsylvania, New Jersey, and Delaware were familiar to me from past writing and personal weekending, yet I discovered new pleasures each time I returned. Maryland, Virginia, and West Virginia were new territory for me, and each visit was a treat. I've become addicted to Virginia ham biscuits and Maryland crabcakes, acquired beautiful mountain crafts, discovered the sparkle of Chesapeake Bay in springtime, the bounty of Delaware's beaches in summer, the glory of autumn in the Shenandoah Valley, and the stunning beauty of the West Virginia mountains cloaked in winter white. I've also had a refresher course in American history, made all the more meaningful by standing on the grounds where it was made. And everywhere, I've found warm hospitality, southern and northern, and helpful friends to make my job easier and my travels pleasanter.

I hope that my very real enthusiasm for these places and pleasures comes through to inspire you to share my discoveries—and to make some of your own.

State Tourist Offices

All of the offices listed below will provide maps as well as information and literature on attractions throughout their states:

Delaware Tourism Office
99 Kings Highway
Dover, DE 19901
Toll free: (800) 441-8846
In Delaware: (800) 282-8667

Maryland Office of Tourist Development
217 East Redwood Street
Baltimore, MD 21202
(301) 333-6611
Toll free: (800) 543-1036

New Jersey Travel and Tourism
CN-826
Trenton, NJ 08635
(609) 292-2470
Toll free: (800) JERSEY-7

Pennsylvania Bureau of Travel Development
Department of Commerce
Forum Building
Harrisburg, PA 17120
(717) 787-5453
Toll free: (800) VISIT-PA

Virginia Division of Tourism
1021 East Cary Street
Richmond, VA 23219
(804) 786-2051

West Virginia Department of Commerce
2101 Washington Street
Capitol Complex, Building 17
Charleston, WV 25305
(304) 348-2286
Toll free: (800) CALL-WVA

Bed-and-Breakfast Registry Services

The reservation services listed here offer many listings of individual homes offering bed-and-breakfast hospitality in the locations noted. Rates for these accommodations can vary from $50 to $75 or more, depending on the size and luxury of the accommodation and whether there is a private bath. You have a better chance of being happy with your lodgings if you are very specific about what you are seeking—economy or luxury, privacy or congeniality, location in town or in the country, swimming pools or any other special needs. Most state tourist offices also keep listings for their own states; write for the latest update.

DELAWARE
Bed and Breakfast of Delaware
P.O. Box 177
3650 Silverside Road
Wilmington, DE 19810
(302) 479-9500
(entire state)

MARYLAND
Maryland Reservation Center, Inc.
66 Maryland Avenue
Annapolis, MD 21401
(301) 269-7550
Out of state: (800) 654-9303

The Traveller in Maryland, Inc.
P.O. Box 2277
Annapolis, MD 21404
(301) 269-6232
From D.C.: (301) 261-2233
(entire state)

*Amanda's Bed & Breakfast
Reservation Service*
1428 Park Avenue
Baltimore, MD 21217
(301) 225-0001
(Maryland and neighboring states)

NEW JERSEY
Bed and Breakfast of New Jersey
103 Godwin Avenue, Suite 132
Midland Park, NJ 07432
(201) 444-7409

PENNSYLVANIA
Bed and Breakfast of Philadelphia
P.O. Box 252
Gradyville, PA 19039
(215) 358-4747 or
800-733-4747
(center city plus Main Line, Bucks and Chester counties, Brandywine Valley, and Valley Forge)

Bed and Breakfast, Center City
1804 Pine Street
Philadelphia, PA 19103
(215) 735-1137 or (215) 923-5459
(Philadelphia)

All About Town—Bed and Breakfast in Philadelphia
P.O. Box 562
Valley Forge, PA 19481
(215) 783-7838

Bed and Breakfast Connections
P.O. Box 21
Devon, PA 19333
(215) 687-3565
(Philadelphia and suburbs)

Guesthouses
RD 9
West Chester, PA 19380
(215) 692-4575
(Brandywine Valley and Philly Main Line)

Bed and Breakfast of Chester County
P.O. Box 825
Kennett Square, PA 19348
(215) 444-1367 or (215) 444-5291
(Chester County, Brandywine Valley, and Pennsylvania Dutch Country)

Hershey Bed and Breakfast
P.O. Box 208
Hershey, PA 17033
(717) 533-2928
(Hershey, Lancaster, and Gettysburg)

Bed & Breakfast of Southeast Pennsylvania
146 West Philadelphia Avenue
Boyertown, PA 19512
(215) 367-4688
(Bethlehem, Kutztown, Reading, Hershey, and Lancaster)

Bed & Breakfast of Valley Forge
P.O. Box 562
Valley Forge, PA 19481
(215) 783-7838
(Valley Forge area)

VIRGINIA
Bed & Breakfast of Tidewater Virginia
P.O. Box 3343
Norfolk, VA 23514
(804) 627-9409 or (804) 627-1983
(Norfolk, Virginia Beach, Eastern Shore, and Northern Neck)

Bensonhouse of Richmond & Williamsburg
2036 Monument Avenue
Richmond, VA 23220
(804) 648-7560
(Richmond, Williamsburg, Fredericksburg, and Northern Neck)

Bed & Breakfast on the Hill
2304 East Broad Street
Richmond, VA 23223
(804) 780-3746
(Lodgings on Richmond's historic Church Hill)

Blue Ridge Bed & Breakfast
Rock & Rills, Route 2
Box 3895
Berryville, VA 22611
(703) 955-1246

Guesthouses—Charlottesville
P.O. Box 5737
Charlottesville, VA 22905
(804) 979-7264
(Charlottesville, Luray, and Staunton)

Rockbridge Reservations
Sleepy Hollow
Brownsburg, VA 24415
(703) 348-5698
(Lexington area)

SPRING

Overleaf: **Daffodils in bloom at Winterthur.** *Photo courtesy of Winterthur Museum and Gardens, Winterthur, Delaware.*

Apple Blossom Time in Winchester

Spring steals softly into the Shenandoah Valley, carrying her palette of pastels—and before you know it, brown hills are tinted with soft new greens, and barren branches are crowned with blossom clouds of pink and pearly white.

In Winchester, Virginia's self-proclaimed "Apple Capital," the appearance of snowy blossoms in the countryside means the renewal of the apple orchards—and cause for celebration. Ever since 1927, the first weekend in May here has been set aside for the Shenandoah Apple Blossom Festival, an event that seems to grow more gala every year.

Banners in spring shades of pink and white and green float from every lamppost and windowsill in town for this four-day extravaganza. A Friday night parade boasting the nation's largest display of firefighting equipment is a highlight, and the Saturday parade is a knockout—a five-hour spectacular featuring big-time floats and as many as 100 marching bands, plus a celebrity marshal and the newly crowned Queen Shenandoah, an honor that has been shared by many daughters and granddaughters of presidents.

The festival features the annual Sports Breakfast, which has attracted luminaries such as Hank Aaron and Jim Plunkett, and there are air shows, circus acts, and dances to keep things humming throughout the weekend. The grand finale, Sunday in the Park, offers an apple-crate derby, a mock Civil War battle, crafts, and lots of food.

It's a festive way to greet the season, and a good reason to visit a small city with a large share of history to its credit. You can top things off with some antiquing and a look at the Skyline Drive aglow in its best spring finery.

Winchester's modern malls and motels mask the fact that this is the oldest city west of the Blue Ridge. The three major sightseeing attractions in town, all maintained by the local historical society, mark the main events in a long history, starting with the first settlements in the 1730s. One of the first settlers was a Quaker, Abraham Hollingsworth, who came to the valley from southern Maryland, buying up 532 acres from the resident Indians for a cow, a calf, and a piece of cloth. In 1754, his son Isaac built a limestone house with walls two and a half feet thick, which he named Abram's Delight. It has been authentically restored, along with a log cabin on the site, to show what life was like in the town's earliest years. The adjacent visitors center has a free 18-minute video on the Winchester area.

Winchester proper had its beginnings in 1735, when an English colonel, James Wood, came into the Shenandoah Valley with a handful of English, Scottish, and Welsh followers to start a tiny colony that was eventually named in honor of Wood's birthplace in England. The land Wood's followers settled, however, was not their own. It was part of a six-million-acre tract belonging to Thomas, Lord Fairfax, who is buried in the Episcopal church courtyard at the corner of Boscawen and Washington streets in Winchester. In 1748, Fairfax hired his 16-year-old friend, George Washington, to help survey his holdings. Washington returned ten years later as a colonel of the Virginia militia in the French and Indian War, occupying an office in a log-and-stone structure at the corner of Cork and Braddock streets while Fort Loudoun was being constructed on a high hill at the north end of town. The office has been maintained as a museum.

George Washington lived in Winchester from 1755 to 1758, and some credit him with helping to foster the planting of the apple orchards. It was from this area that Washington was first elected to the Virginia House of Burgesses.

Perhaps the most famous of the historic structures is the house where Thomas "Stonewall" Jackson was quartered in 1861 and 1862 while he planned the brilliant "Valley Campaign," which defeated Union troops despite overwhelming odds. His Hudson River Gothic home on North Braddock Street still looks much as it did in 1861; the airy upstairs bedroom that Jackson shared with his wife and his first-floor office are still intact. The house contains much Civil War memorabilia.

Within a few blocks of the house is Stonewall Cemetery, where the Confederate dead are buried, and National Cemetery, where thousands of Union soldiers are at rest, moving testaments to the devastation Winchester witnessed during the Civil War. The town was of great strategic importance to both sides, providing access to the crops, cattle, and mills of the Shenandoah Valley. It changed hands more than 70 times during the war, sometimes two or three times a day, and was the site of five major battles.

Although it was left in ruins, Winchester was soon rebuilt and prospered once again as a commercial and industrial center of the upper valley, and as a processing center for the burgeoning local apple industry. Lately, electronics and pharmaceutical firms have moved into the area as well.

Preservationists are working hard to hold on to the reminders of the town's historic past in the midst of its present growth. About 130 original eighteenth-century buildings remain, and a number of them have been rehabilitated through the efforts of the Preservation of Historic Winchester group, which is constantly adding to its roster. You can see some of their handiwork on 'Tater Hill on South

Loudoun Street, a onetime tenement that is rapidly regaining its lost glory.

If you follow the free self-guided tour sheet available at the historical society sites, you'll find still more of the past in Winchester. On Amherst Street alone are three prize properties: James Wood's 1794 home, Glen Burnie, still occupied by one of his direct descendants; Hawthorne, the 1765 house lived in by Governor James Wood, Jr.; and the 1786 home of General Daniel Morgan, a Revolutionary War hero.

Much of the old downtown has been declared a historic district. Sights here include the Red Lion Tavern at Loudoun and Cork, the recently restored 1840 Court House, and Logan House, from where General Philip H. Sheridan rode out to Cedar Creek in 1864 to defeat the Confederates.

The main downtown artery, Loudoun Street, has been turned into a pedestrian shopping mall, and many of the old stores are turning into interesting shops and galleries. Handworks Gallery is notable for its quality American handcrafts, and Olde Towne Antiques is one of a growing number of antique shops. More antiques are to be found in several stores on Cameron Street, one block above Loudoun, and at Apple Blossom Antiques on nearby West Piccadilly. Millwood Crossing, at 381 Millwood Avenue, near Abram's Delight, is a collection of quality shops in a renovated apple-packing warehouse.

Continue south on Route 11 for more choice antiquing all the way to Strasburg. In Stephens City you'll find Valley Furniture, with a sign promising "country antiques, oak, pine, walnut, and wicker." Inside is a pleasant country-store ambience and a mix of old and new. Follow the signs to Route 631 two miles west of Stephens City for Whitneys, two rooms filled with some 60 clocks.

If you can get here on a weekday, a worthwhile detour to Route 277 will bring you to White Post Restorations and a fascinating tour of the shop where classic antique cars are restored. Tours are given Monday to Friday. Even if you don't know a Ferrari from a Ford, you may want to come to White Post for dinner at L'Auberge Provençale, the best French restaurant in the area. There are a few rooms to let here as well. Winchester food is improving, but many people still head south or across the nearby West Virginia border for dinner. The delightful eighteenth-century Wayside Inn has been a landmark on Route 11 in Middletown since stagecoach days, and it is top choice for dinner and lodging in the Winchester vicinity. Since Winchester in-town accommodations are mostly motels, the best bet for charm currently is local bed-and-breakfast hospitality.

One of the area's handsomest attractions is just a mile south of Middletown. Beautiful Belle Grove Plantation served as General Sheridan's main headquarters during his valley battles. The stately home is now maintained by the National Trust for Historic Preservation as a working farm and a center for regional crafts.

If you continue your antiquing tour south to Strasburg, you'll find the Strasburg Emporium, which has 60,000 square feet crammed with anything you can think of, from Victorian bedsteads and 1920s leather couches to old postcards and kitchen tools. Some of it is good, some is just plain junk—it's a little like poking through someone's giant attic. You'll recognize some of the Victorian pieces if you stop at the Strasburg Hotel, which looks as if it were decorated by the Emporium. It's a recommended stop for lunch or dinner.

From here it's easy to end an apple blossom weekend by turning east on Route 55 to Front Royal and taking a spin south on the Skyline Drive. Bring the camera—or the easel. Whether you drive for two miles or twenty, the pastel panorama of dogwoods, apples, and "red buds" in bloom is worth remembering.

Area Code: 703

DRIVING DIRECTIONS Winchester is at the intersection of routes I-81, 50, 7, 11, and 522. From the D.C. area, take Route 7 west. Approximate distance from D.C., 75 miles.

ACCOMMODATIONS *Best Western Lee-Jackson Motor Inn,* 711 Millwood Avenue (US 50 and I-81), Winchester, 22601, 662-4154, $ ● *Holiday Inn-East,* US 50 and I-81, Winchester, 22601, 667-3300, $$ ● *Wayside Inn,* 7783 Main Street (Route 11 and I-81, Exit 77), Middletown, 22645, 869-1797, $$$. (See also Harpers Ferry, WV, page 145.)

BED AND BREAKFAST *Blue Ridge Bed & Breakfast,* Rock & Rills, Route 2, P.O. Box 3895, Berryville, VA 22611, 955-1246.

DINING *Gaspards,* 200 North Braddock Street, Winchester, 662-5350, best bet in town, in old post office, casual fare in bar, $– $$; main dining room $$$ ● *Courthouse Cafe,* 21 East Boscawen Street, Winchester, 662-3300, delightful for lunch, $; serves gourmet dinners once a month on Saturdays, $$$$ ● *Foxcross Ltd.,* 25 South Indian Alley, Winchester, 667-9463, informal, $$ ● *Cork Street Tavern,* 8 West Cork Street, Winchester, 667-3777, pub atmosphere, $–$$ ● *Cafe Sofia,* 688 North Loudoun Street, Winchester, 667-2950, change of pace, Bulgarian, $–$$ ● *Ice Cream Factory,* 383 Millwood Avenue at Millwood Crossing, Winchester, 665-0219, salads, sandwiches, ice cream, $ ● *L'Auberge Provençale,* Route 340, 1 mile east of Route 50, White Post, 837-1375,

$$$ • *Strasburg Hotel*, 201 Holiday Street, Strasburg, 465-9191, $-$$ • *Wayside Inn* (see above), $$-$$$. See also Harpers Ferry, WV, page 145.

SIGHTSEEING *Shenandoah Valley Apple Blossom Festival*, 4-day event held annually the first weekend in May. Information from Publicity Department, P.O. Box 3099, Winchester, VA 22601, or from Chamber of Commerce • *Washington's Office-Museum*, Cork and Braddock streets, 662-4412. Hours: April to October, daily 9 A.M. to 5 P.M. Adults, $1.50; children, $.75 • *Stonewall Jackson's Headquarters*, 415 North Braddock Street, 667-3242. Hours: April to October, daily 9 A.M. to 5 P.M. Adults, $3; children, $.75 • *Abram's Delight*, 1340 South Pleasant Valley Road, 662–6519. Hours: April to October, daily 9 A.M. to 5 P.M. Adults, $3; children, $1.50; combination ticket to all 3 attractions, $6.50 and $3.25. Be sure to check hours of historic sites for Festival Weekend; most are closed on Saturday and have shorter Sunday hours.

INFORMATION Winchester-Frederick County Chamber of Commerce, 1360 South Pleasant Valley Road, Winchester, VA 22601, 662-4118.

Crossing the Delaware to New Jersey

When George Washington crossed the ice-clogged Delaware River in a rowboat on a frigid Christmas night back in 1776, he was headed from Pennsylvania to Trenton, New Jersey, where his troops won a battle that helped turn the tide of the Revolutionary War.

Nowadays travelers to New Jersey's Delaware Valley have more peaceful pursuits in mind, things like country inns, antiques and art, bargain hunters' havens in Flemington, and a visit to Princeton, one of America's most beautiful and historic college towns—more than enough reasons to warrant the trip. And while you're in the neighborhood, you can check out the spot where George made history.

The first happy order of business when you plan your crossing is to find a home base among the appealing small inns on the Jersey side of the valley. Lambertville, just a footbridge across the Delaware from busy New Hope, Pennsylvania, used to be a sleepy place, best known for its small Victorian row houses with pointy roofs. But lately Lambertville has begun to attract galleries and antique shops that can't afford the rents across the water, and with the influx of browsers have come new and choice lodgings in and around the town. Chimney Hill Farm, an 1820 stone house high on a hill, is especially noteworthy.

Two more inviting lodgings are right next door in Stockton. Colligan's Stockton Inn is said to be the inspiration for the old song "There's a Small Hotel," and it does, indeed, have a wishing well. The upstairs, as well as a series of historic adjacent homes and buildings, including the carriage house and the wagon house, has been furnished in high Federal style, with canopy beds and pretty decorator fabrics. Many rooms have working fireplaces, making them perfect places to come home to on a chilly spring night.

Another Stockton standby is the Woolverton Inn, a very private, mellowed stone country house tucked away high on a hill and surrounded by lawns and gardens. The Victorian queen of the area is the Old Hunterdon House, up the river a bit in Frenchtown, a village that has itself begun to bloom with charming cafes and shops. Chestnut Hill in Milford is another small charmer on the river.

Having made your choice and settled in, you might plan Saturday for shopping or sightseeing and Sunday for the many pleasures of Princeton. Lambertville is easy to cover, since everything is within about four square blocks. One of the choicest stops is the Porkyard on Coryell Street, an attractively renovated former sausage factory, which now holds a potpourri of country furniture, paintings, and antiques. The Genest Gallery on North Union is the area's most elegant art showcase, and Goldsmiths on North Union Street has award-winning hand-fashioned jewelry. Antiquers will find two dealers' cooperatives with dozens of vendors to choose from: the People's Store, also on North Union, and Bridge Street Antiques. While you are on Bridge Street, stop in at the Lambertville Trading Company for gourmet foods, including raspberry jam that is billed as "the best in the universe."

Stockton's main attraction is Country Tiles, which features a wide selection of decorative tiles from Mexico, Brazil, Holland, France, and Italy, and farther upriver in Frenchtown, there are several enticing small shops and galleries along Bridge and Race streets.

Stop for lunch at the Race Street Café, a gourmet's favorite in Frenchtown, and you'll be well fortified to follow Route 12 west for some serious shopping among the discount bargains in Flemington. Dansk, Stangl pottery, Mikasa china, Corningware, and Revereware are just a few of the dozens of brand names with their own outlet stores, many of them clustered around the Turntable Junction complex or Liberty Village, a shopping village with an eighteenth-century motif. You'll find everything from luggage to furs to clothing offered here at discount prices. You can write ahead for a free guide to the many shops, or pick one up at almost any of the stores in town.

If shopping is not your thing, you might choose instead to visit Washington Crossing State Park, several miles south on the Delaware. The park, commemorating the famous crossing, runs along both sides of the river. The New Jersey half includes the Ferry House, a restored Colonial inn where Washington and his men spent the night, and the Flag Museum, showing the evolution of the nation's flag. Across the river are the McConkey Ferry Inn, where Washington held his final meeting before the crossing, replicas of the boats rowed by his men, and Bowman's Hill and Tower, the observation site used by the army. (It is 121 steps up for the view.) Should you be in the neighborhood on Christmas Day, you can watch the annual re-creation of the stormy crossing.

But there is more than military history to lure you across the river. The restored and operating Thompson Grist Mill and its barn are interesting examples of nineteenth-century life. And what could be nicer on a fine spring day than a ramble through the 100-acre wildflower preserve?

To see where Washington's daring raid surprised the British Hessian troops, continue south to New Jersey's capital city of Trenton. The Old Barracks Museum here is the finest remaining example of a Colonial barracks. Guides in period costumes will show you the re-created soldiers' squad room and point out the best of the museum's furniture and decorative arts collections.

New Jersey's State Museum and the 1719 William Trent House are other local attractions.

Come Sunday, different pleasures await. If Hollywood were to construct a set for the world's most perfect college town, it would probably look like Princeton, New Jersey. Not only does Princeton boast the fine campus and cultural facilities of an outstanding university, but it is also a town of historic importance and outstanding architecture.

Stop at the Maclean House, to the right just inside the university's main campus gate, where you can sign up for one of the free hourlong guided tours, or pick up literature for your own stroll around the Princeton campus.

Either way, the place to begin is where Princeton began—at Nassau Hall, which constituted the entire college for some 50 years beginning in 1756. Nassau Hall was one of the largest buildings in the colonies and played an important part in the nation's history, serving as home of the Continental Congress for six months in 1783. George Washington, who routed the British here in 1777, returned six years later to receive the thanks of that congress.

Aside from its history, the Georgian-style hall can be appreciated for its beauty. Some say the vines climbing up its mellowed walls inspired the term "Ivy League," though a few New England campuses might dispute that claim. The faculty room, modeled after the British House of Commons, contains some interesting paintings, including one of George Washington at the battle of Princeton by Charles Willson Peale.

The next stop is Firestone Library, where students need road maps and compass points on the floor to find their way around the three million volumes on the shelves. The library contains many rare manuscripts and usually has a special exhibit on display on the main floor.

Two eighteenth-century undergraduates who honed their debating skills at Princeton were James Madison and Aaron Burr. Whig and Clio halls, twin Greek temples west of the library, are reminders of the societies where they competed.

University Chapel, just south of the library, is one of the most magnificent to be found on any college campus. The glowing stained-glass windows, oak pews, and sixteenth-century pulpit were brought from France. It took 100 men one year to carve the choir and clergy stalls, which are made of wood from England's Sherwood Forest.

To see some of the vast Princeton art collection, you need only stroll the campus past the many stunning outdoor sculptures by the likes of Nevelson, Moore, Calder, Lipchitz, and Noguchi. A Picasso sculpture, *Head of a Woman,* stands at the entrance to the University Art Museum, which houses a vast collection ranging from Egyptian sculptures to modern art. Chinese paintings and prints and drawings are among the museum's special strengths.

Save time for some of Princeton's many off-campus sights, including Rockingham, George Washington's onetime headquarters; Morven, the former official residence of the governor of New Jersey; and Drumthwacket, the present governor's mansion. Then there are the homes of Woodrow Wilson, Albert Einstein, and Aaron Burr, and literally hundreds of fine eighteenth- and nineteenth-century homes to be found on Nassau Street and the surrounding side streets, such as Alexander, Mercer, and Stockton.

The traditional place to dine in Princeton is the Nassau Inn on Palmer Square across from the campus. It isn't as old as you might expect, having been built in 1937 to replace the original inn, which was torn down to make way for the new square. Nevertheless, the beamed ceilings, paneled lobby, and enormous fireplace seem right for the town. Or you may choose to splurge at the highly rated Black Swan in a modern hotel complex outside town. Either is a fine way to end a visit to the ivied halls of Nassau.

Area Code: 609

DRIVING DIRECTIONS From the south, take I-95 north to Yardley, Pennsylvania. Cross the Delaware River here and proceed north on New Jersey Route 29 to Lambertville. Approximate distance from D.C., 180 miles. Route 29 also intersects with Routes 78 and 202 from the north and I-95 from the east.

PUBLIC TRANSPORTATION   Amtrak and bus service to Trenton; air service to Trenton/Princeton's Mercer County Airport.

ACCOMMODATIONS   *Colligan's Stockton Inn,* Route 29, Stockton, 08559, 397-1250, $$–$$$$ ● *Woolverton Inn,* RD 3, P.O. Box 233, Stockton, 08559, 397-0802, $$–$$$ CP ● *The Old Hunterdon House,* 12 Bridge Street, Frenchtown, 08825, (201) 996-3632, $$–$$$ CP ● *Chestnut Hill,* 63 Church Street, Milford, 08848, (201) 995-9761, $$–$$$ CP ● *York Street House,* 42 York Street, Lambertville, 08530, 397-3007, Colonial mansion turned B&B, $$–$$$ CP ● *Chimney Hill Farm,* Goat Hill Road, RD 3, P.O. Box 150, Lambertville, 08530, 397-1516, a real beauty, $$$–$$$$ CP.

DINING   *Frenchtown Inn,* Bridge Street, Frenchtown, (201) 996-3300, excellent continental menus, $$$–$$$$ ● *Race Street Cafe,* 2 Race Street, Frenchtown, (201) 996-3179, creative menu, $$–$$$ ● *Colligan's Stockton Inn* (see above), $$–$$$ ● *Hamilton's Grill,* 8½ Coryell (adjoining the Boat Yard), Lambertville, 397-4343, current favorite in the area, $$–$$$ ● *Swan Hotel,* Swan and Main streets, Lambertville, 397-1418, great setting for pub food and drinks, $–$$ ● *Sergeantsville Inn,* Main Street, Sergeantsville, 397-7000, romantic candlelit Colonial charmer north of Stockton, $$$–$$$$ ● *Omni Nassau Inn,* Palmer Square, Princeton, 921-7500, $$–$$$ ● *Black Swan,* Scanticon-Princeton, 100 College Road East (off US 1), Princeton, 452-7800, $$$–$$$$.

SIGHTSEEING   *Princeton University,* guided tours from Maclean House. Hours: Monday to Saturday 10 A.M., 11 A.M., 1:30 P.M., 3:30 P.M.; Sunday afternoons only. Free ● *Washington Crossing State Park,* visitors center, Route 29, 737-0263, picnicking, arboretum, Ferry House, and Flag Museum. Hours: Wednesday to Sunday 8:30 A.M. to 4:30 P.M.; summer daily till 5 P.M. $1 per car weekends and holidays in summer, free rest of year ● *Old Barracks Museum,* South Barrack Street, Trenton, 396-1776. Hours: Monday to Saturday 10 A.M. to 5 P.M.; Sunday 1 P.M. to 5 P.M. Adults, $1; children, $.50.

INFORMATION   Princeton Chamber of Commerce, 44 Nassau Street, P.O. Box 486, Princeton, NJ 08540, 921-7676; Historical Society of Princeton, Bainbridge House, 158 Nassau Street, Princeton, NJ 08540, 921-6748. For Flemington shopping list, write to F.T.A. INFO, P.O. Box 686, Flemington, NJ 08822, or Flemington

Chamber of Commerce, 76 Main Street, Flemington, NJ 08222, (201) 782-7456.

Garden Hopping in Virginia

Historic Garden Week is a longtime Virginia tradition, a once-a-year event that opens many private doors to visitors throughout the state. But nowhere are more hidden treasures awaiting than on the little-explored peninsula known as the Eastern Shore.

Insulated from the world by water on three sides, this peaceable world of farmers and fishermen has been slow to give in to change. Even if you've lived your entire life on the narrow 70-mile stretch between the Atlantic Ocean and Chesapeake Bay, you're still considered a "Come Here" by the natives unless your family goes back at least a generation.

The Eastern Shore was even more isolated until 1964, when the construction of the remarkable 17.6-mile Chesapeake Bay Bridge Tunnel provided a link to Norfolk and Virginia Beach. Now Eastern seaboard motorists travel through, but few get beyond Route 13—the boring main highway—unless they are fishermen or nature lovers bound for Chincoteague Island's beaches and wildlife preserves.

Venture off onto the back roads, however, and you will discover an area rich in history and rustic charm. Along the bountiful creeks and streams that weave through the countryside and out to sea are fine old homes dating back to the early eighteenth century; some have been in the same family for generations. Distinctive in their architecture and delightful in their settings, they have a look all their own—multileveled, steep-roofed frame structures with dormer windows and two or more chimneys. A typical Eastern Shore home is one room deep and might have four different roof levels for the "big house," "little house," colonnade, and kitchen.

A selection of these privately owned and often secluded properties is opened to visitors just once each year for Historic Garden Week, and it is well worth a trip to see them. The selection changes with the years, but a recent roster gives a typical sampling: an eighteenth-century home—owned by the same family since 1832—noted for its woodwork and wainscoting, surrounded by water views, groves of native trees, English boxwood, and a rainbow of spring bulbs; a story-and-a-half farm overlooking Still Pond, handsomely furnished with American, French Provincial, and English antiques; a 1745 plantation house and rose garden set along the

shore of Deep Creek, filled with fine needlework and exquisite miniature bird carvings made by the owners.

A perennial on the tour is Eyre Hall, built in 1730 and recognized
as one of the great houses of the Eastern Shore. The present owner
is the tenth successive generation of the Eyre family to own the
property. Located on Cherrystone Creek, the white frame home
boasts fine woodwork and paneling, early French wallpapers, and
heirloom furnishings including Queen Anne, Chippendale, Hep-
plewhite, and Chinese export pieces. Outside, mellow brick walls
enclose a magnificent boxwood garden with ancient plantings of
yew, crepe myrtle, holly, magnolia, and laurel. Neatly raked sandy
walks thread through the borders for views of old roses and unusual
trees and shrubs. Nearby, through a garden gate, is the family cemetery, where generations of Eyres are buried.

Kerr Place, located in the old port town of Onancock, is another
home always included on the tour and the only one you can count on
seeing anytime you are in the area. A late-eighteenth-century Federal brick mansion, it was purchased by the Eastern Shore of Virginia Historical Society and beautifully restored and furnished with
choice antiques and Oriental rugs. The house also contains interesting collections of quilts, costumes, and local memorabilia. The
landscaping of the grounds with period plants and trees was a Garden Club of Virginia restoration project, one of many the Garden
Club has funded for more than 50 years through its annual spring
tours.

Take time in Onancock for a look at Hopkins & Brothers store, a
general store dating back to 1839 that still retains its old-fashioned
air and antique cash register. In addition to a pleasing ambience, it
offers a little cafe and handmade crafts and gifts. The store is also
ticket headquarters for summer excursion boats to Tangier Island,
an oystering enclave where life has changed little over the past three
centuries, and many of the natives still speak with accents more
Elizabethan than American.

As you drive from house to house on the Garden Week tour,
you'll find other interesting sights tucked away in the small villages
of the Eastern Shore. The Eastville Courthouse has the oldest continuous set of records in the country, dating from 1632. The old
courthouse, built in 1731, is part of a complex that includes a 1731
clerk's office and an 1814 debtors' prison. Another debtors' prison,
circa 1782, can be found in Accomac, and historic white-spired
churches dot the area. Some that date back to the eighteenth century
are Hungars Episcopal (1742) in Bridgtown, St. George's Episcopal
(1738) in Pungoteague, and Cokesbury (1784) in Onancock. Even
the Greek Revival St. James Church in Accomac has a history much
older than the façade might lead you to believe. The bricks in the
building come from the original church built on this site in 1767,

paid for with taxes levied in pounds of tobacco. Of special interest is the handsomely painted interior, with columns and an archway creating an optical illusion. The church has been named a National Historic Landmark.

The 100-year-old Shore Railroad in Cape Charles is also a curiosity for railroad buffs. Its tracks run directly on to carfloat barges for transporting railroad cars on a 26-mile water route between Cape Charles and Little Creek. Another attraction for railroad buffs is the Eastern Shore Railway Museum in Parksley, consisting of the restored station plus two vintage cabooses and a baggage car containing a model railroad exhibit.

The Chincoteague Wildlife Refuge, with its wild ponies and many species of birds, is a well-known attraction up in the northern corner of the area and definitely merits a driving tour. Chincoteague is only one of a whole chain of barrier islands on the Atlantic side of the Eastern Shore, an untouched world said to have the richest assortment of bird life in the mid-Atlantic. Dedicated naturalists and bird-watchers may want to splurge for an excursion to the solitude of the wild undeveloped islands that can be reached only by boat. Trips through the tidal marshes are run for parties of from one to six people by the Virginia Coast Reserve, but advance reservations are essential, and the cost is over $100 per person.

Should you want to take a break from sightseeing, there are public tennis courts at many local schools along the peninsula and golf at the Northampton County course in Cape Charles. Fishing here is superb, and charter boats go out from many local docks, including the Wachapreague Marina and Kings Creek Marina in Cape Charles.

Accommodations on the Eastern Shore are mostly limited to modest bed-and-breakfast homes and motels. Among the latter, America House in Cape Charles offers the most comfortable accommodations, unless you choose to head up to Chincoteague. Others are clean but strictly no-frills, used mainly by fishermen. A promising newcomer is The Garden and the Sea Inn in New Church, a small Victorian inn with a restaurant featuring seafood and seasonal specialties.

On the whole, dining is far from fancy in this area, but the seafood is deliciously fresh and the prices refreshingly reasonable— another bonus for those who take the time to explore the hidden treasures of Virginia's Eastern Shore.

Area Code: 804

DRIVING DIRECTIONS   Route 13 runs the length of the Delmarva peninsula, from Delaware and Maryland through the Eastern

Shore, connecting to the Chesapeake Bay Bridge Tunnel to Norfolk at the southern tip of Virginia. From D.C., take Route 50/301 east toward Annapolis, cross the Chesapeake Bay Bridge, follow Route 50 to Salisbury, and connect to Route 13 south. Total distance to Onancock (approximately midway on the shore), 185 miles from D.C.

ACCOMMODATIONS   *The Garden and the Sea Inn,* P.O. Box 134, New Church, 23415, 824-0672, $$ CP ● *Colonial Manor Inn,* 84 Market Street, Onancock, 23417, 787-3521, $ ● *America House,* US 13 near the Chesapeake Bay Bridge Tunnel, Cape Charles, 23310, 331-1776, $$ ● *Wachapreague Motel and Marina,* Route 180, Wachapreague, 23480, 787-2105, $ ● *Anchor Motel,* Route 13, Nassawadox, 23413, 442-6363, $.

DINING   *The Garden and the Sea Inn* (see above), $$–$$$ ● *Island House Restaurant* (see *Wachapreague Motel* above), $–$$ ● *Wright's Seafood Restaurant,* Route 766, Atlantic, 424-4012, $–$$.

SIGHTSEEING   *Historic Garden Week on the Eastern Shore of Virginia,* usually held the last weekend in April. Hours: Friday and Saturday 10 A.M. to 5 P.M. Block tickets, $10; single admissions, $2. Information for the current year is available from the chamber of commerce. Since sightseeing sites are small and hours change, it's best to check them also with the chamber of commerce. *Barrier Island Tours,* Virginia Coast Reserve, Brownsville, Nassawadox, 442-3049. Hours: April through October, Monday to Friday and selected weekends 9 A.M. to 2:30 P.M., weather permitting. Call for current prices.

INFORMATION   Eastern Shore of Virginia Chamber of Commerce, Inc., Box 147, Accomac, VA 23301, 787-2460.

Celebrating Spring in Salisbury

Salisbury, Maryland, is a town that might well have an inferiority complex if it didn't have so much going for it. Lots of tourists come to Salisbury—but they keep right on going, east on Route 50, north or south on Route 13, usually headed for the beach.

That's because Salisbury is known mostly as the commercial center of the Eastern Shore, and the heart of Perdue chicken country. Many people don't realize that it is also an attractive small city with a river meandering through the middle, not to mention home to an unmatched museum holding the world's largest collection of bird carvings, and site of one of the finest small zoos in the country. It is also a place with some lovely neighborhoods for strolling on a fine spring day.

Salisbury merits a visit on its own, and an excellent time to get acquainted is in early May, when spring is welcomed with a fun-packed annual festival that fills the streets with music and entertainment, arts and crafts, an antique car meet, and lots of good eating. As a bonus, there are tours of the residential streets lined with dogwood trees at their peak bloom.

Bring the kids along—there's always plenty of pint-size activity planned, and since this is essentially a small-town affair, the crowds never overwhelm the fun. You can round out the weekend with a visit to charming eighteenth-century Eastern Shore villages nearby or with a preseason stroll on the boardwalk in Ocean City, a far more serene scene before the summer throngs arrive.

Though Salisbury was laid out by a charter granted in 1732, you'll find today's town Victorian in feel. It was rebuilt after two 1860s fires all but leveled the downtown, the reason why so many of the buildings today are of fire-resistant red brick.

The center of Main Street is a tree-lined pedestrian walk, turning the heart of town into an attractive open-air plaza known as the Downtown Plaza Historic District. To the east along East Market Street near the Sheraton Inn is Riverfront Walk, a green oasis that is being extended along the entire east prong of the Wicomico River.

For festival weekend, both the riverfront and the Downtown Plaza are filled with activity. Things get rolling on Friday night with jazz and Dixieland, hayrides for the small fry, paddleboat rentals on the river, and food galore, from hickory-pit barbecue to oyster sandwiches.

On Saturday, the music plays on for every taste from bluegrass to baroque. Booths display decoys, baskets, stoneware, herb wreaths, watercolors, and almost any other art or craft you can name. Meanwhile, there is continuous entertainment, including dance demonstrations, concerts, sing-alongs, and a long list of special amusements for youngsters, from clowns and pony rides to puppet shows and magicians.

When hunger strikes, choose from Eastern Shore raw bars and crab cakes and down-home favorites like Maryland fried chicken, chitlins, corn bread, and sweet potato pie. The International Food Alley features more exotic fare, such as Liberian skewered beef, Filipino sesame chicken, and Indian gulab and jaleby.

Bike and foot races on land and raft and shell races on the water add to the excitement. And you'll want to set aside time for a narrated sightseeing cruise on the Wicomico aboard the sidewheeler *Maryland Lady*.

Come dinnertime, if you want to sample the best local fare and lots of it, call for driving directions to the Red Roost in Whitehaven, where you can get in line for a nonstop orgy of fried shrimp and clams, hush puppies, delectable fried chicken, corn on the cob, and steamed hard-shell crabs that keep coming as long as you can keep eating. The wait can be long, but nobody complains, especially after seeing the amazingly low tab.

A fine start to a Sunday in Salisbury is a visit to the charming Salisbury Zoo, set in the lush green City Park by the river and enhanced by tall shade trees and lovely plantings. Close to 400 mammals, birds, and reptiles are found here in naturalistic habitats. The exhibits include spectacled bears, monkeys, jaguars, bison, bald eagles, Chincoteague ponies, and a fine assortment of waterfowl. The zoo is just the right size for young children—and a guaranteed hour's fun for all ages.

A walking tour will give you a better look at the handsome houses in the historic district, called Newtown, beginning at Elizabeth and Poplar Hill avenues. East Isabella Street and East William Street off Poplar Hill have the finest homes, and at 1 P.M. tours begin at the 1805 Poplar Hill Mansion, the oldest house in town. It boasts impressive woodwork and mantels, original heart pine floors, and Palladian windows, as well as fine eighteenth- and nineteenth-century furnishings.

One P.M. is also opening time for Salisbury's chief claim to fame, the Ward Foundation Art Museum, named for two brothers, Steve and Lem Ward, who are considered pioneers in decorative carving. Featuring the world's largest collection of decorative bird carvings, the extraordinary exhibits present a history of the carver's art, including more than 100 examples of decoys carved by the Ward brothers. Highlights are displays of works by the finest contemporary carvers, the winners of the annual world championship bird-carving competition. You need not be a bird lover to appreciate the skill and beauty of these exquisite carvings, and you will almost surely leave with a new appreciation of this special branch of American folk art.

There are several nice options to fill out the rest of a Sunday on the Eastern Shore. You might choose to stock up and head for City Park's Picnic Island and a meal under the loblolly pines. Pemberton Historical Park near Salisbury gives you the chance to see a restoration in progress at Pemberton Hall, a brick gambrel-roofed eighteenth-century Eastern Shore plantation house in a 61-acre park setting.

A drive 14 miles south on Route 13 brings you to Princess Anne, a village laid out in 1733 that is filled with homes dating back to its early days. Two interesting stops are the Washington Hotel in the center of town, which has been an inn since 1797, and the Treackle Mansion, an 1801 Georgian home furnished with period pieces that now serves as headquarters of the Somerset County Historic Society.

Heading south on Route 12 instead will take you to Snow Hill. Founded in 1642, it is one of the oldest of the Eastern Shore communities, and yet another place where many early homes remain intact. Snow Hill is a river town (*Tillie the Tug* gives rides here in summer on the Pocomoke River), and you can learn about its prosperous early history and way of life at the Julia A. Purnell Museum, housed in a historic church.

Or, if the weather is cooperative, you may choose to forget about history and simply head for the shore. It's a half-hour drive east on Route 50 from Salisbury to Ocean City, and you'll hardly recognize the wide open empty beach if you know this resort area only in season. On the right day, a rejuvenating sniff of sea air and a stroll on the boardwalk can be a genuine spring tonic.

Area Code: 301

DRIVING DIRECTIONS   Salisbury is at the intersection of routes 50 and 13. From D.C., follow Route 50/301 east across the Chesapeake Bay Bridge and follow Route 50 directly into town. Approximate distance from D.C., 119 miles.

ACCOMMODATIONS   *Sheraton of Salisbury,* 300 South Salisbury Boulevard, 21801, 546-4400, (800) 325-3535, by far the best location in town, $$–$$$ ● *Best Western Statesman Motel,* 712 North Salisbury Boulevard (Business Route 13), 21801, 749-7155, $$ ● *Holiday Inn,* US 13 north, 21801, 742-7194, (800) HOLIDAY, $–$$ ● *Days Inn,* US 13 north, 21801, 749-6200, (800) 325-2525, $.

BED AND BREAKFAST *The Traveller in Maryland, Inc.,* P.O. Box 2277, Annapolis, MD 21404, 269-6232 ● *Amanda's Bed & Breakfast Reservation Service,* 1428 Park Avenue, Baltimore, MD 21217, 225-0001.

DINING You'll probably eat hearty at the festival and at *Red Roost,* Clara Road (Route 349 east from Salisbury, south on Route 352, then left to Clara Road), Whitehaven, 546-5443, $–$$ ● *Johnny and Sammy's Alpine Room,* 670 South Salisbury Boulevard (Route 13), seafood and prime ribs, $–$$$ ● *Basil,* 1137 South Division Street, 548-2660, fish, chicken specialties, $$–$$$ ● *Nick Idoni's House of Ribs,* 1306 South Salisbury Boulevard, 742-7427, $$.

SIGHTSEEING *The Salisbury Festival* is usually the first weekend in May, Friday night and Saturday. Current schedule from Salisbury Chamber of Commerce, 300 East Main Street, P.O. Box 510, Salisbury, MD 21801, 749-0144 ● *Ward Foundation North American Wildfowl Art Museum,* Holloway Hall, Salisbury State University, 655 South Salisbury Boulevard (US 13 south), 749-6104. Hours: Tuesday to Saturday 10 A.M. to 5 P.M.; Sunday 1 P.M. to 5 P.M. Adults, $2; children under 12, free ● *Salisbury City Zoo,* City Park, 750 South Park Drive, 548-3188. Hours: daily 8 A.M. to 5 P.M. Free ● *Poplar Hill Mansion,* 117 Elizabeth Street, 749-1776. Hours: Sunday 1 P.M. to 4 P.M. Free ● *Maryland Lady Cruises,* Second Floor, City Center, P.O. Box 4062, 543-2466 or 800-654-5440. Check for current prices.

INFORMATION Wicomico County Convention & Visitors Bureau, Wicomico Youth and Civic Center, Glen Avenue Extended, Salisbury, MD 21801, 548-4914.

Renaissance in Richmond

It isn't every Southern belle who wants the world to know about a face-lift, but in Richmond, Virginia, they are caroling the news.

Tradition-conscious Richmond for years was accused of steadfastly looking backward. An old joke needled that it took three people to change a light bulb here, one to remove the bulb and two to talk about what a fine old bulb it was.

Now Richmond is in the midst of a billion-dollar building boom, a virtual renaissance that is changing the face of downtown and infusing new pride and spirit into this born-again belle.

Old Southern hospitality, Civil War monuments, and plantation houses still abound, but today visitors also find a growing downtown, a smashing modern wing on the Virginia Museum of Fine Arts, shops and lively cafes in the old tobacco warehouses along Shockoe Slip, city residential neighborhoods coming back to life, and a riverfront being transformed into an urban park.

Rejuvenated Richmond is definitely a lady worth calling on, especially in springtime when this city of 200,000 trees is aglow with dogwoods, crepe myrtle, and azaleas in bloom. To see how the old is blooming anew here, check into the magnificently restored Jefferson Hotel with its fabulous Palm Court and staircase, or try either the Catlin-Abbott House or Carrington Row Inn, both 1800s town houses up on Church Hill that have been transformed into elegant bed-and-breakfast inns.

For first-timers, a must to visit is Court End, the remarkable six-block area containing seven National Historic Landmarks and twelve buildings on the National Register of Historic Places. It shows in a nutshell why the city has good reason to take pride in its past.

Most imposing is the graceful columned Virginia State Capitol building constructed in 1785. The Virginia legislature, America's oldest continuous English-speaking legislative body, still meets here. The design was chosen by Thomas Jefferson based on the Maison Carrée, a Roman temple he considered a perfect example of classical style. The building includes a remarkable rotunda dome placed 20 feet below the roof so as not to spoil the outside roof line.

Inside are tributes to two beloved native sons, a life-size statue of George Washington (the only one he ever posed for and said to be the nation's most valuable piece of marble art), and a warm bronze likeness of Robert E. Lee, placed on the spot where Lee stood in 1861 while accepting command of the Confederate forces. Busts placed around the rotunda portray the other seven Virginia-born presidents.

More statues of Virginia heroes can be found in the shady park surrounding the capitol, including one of Edgar Allan Poe, who grew up in Richmond. The grounds were laid out in 1816, the wrought-iron fence added in 1819 to keep out cattle and pigs. Picnickers are welcome on the lawn and lunch-hour entertainment takes place frequently in spring and summer in front of the 1824 Bell Tower west of the capitol. To the east is the gracious white executive mansion, the residence for Virginia's governors since 1813.

From here, Civil War buffs will want to head directly to the Museum of the Confederacy, which contains the nation's largest collection of Confederate memorabilia, including the gray frock coat Jefferson Davis wore when he was taken prisoner toward the end of the war, Jeb Stuart's boots, and the sword of surrender and gold-braided uniform General Lee wore at Appomattox.

Richmond Battlefield Park, site of seven Civil War battles, can also be visited. It is maintained by the National Park Service.

Next to the Museum of the Confederacy is the Confederate White House, the 1818 John Brockenbrogh home. Interior restoration should now be complete, returning the house to its 1861 appearance. Also nearby is the John Marshall House, built by the Chief Justice in 1790 when he was a young lawyer, and filled with Marshall family furnishings and mementos.

Take time for a look at the neoclassical Wickham Valentine House, built in 1812 by Richmond's wealthiest resident. It is now a museum showing the history of the city and noted for its fine period costume collection.

Having seen some of the old, you can begin to appreciate some of Richmond's newer claims to fame. The Virginia Museum of Fine Arts, the largest art museum in the Southeast, is known for its fabulous collection of Russian Imperial jewels, including some of the famous Fabergé Easter eggs. But the museum entered the big leagues of the art world in 1985 with a soaring new wing housing two major private collections. Five hundred nineteenth- and twentieth-century masterpieces including works by Manet, Monet, Renoir, Van Gogh, Cézanne, Picasso, Homer, and Eakins are the donation of Mr. and Mrs. Paul Mellon, and contemporary works by Johns, de Kooning, Lichtenstein, and Rauschenberg are the stars of the Sydney and Frances Lewis collection.

Visiting the museum brings you to the Fan, a gracious neighborhood bordered by grand Monument Avenue, canopied by sugar maples and studded with statues of Confederate heroes. Trendy new shops and cafes are bringing new life to this area, places like Charlie's or Humphrey's, where Richmonders go to listen to jazz.

More dramatic signs of change are found in the center of the city. The 6th Street Marketplace, stretching three blocks in the heart of downtown and anchored by the city's two major department stores, is centered by the "Crystal Palace," a 96-foot-high glass-enclosed structure containing food stalls, a city market, open seating, and a stage for frequent free entertainment. There are dozens of shops and vendors here, from standards like Benetton and Caswell-Massey to pushcarts selling handmade crafts. The complex is near both the Richmond Coliseum and the newly restored Carpenter Center for the Performing Arts, tying downtown's main attractions into a convenient package.

The Marketplace is more than a commercial enterprise. For years there had been a visible rift in black-white relations in Richmond, symbolized by Broad Street, which served as a virtual divider be tween black and white shoppers. The Marketplace deliberately was planned with a sky deck spanning Broad as a gesture of unity in the city. Its construction also was accompanied by a unique minor ity entrepreneur development program, teaching basics of managing and operating businesses to encourage black participation in the new development.

Another recent shopping center of note just outside the center of town is Main Street Station, housed in a restored railroad depot. It is near the 17th Street Farmers' Market, a fixture throughout the city's long history.

From its earliest days Richmond's history has revolved around the James River. The rejuvenation in progress on the north bank of the James is one of the city's most expansive and expensive projects, a plan that eventually envisions boat ramps, nature trails, hiking and bicycle trails, footbridges to river islands with open meadows, and a historic walk, all easily adjacent to downtown. Another ambitious commercial complex under construction is the $350 million James Center overlooking the river's falls. It will include offices, retail shops, condominiums, and a hotel in a glittery series of towers.

Down by the river to the south is the Kanawha Canal, designed by George Washington in 1787 in the hope of linking the James and Kanawha rivers. The dream was never realized, but the canals and locks have been restored and picnickers and strollers are welcome.

Shockoe Slip, the old cobblestoned warehouse district running uphill here from the James, is receiving its own $70 million renovation, adding fine shops and more restaurants to an area that is already a center for nightlife in the city. Visit the Old Tobacco Company to sample the local action.

Save one Richmond evening for the drive to neighboring Hanover and the Barksdale Theatre, where the historic 1723 Hanover Tavern houses a talented local dinner-theater troupe. The theater has been a favorite local tradition for more than thirty years. The buffet dinner is optional, but if you do decide to come early, you can join owner Nancy Kilgore's 6:30 P.M. tour of Hanover Courthouse and Jail just across the road and get a brief history of the tavern itself. You'll learn that Patrick Henry, who grew up nearby, married the innkeeper's daughter and spent three years here helping tend bar and arguing his first cases in the local courthouse.

On Sunday, you can pick and choose your pleasures in Richmond. Up on Church Hill, you can visit St. John's, the little white church where Patrick Henry made his impassioned ''Give me liberty or give me death'' speech, an event reenacted on Sunday after-noons in the summer. You'll find yourself in the midst of a charm-ing nineteenth-century residential area now blooming anew with more than 300 restored homes.

The Jackson Ward Historic District was home to many prominent blacks, and is a treasure trove of nineteenth-century building styles adorned with intricate cast-iron work.

Historic homes abound in the city. Maymont is the queen, the ultimate Victorian mansion set amid a vast park that includes exten-sive formal gardens, a children's zoo, and a museum of antique carriages. Carriage rides are one of the highlights of a visit here.

Wilton House, a stately 1750 Georgian brick mansion, was built by William Randolph III, descendant of one of the great families of Virginia. The parlor is included in a book featuring the hundred most beautiful rooms in America. Agecroft is something of a sur-prise, a fifteenth-century timbered Renaissance home that was dis-mantled and transplanted alongside the James River, and set off by Elizabethan gardens. And a short drive outside of town will take you to Tuckahoe Plantation, the boyhood home of Thomas Jeffer-son, or to Patrick Henry's Scotchtown, one of Virginia's oldest plantation houses.

For ''Raven'' fans, there is the Edgar Allan Poe Museum, a com-plex including the Old Stone House, the oldest in Richmond, fur-nished with mid-eighteenth-century pieces and with the Raven Room, containing 43 illustrations for the poem.

If children are along, the Science Museum of Virginia, hand-somely housed in a vintage railroad station, has an I-MAX theater and many hands-on exhibits, as well as a Children's Museum espe-cially for the under-13 set. A new wing, the Thalhimer Hall of Sci-ence Exploration, opened in 1989 with some fascinating exhibits. The aerospace portion includes planes from a reproduction of the Wright glider to the Solar Challenger, which actually crossed the English Channel. On ground level, a spin tunnel illustrates how NASA scientists test future aircraft, and flight simulators put vis-itors at the controls. *Electriworks* has many participatory exhibits, including a laser oscilloscope that creates giant laser ''waves'' through voice and hand commands.

For a real change of pace, get out on the river with Richmond Raft Company. There's plenty of excitement tackling the white water through the falls of the James. Or, if calmer waters are more your style, a perfect end to a Richmond visit is a twilight cruise on the paddle wheeler *Annabel Lee,* down the James River where it all began. There's no better way to see the contrast of old and new than along the riverbanks, or to appreciate the dual spirit of a city main-taining pride in yesterday while facing squarely toward tomorrow.

Area Code: 804

DRIVING DIRECTIONS   Richmond is at the intersection of routes 95 and 64. From D.C. and points north, take I-95 south into town. Approximate distance from D.C., 111 miles.

PUBLIC TRANSPORTATION   Excellent Amtrak connections, Greyhound and Trailways buses, and many airlines serve Richmond. Downtown trolleys make it easy to get around.

ACCOMMODATIONS   *Jefferson Sheraton Hotel,* Franklin and Adams streets, 23220, 788-8000, $$$–$$$$ ● *Catlin-Abbott House,* 2304 East Broad Street, 23223, 780-3746, $$$ CP ● *Carrington Row Inn,* 2309 East Broad Street, 23223, 343-7005, $$ CP ● *Richmond Marriott,* 500 East Broad Street, 643-3400, adjacent to 6th Street Marketplace, 23219, $$$–$$$$ ● *Commonwealth Park Suites Hotel,* 9th and Bank streets, 23203, 343-7300, across from the state capitol, $$$–$$$$ ● *Hyatt Richmond,* West Broad Street, 23230, 285-1234, attractive resort-motel just outside the city, $$–$$$ ● *Omni Richmond,* 100 South 12th Street, 23219, 344-7000 or (800) THE-OMNI, $$–$$$$ ● *Linden Row Historic Inn,* 100 East Franklin Street, 23219, 783-7000, $$–$$$$ CP ● *The Berkeley Hotel,* 12th and Cary streets, 23219, 780-1300, classy small downtown hotel on nearby Shockoe Slip, $$–$$$.

BED AND BREAKFAST   *Bensonhouse of Richmond,* P.O. Box 15131, Richmond, VA 23117, 321-6277.

DINING   *Tobacco Company,* 1201 East Cary Street, 782-9431, restored warehouse and local landmark, $$–$$$ ● *Traveller's,* 707 East Franklin Street, 644-1040, historic home where Mrs. Robert E. Lee lived briefly during the war, named for Lee's horse, $$$–$$$$ ● *Aviary,* 1 James Center, 901 East Cary Street, 225-8219, attractive contemporary decor, continental choices, $$–$$$ ● *Linden Row Historic Inn* (see above), $$–$$$ ● *Lemaire,* Jefferson Sheraton Hotel (see above), Continental with a Southern accent, elegant room, $$–$$$ ● *Blue Point Seafood,* 6th Street Marketplace at the Carpenter Center, 783-8138, $$–$$$ ● *Sam Miller's Warehouse,* 1210 East Cary Street, Shockoe Slip, 644-5465, seafood and beef, entertainment, $$–$$$ ● *DeFazio's Church Hill Restaurant,* 9 North 17th Street, in Shockoe Bottom, 780-3843, newly emerging nightlife area, $–$$$ ● *Commercial Cafe,* 111 North Robinson Street, 353-7110, hickory-smoked barbecue, in the Fan district, $$–$$$ ● *Strawberry Street Café,* 421 North Strawberry Street, 353-6860, another Fan location, casual, $–$$ ● *La Petite France,* 2912 Maywill Street, 353-8729, fine French, $$$ ● *du Jour,* 5806

Grove Avenue, 285-1301, international menu, $$–$$$ ● *The But-tery*, 6221 River Road Shopping Center, 282-9711, country French, $$$.

For a rundown on what's new in Richmond nightlife, look for the free weekly publication *Style*.

SIGHTSEEING *Virginia State Capitol,* Capitol Square, 9th and Grace streets, 786-4344. Hours: April to November, daily 9 A.M. to 5 P.M.; December to March, Monday to Saturday 9 A.M. to 5 P.M.; Sunday 1 P.M. to 5 P.M. Free ● *Museum of the Confederacy,* 1201 East Clay Street, 649-1861. Hours: Monday to Saturday 10 A.M. to 5 P.M.; Sunday 1 P.M. to 5 P.M. Adults, $3; children, $1.75 ● *White House of the Confederacy,* 12th and Clay streets, 649-1861, Monday to Saturday, 10 A.M. to 5 P.M.; Sunday 1 P.M to 5 P.M. Adults, $3; ages 7–12, $1.25. Combination Confederacy Museum and White House tickets, adults, $5; children, $2 ● *Valentine Museum,* 1015 East Clay Street, 649-0711. Hours: Monday to Saturday 10 A.M. to 5 P.M.; Sunday 12 P.M. to 5 P.M. Adults, $3.50; ages 7–12, $1.50 ● *John Marshall House,* 818 East Marshall Street, 648-7988. Hours: Tuesday to Saturday 10 A.M. to 5 P.M. Adults, $3; ages 7–12, $1.25 ● *Virginia Museum of Fine Arts*, Boulevard and Grove avenues, 367-0844. Hours: Tuesday to Saturday 11 A.M. to 5 P.M.; Thursdays to 10 P.M. Adults, $2; under 16, free ● *Edgar Allan Poe Museum,* 1914 East Main Street, 648-5523. Hours: Tuesday to Saturday 10 A.M. to 4 P.M.; Sunday, Monday 1:30 P.M. to 4 P.M. Adults, $3; students, $1 ● *Barksdale Theatre,* Hanover, 537-5333. Hours: Wednesday to Saturday, dinner 6:45 P.M., theater 8:30 P.M. Call for current attraction and prices ● *St. John's Church,* 24th and Broad streets, 648-5015. Guided tours: Monday to Saturday 10 A.M. to 3:30 P.M.; Sunday 1 P.M. to 3:30 P.M. Adults, $2; children, $1 ● *Maymont,* 1700 Hampton Street at Pennsylvania Avenue, 358-7166. Exhibits: Tuesday to Sunday noon to 5 P.M. Grounds open: 10 A.M. to 7 P.M. April to October; to 5 P.M. rest of year. Free ● *Maymont Carriage Collection.* Hours: Tuesday to Sunday noon to 5 P.M. Donation. Carriage rides: April to mid-December, Saturday and Sunday 1 P.M. to 5 P.M. Adults, $1.50; children, $1 ● *Wilton,* South Wilton Road off Cary Street, 282-5936. Hours: September to July, Tuesday to Saturday 10 A.M. to 4:30 P.M.; Sunday 1:30 P.M. to 4:30 P.M.; closed Sunday in July. Adults, $2.50; children, $2 ● *Scotchtown,* Route 2, P.O. Box 168, Beaverdam, 227-3500. Hours: Monday to Saturday 10 A.M. to 4:30 P.M.; Sunday 1:30 P.M. to 4:30 P.M. Adults, $3; students, $1 ● *Tuckahoe Plantation,* River Road, 784-5736, by appointment only ● *Agecroft Hall,* 4305 Sulgrave Road, 353-4241. Hours: Tuesday to Saturday 10 A.M. to 4 P.M.; Sunday 2 P.M. to 5 P.M. Adults, $2; students, $1 ● *Science Museum of Virginia,* 2500 West Broad Street 367-1013.

Hours: Monday to Thursday and Sunday 11 A.M. to 5 P.M.; Friday and Sunday 11 A.M. to 8 P.M. Adults, $3; children, $2.50. Additional charge for I-MAX films ● *Richmond Children's Museum,* 740 North 6th Street, 788-4940. Hours: Tuesday to Friday 10 A.M. to 4:30 P.M.; Saturday and Sunday 1 P.M. to 5 P.M. Adults, $2; age 3–12, $1.50 ● *Bloemendaal,* the Lewis Ginter Botanical Garden, 7000 Lakeside Avenue, 262-9887. Daily 9:30 A.M. to 4:30 P.M. Adults, $1.50; children, $.50 ● *Richmond Raft Company,* 4400 East Main Street, 222-RAFT, rafting trips on the James. Call for current schedules and rates ● *Annabel Lee,* river cruises, 104 Shockoe Slip, 787-0107. Check for current schedule and prices.

INFORMATION Metropolitan Richmond Convention and Visitors Bureau, 300 East Main Street, Richmond, VA 23219, 782-2777 or (800) 365-7272.

House Hunting in Old New Castle

You can always spot a first-time visitor to New Castle, Delaware. Open-mouthed ''oohs'' of delight are easy clues that someone new has discovered Delaware's first capital, a tiny riverside charmer whose brick sidewalks, white cupolas, Georgian town houses, and Colonial gardens have hardly changed a whit in appearance in 200 years.

Normally, New Castle is almost a chance discovery, for though a handful of buildings are open to the public, this is not a museum piece but very much a living town. For over 60 years, however, New Castle has held an annual open house, known as A Day in Old Newcastle, when the public is invited in for one day only—the third Saturday in May—to view its exceptional homes and gardens.

There is no better time to become acquainted with this extraordinary pocket of history, followed on Sunday by the discovery of some other little-heralded Delaware gems, including the present capital city of Dover.

In its earlier years, as the seat of government of the ''three lower counties'' of Pennsylvania, which eventually became the state of Delaware, New Castle was a center of trade and travel, and its leading citizens were lawyers, judges, and government officials—people of taste and distinction whose homes reflected their wealth and position.

But fate took the spotlight away from New Castle. In 1777 the capital was moved to Dover, safer from the guns of the British fleet. By the mid-1800s Wilmington had overshadowed New Castle as a railroad and commercial center, and in 1881 even the county offices and court were removed, leaving the town to settle into mellow obscurity.

The whims of fate and the resulting relative poverty of New Castle's residents kept building alterations to a minimum, leaving the town much the way earlier generations had known it. Today, a walk through the streets is a rare journey back in time.

Flags of the Netherlands, Sweden, Great Britain, and the United States are still displayed on the balcony of the Old Court House to honor the history of the town, which was founded by the Dutch back in 1651 at a strategic point on the edge of the New World. It changed hands five times and had four names over the next 30 years. When William Penn claimed it as part of his land grant in 1682, it became a colonial capital.

New Castle streets boast examples of Dutch, Colonial, French, Georgian, Federal, and Empire architecture. Some buildings are made of clapboard, stone, or stucco, but the look of the town is predominantly Georgian- and Federal-style red brick. The homes on the tour vary each year, but you can count on seeing fine mantels, paneling, staircases, and fireplaces, as well as woodwork and flooring of note, and rare and beautiful examples of the colonial furniture-maker's art.

The gardens tucked behind the homes are long and narrow and represent a charming variety of formal and informal. Dressed in their mid-May colors, they make a happy addition to the day's touring.

In all there are more than 50 sights on the open-house roster each year, including the historic public buildings and spaces that are customarily open to everyone. If you can't make it for the house tour, the public buildings are worth seeing anytime.

Chief among them is the beautiful Old Court House, whose cupola is a town landmark. The town green, according to local tradition, was pegged out as common land by Peter Stuyvesant back in 1655. The Market Place was used for trade as early as 1682, and the Old Town Hall, built in 1823 with a unique arch connecting Delaware Street with the Market Place, has served as both firehouse and federal courthouse during its long life.

A small building with an impressive history is the 1832 ticket office of the New Castle–Frenchtown Railroad, one of the nation's first steam railroads, which brought many prominent passengers to New Castle before the Civil War.

Immanuel Episcopal Church, the sponsor of the annual Day in Old New Castle, originally was built on the town green in 1703.

When the building burned in 1980, it was reconstructed with the remaining original wall materials. George Read, a signer of the Declaration of Independence, and other prominent Delaware statesmen are buried in the graveyard here.

A few lovely historic homes also are open to the public. The Old Dutch House, the oldest brick dwelling in the state, was built before 1700. The 1730 Amstel House had the honor of George Washington's presence as a guest at a wedding held in the home in 1784. The George Read II House, an outstanding Georgian mansion with a handsome formal garden, was recently restored to its early splendor by the Historical Society of Delaware.

Stroll down Delaware Street to see the fine home of Senator Nicholas Van Dyke at number 400 and, at number 300, the home where the Marquis de Lafayette attended the wedding of Dorcas Van Dyke and Charles I. Du Pont in 1824. Near the end of the street is the spot where William Penn first set foot on New World soil in 1682. The Strand, along the Delaware River, is also lined with many fine residences.

To fortify you during your touring, lunch is served at the Immanuel Parish House, high tea at the academy building, and sandwiches at several town locations. New Castle lodgings help maintain the spirit of the past. The little David Finney Inn occupies a structure that has stood on this site in one form or another since 1688, while the William Penn Guest House is a tiny, elegantly furnished historic brick town house right across the street from the courthouse. You can also dine in historic surroundings at the New Castle Inn, once an arsenal, just behind the courthouse. The house specialty is chicken and oyster pie, and a hearty Sunday brunch is served beginning at 11 A.M.

Following brunch, having spent Saturday under the colonial spell of Old New Castle, you can move south on Sunday for some further early Delaware charm in the little historic cluster known as Odessa, and then on to Dover, the state capital.

Located midway between Wilmington and Dover, Odessa was once a thriving commercial center. Today it is a small village remarkable for its aura of that earlier time and for its rich architecture. Two of the finest homes, the Corbit-Sharp House and the Wilson-Warner House, were given to the Winterthur Museum and are maintained by this noted institution as examples of eighteenth-century elegance. The 1822 Brick Hotel has been restored as a gallery with changing exhibits.

It is 26 miles farther to Dover, a town of broad tree-lined avenues and many fine homes. The expansive lawns of Capital Square and the original Town Green, lined with redbrick government buildings, give the center of town more the look of a colonial college campus than a government seat.

Stop at the visitors center at the head of the square on Federal Street for a printed tour to guide your wanderings, or make advance arrangements with the Dover Heritage Trail for a guided walking tour.

From your brochure, you'll learn that Dover, the center of Kent County, was formally laid out in 1717 according to a plan set forth by William Penn shortly after he arrived in America. He named the town after Dover in Kent, England.

A bit of early American history was made here when Caesar Rodney, a favorite Delaware hero, galloped off to Philadelphia to sign his name to the Declaration of Independence, assuring his state's adoption of the document. It was also from Kent County that the famous Delaware Battalion marched to join Washington's main army, winning the respect of all Americans and the nickname "Blue Hen Chickens" for the spirited fighting cocks the men carried with them to war. The Blue Hen became the state bird, perhaps an omen that one day the Delmarva Peninsula would become the heart of the nation's chicken-raising industry.

Among the major sights in Dover is the Georgian-Revival State House on the Green, one of the nation's oldest. It is now used only for ceremonial occasions, and its courtrooms, legislative chambers, and governor's office were nicely restored for the bicentennial in 1976. A larger-than-life 1802 portrait of George Washington hangs in the senate chamber.

Also open to visitors is the eighteenth-century State Museum complex, whose diverse exhibits include an 1880 gallery of turn-of-the-century crafts and commercial shops; the Johnson Memorial Building, which highlights the men, machines, and music of the golden age of the American phonograph; and the Meeting House Gallery. The last is actually the restored 1790 Presbyterian church and is of interest for its circular stair and belfry and changing displays of local history.

Dover is rightfully proud of its historic homes. Many dating from the eighteenth century are clustered on South State Street near the Green. The nineteenth-century Victorian homes are farther north on South State and on South Bradford. Many of them are open for Old Dover Days early in May. The governor's lovely 1790 Georgian home on Kings Highway is also sometimes open for tours. Check for current schedules.

Dover's other showplace is the John Dickinson Mansion, a 1740 residence that was the boyhood home of one of the state's foremost early patriots, the man known as the Penman of the Revolution for his many political pamphlets and articles. The seat of a 5,000-acre plantation, the mansion faces the St. Jones River across the fields and is a fine sight in its rural setting. A fire in 1804 destroyed much of the original woodwork, but the interior has been restored with comparable period paneling.

One final attraction in Dover recommended for children is the little Delaware Agricultural Museum, where farm equipment is displayed and exhibits illustrate the evolution of the state's dairy and poultry industries. (You won't need to be told it is across the street from Dover Downs when you hear the roar of the stock-car racers.) Beside the main building there is a one-room schoolhouse, a grist mill, a sawmill, a blacksmith shop, and a typical farmhouse with outbuildings. The buildings and their contents show farm life in the late nineteenth century. It's another part of the past in a little state with a big share of history.

Area Code: 302

DRIVING DIRECTIONS   New Castle is on routes 9 and 141, both exits off I-95 a few miles southeast of Wilmington. From D.C., take I-95 north, turning off at Route 141 east. Approximate distance from D.C., 110 miles.

PUBLIC TRANSPORTATION   Amtrak, Greyhound, or Trailways to Wilmington.

ACCOMMODATIONS   *David Finney Inn,* 216 Delaware Street, New Castle, 19720, 322-6367, $$–$$$ CP ● *William Penn Guest House,* 206 Delaware Street, 19720, 328-7736, $ (no private baths) ● If no room at the inns, try these motels or go into Wilmington (see page 44): *Quality Inn–Dutch Village,* 111 South Du Pont Highway, 19720, 328-6246, $–$$ ● *Ramada Inn,* south of Delaware Memorial Bridge at US 13, 19720, 658-8511, $$.

BED AND BREAKFAST   *Bed & Breakfast of Delaware,* 1804 Breen Lane, Wilmington, DE 19810, 475-0340.

DINING   *New Castle Inn,* 1 Market Street (behind the courthouse), 328-1798, $$–$$$ ● *David Finney Inn* (see above), pleasant garden, $$–$$$ ● *Lynnhaven Inn,* 154 North Du Pont Highway, New Castle, 328-2041, early American decor, $$–$$$ ● *Blue Coat Inn,* 800 North State Street, north of town, Dover, 674-1776, seafood and colonial recipes, $$–$$$ ● *Dinner Bell Inn,* 121 South State Street, Dover, 678-1234, popular local spot, $$–$$$.

SIGHTSEEING   *A Day in Old New Castle,* P.O. Box 166, New Castle, DE 19720, 323-4453. Open House: held annually third Saturday in May 10 A.M. to 5 P.M. Adults, $10; students, $8.50 ● *George Read II House,* 42 The Strand, New Castle, 322-8411. Hours: March 1 to December 21, Tuesday to Saturday 10 A.M. to 4 p.m.; Sunday noon to 4 P.M. Adults, $3; children, $1.50 ● *Amstel House Museum*, 2 East 4th Street at Delaware Street, New Castle, 322-2794. Hours: April 1 to November 30, Tuesday to Saturday 11 A.M. to 4 P.M.; Sunday 1 P.M. to 4 P.M. Adults, $1; children, $.50 ● *Old Dutch House*, 32 North 3rd Street, 322-9168. Hours: April through November, Tuesday to Saturday 11 A.M. to 4 P.M.; Sunday 1 P.M. to 4 P.M. Adults, $1; children, $.50 ● *Old Court House*, 2nd and Delaware streets, New Castle, 323-4453. Hours: Tuesday to Saturday 10 A.M. to 4:30 P.M.; Sunday 1:30 P.M. to 4:30 P.M. Free ● *Corbit-Sharp House*, *Wilson-Warner House*, and *Brick Hotel Gallery*, Odessa. Hours: Tuesday to Saturday 10 A.M. to 4:30 P.M.; Sunday and holiday Mondays, 1 P.M. to 4:30 P.M. Adults, $3 per building, $5 for two, $6 for all three; students, $2.25, $4, and $5; under 12, free ● *Margaret O'Neill State Visitor Center*, Federal and Court streets, Dover, 736-4266. Center and all Dover historic sites open Monday to Saturday 8:30 A.M. to 4:30 P.M.; Sunday 1:30 P.M. to 4:30 P.M. Sites include *State House*, the Green; *State Museum Complex*, 316 South Governors Avenue; *John Dickinson Plantation*, Kitts Hummock Road, south of Dover. All free ● *Delaware Agricultural Museum*, 866 North Du Pont Highway, Dover, 734-1618. Hours: May to October, Tuesday to Saturday 10 A.M. to 4 P.M.; Sunday 1 P.M. to 4 P.M. Adults, $3; ages 10–16, $2; under 10, free ● *Dover Heritage Trail Walking Tours*, P.O. Box 1628, Dover, DE 19903, 678-2040.

INFORMATION Delaware Tourism Office, 99 Kings Highway, P.O. Box 1401, Dover, DE 19903. Toll free: (800) 441-8846.

Saluting the Generals in Lexington

The horse-drawn carriages trotting tourists around town seem perfectly at home on the quaint streets of Lexington, Virginia.

The feel of the past remains strong here among the brick sidewalks, nineteenth-century façades, and gracious college greens. Wherever you go, you find yourself following the paths of four great American generals, George Washington, Robert E. Lee, Thomas J. "Stonewall" Jackson, and George C. Marshall.

Thanks to the exploits of those generals, Lexington, a modest town of 4,500, attracts visitors from all over the country. In one recent month alone, there were guests from every one of the 50 states touring the home of Stonewall Jackson and the picturebook campuses of Washington and Lee and the Virginia Military Institute (VMI), where these leaders played important roles.

Yet there's more than history to lure you to Lexington in the spring. There is the lush beauty of the lower Shenandoah Valley, cradled by the Blue Ridge and Allegheny mountains—and locals will tell you it's at its loveliest in May, when the laurels burst into bloom along the Maury River.

The carriages leaving from the Historic Lexington Visitors Center are a fine way to get the lay of the land and learn some of the local lore, or you can do it on your own with walking tours provided by the visitors center. Either will take you past some two dozen fine nineteenth-century homes along Washington Street and Lee and Jackson avenues, then to the redbrick buildings and white colonnades of Washington and Lee, and finally to the austere white neo-Gothic stone façades of VMI, "the West Point of the South."

Washington and Lee, the nation's sixth-oldest college and the oldest one established inland, was an impoverished school when George Washington saved it in 1796 with a gift of $50,000 in stock. Grateful trustees immediately renamed the school Washington Academy.

It became Washington and Lee after Robert E. Lee assumed the presidency after the Civil War, with the goal of transforming a classical academy into a university that could prepare its graduates for the formidable task of rebuilding the ravaged South.

Lee turned the school into a university of national prominence. He made many advances in the curriculum, adding a school of law, introducing courses in science and engineering, laying plans for a school of commerce, and initiating the first course in journalism at an American college. His presence attracted outstanding teachers and endowments from prominent citizens, such as inventor Cyrus H. McCormick, whose farm was north of Lexington. Lee's name was added by the school in appreciation after his death.

Many of the campus landmarks are due to Robert E. Lee as well. The beautiful redbrick Lee Chapel, where he attended daily services with his students, was designed and built under his supervision in 1867. The lower level, where Lee's office stood, is now a museum whose most famous exhibit is Edward Valentine's remarkable recumbent statue of Lee. The noted Washington–Custis–Lee portrait collection is also here. In the chapel itself are the famous Charles Willson Peale portrait of George Washington as a colonel in the British army and a Pine portrait of Lee in Confederate uniform. The general and his family are buried in the crypt on the museum level.

Lee's office remains, preserved just as he left it for the last time on September 28, 1870, with papers in disarray on the desk. His faithful horse, Traveller, rests in a marked plot just outside.

By extraordinary coincidence, the Lee–Jackson House was the residence of both these Southern heroes at different times. Jackson lived in the east wing before the Civil War while he was married to Elinor Junkin, daughter of the college president. She died in childbirth, and he later remarried and moved into town.

Lee lived in the house while the President's House was being built, with a wraparound veranda where his wheelchair-bound wife could enjoy the outdoors, and a stable for Traveller. The presidents of Washington and Lee continue to live in this home.

Both the chapel and the front campus of Washington and Lee have been declared national landmarks. The long colonnade, with its wooden statue of George Washington, tempts almost everyone to whip out a camera. The statue is usually white, but has been known to take on a brighter hue after a nocturnal raid by cadets from rival VMI next door.

It is Stonewall Jackson whose statue stands on the Parade Grounds at VMI. Founded in 1839, this is the oldest state-supported military college in the nation, and the entire campus around the 12-acre Parade Grounds has been named a National Historic District. The dress parades held usually on Fridays are a treat to see; check the visitors center for the current schedule.

It was here that General Jackson taught philosophy and artillery tactics for ten years before he went off to defend his beloved Shenandoah Valley and enter the annals of America's greatest military heroes. In those days, he was known only as a stern teacher and a devout man who started a local Sunday school for blacks.

A few decades later, George C. Marshall, VMI class of 1901, began a remarkable career in Lexington that culminated in the Marshall Plan to rebuild World War II–torn Europe, making him the only professional soldier ever to earn the Nobel Peace Prize.

VMI's Military Museum in Jackson Memorial Hall holds exhibits of cadet life past and present, a kind of minihistory of the nation's past 140 years. One of the most fascinating exhibits is a replica of the cramped barracks rooms, where cadets' sleeping bags are rolled almost as compactly as their neatly folded socks. Uniforms and weapons as they changed over the years are also featured, and there is an explanation of the venerable VMI Honor Code, which inspired the movie *Brother Rat,* starring actor Ronald Reagan.

Prize exhibits in the museum are the uniform coat worn by Stonewall Jackson as a professor as well as the bullet-pierced raincoat he was wearing when he was fatally wounded at Chancellorsville. His horse, Little Sorrel, also has been mounted as a museum display.

Two small butternut jackets in the museum suggest the youthfulness of the "boy soldiers" who in 1864 marched from VMI some 80 miles north to New Market to help General Breckenridge defend the Shenandoah Valley. Ten of them lost their lives. The Cadet Chapel in Jackson Hall features a striking oil painting depicting the brave cadet charge, an event that is reenacted every year on the second Sunday in May at New Market Battlefield. The New Market museum, known as the Hall of Valor, traces all the Civil War battles in Virginia, including Stonewall Jackson's brilliant defense of the strategic Shenandoah Valley, which was the major highway between North and South, as well as the breadbasket that fed Confederate troops. His success here against overwhelming odds is one of the legendary chapters of military history.

If you go to New Market, consider a stop in Staunton for a visit to Woodrow Wilson's birthplace, and a dinner or an overnight at the Belle Grae Inn, a Victorian charmer, or at the Buckhorn, a modest country inn known for its bountiful Southern cooking and peanut butter pie. At the Buckhorn, you can ask for the room where Stonewall Jackson and his wife once slept. While you are in the neighborhood, stop at the Museum of American Frontier Culture in Staunton, a unique living museum that re-creates the farms of England, Ireland, and Germany, the cultures that settled this part of Virginia. There is also an American farmstead from the valley, reflecting the blend of European influences.

Jackson's home in Lexington, the only one he ever owned, has been restored to the way it looked when he lived here just before the Civil War, and contains many of his personal possessions. In 1857 the young widower married Mary Anna Morrison and purchased this modest house on Washington Street. They decorated it with the latest in furniture, wood stoves, and carpeting purchased on summer trips to New York and Philadelphia from 1858 to 1860. In 1861, Jackson marched off to war, never to return to the home he loved. An Edward Valentine statue of the hero stands over his grave in Stonewall Jackson Memorial Cemetery.

VMI's George C. Marshall Museum and Library uses photo murals and displays to tell the story of the man who served his country so well. Marshall reached the highest cadet rank of first captain at VMI, served as an aide to General John J. Pershing in World War I, then as army chief of staff in World War II. He was also ambassador to China, secretary of state, and secretary of defense, as well as architect of the plan that brought new life and hope to battered Europe after World War II. A 25-minute electric map presentation tracing the course of World War II shows the progress of the conflict the way the chief of staff might have viewed it.

One of the pleasures of Lexington is the opportunity it affords to alternate history with scenery. Take time out for a picnic at Goshen Pass, a breathtaking mountain gorge outside of town, or a walk along the Chessie trail, a footpath between Lexington and Buena Vista along a scenic old railroad bed beside the Maury River.

The Virginia Horse Center on Route 11 is a draw for horse lovers, with a busy schedule of shows from mid-March to mid-November, and the Lime Kiln Theater offers concerts and plays from May through September in a remarkable outdoor setting, an old kiln with a stage of stone.

A few miles south of town is the natural wonder known as Natural Bridge, whose 215-foot-high stone arch, on property once owned by Thomas Jefferson, is more imposing than its pictures convey. Not far to the west is the Blue Ridge Parkway, the remarkable road across the spine of the mountains connecting Virginia's Shenandoah National Park with the Great Smoky Mountain National Park in North Carolina. The green hillsides along the road are brightened this time of year by pink bouquets of mountain laurel and rhododendron.

You can stay right in the Lexington Historic District at McCampbell Inn or the Alexander-Withrow House, both run by Historic Country Inns of Lexington, or just out of town at their most elegant property, Maple Hall, an 1850 brick-columned mansion.

Or you might choose to drive farther south and spend at least one night at one of the most scenic accommodations anywhere in the valley, the Peaks of Otter Lodge just off the Blue Ridge Parkway. The peaks are doubly lovely, reflected in a mountain lake, and if you take the Park Service bus up to the top of Flat Top Mountain, you'll be rewarded with soaring views. Another scenic choice just off the parkway to the north is Irish Gap Inns, a stylishly furnished retreat with a swimming pond, a population of prize rabbits and bantam chickens, and views that go forever.

A mix of town and country is a perfect combination, giving you the best of both Lexington worlds.

Area Code: 703

DRIVING DIRECTIONS Lexington is at the intersection of routes I-81 north and south, 60 east, and I-64 west. From D.C., take Route 66 west, then I-81 south. Approximate distance from D.C., 193 miles.

ACCOMMODATIONS *Historic Country Inns of Lexington,* 11 North Main Street, 24450, 463-2044, includes *Alexander-Withrow House* and *McCampbell Inn* in town, and *Maple Hall* on Route 11, seven miles north of town, all $$ CP ● *Peaks of Otter Lodge,* Blue Ridge Parkway, Bedford, 24523, 586-1081, $$ ● *Irish Gap Inns,* Route 1, P.O. Box 40, Vesuvius, 24483, (804) 922-7701, $$–$$$

CP ● *Belle Grae Inn*, 515 West Frederick Street, Staunton, 24401, 886-5151, $–$$ CP ● *Buckhorn Inn*, Route 250, Churchville, 24421, 337-6900, $–$$.

BED AND BREAKFAST *Rockbridge Reservations*, Sleepy Hollow, Brownsburg, VA 24415, 348-5698.

DINING *Wilson-Walker House*, 30 North Main Street, 463-3020, fine dining in 1820s period decor, $$–$$$ ● *Southern Inn*, 37 South Main Street, 463-3612, old local standby, Southern and Greek specialties, $–$$ ● *Peaks of Otter Lodge* (see above), $–$$ ● *Belle Grae Inn* (see above), informal menu, $–$$; main dining room prix fixe, $$$ ● *Buckhorn Inn* (see above), $.

SIGHTSEEING *Stonewall Jackson House*, 8 East Washington Street, 463-2552. Hours: Monday to Saturday 9 A.M. to 5 P.M.; Sunday 1 P.M. to 5 P.M. Adults, $3.50; children, $2 ● *Lee Chapel*, Washington and Lee University, 463-8768. Hours: mid-April to mid-October, Monday to Saturday 9 A.M. to 5 P.M.; rest of year to 4 P.M.; Sunday 2 P.M. to 5 P.M. Free ● *The VMI Museum*, VMI campus, 463-6232. Hours: Monday to Saturday 9 A.M. to 5 P.M.; Sunday 2 P.M. to 5 P.M. Free ● *George S. Marshall Research Library and Museum*, VMI campus, 463-7103. Hours: Monday to Saturday 9 A.M. to 5 P.M.; Sunday 2 P.M. to 5 P.M. Free ● *Natural Bridge*, off Route 81, Natural Bridge (803) 336-5727. Hours: daily 7 A.M. to dark. Adults, $5; children, $2.50 ● *Virginia Horse Center*, P.O. Box 1051, Lexington, 463-7060. Write for horse show schedules ● *Museum of American Frontier Culture*, off Route 250 west of Staunton, P.O. Box 810, Staunton, 332-7850. Adults, $4; children, $2.

INFORMATION Historic Lexington Visitor Center, 102 East Washington Street, Lexington, VA 24450, 463-3777.

Back to Bach in Bethlehem

"Its pianissimos are worth going miles to hear and when it cuts loose in a forte the very firmament trembles. . . ."

H. L. Mencken wrote those words in 1928 after hearing the Bach Choir of Bethlehem, Pennsylvania, and thousands of music lovers who throng to Bethlehem's Bach Festival each May affirm that they are still true.

Calling itself the oldest Bach choir in the world, the group traces its origins back to Bethlehem's original Moravian settlers, who brought with them a strong musical heritage when they came to the New World in 1741.

Their Collegium Musicum gave the first full American performance of Haydn's *Creation* back in 1811. A newly formed choir continued to make musical history in the late nineteenth century with "firsts" of two of Bach's "Passions" and in 1900 gave the first rendering in this country of the composer's formidable *Mass in B Minor,* a work that has been repeated and hailed in the major concert halls of the world. The *Mass* is the highlight of the annual Bach Festival held for two weekends in May in the inspired setting of the Packer Memorial Church at Lehigh University, an occasion that is a perennial sellout.

The present Bach Choir, over 100 voices strong, is made up of devoted amateurs who sing only for the love of Bach, and they have reached a level of perfection many a professional chorus might envy. A fine accompanying orchestra that includes many professional musicians adds richness to the performances, and the reverent surroundings of a beautiful church are absolutely right.

Order your tickets early, and you will have not only a musical treat in store, but the chance to discover a community rich in history and Old World charm, with many atmospheric eighteenth- and nineteenth-century buildings, interesting museums, and one of early America's most successful industrial experiments all waiting to be explored.

The Bach Festival, which celebrates its eighty-fifth birthday in 1992, begins on Friday with late afternoon and evening concerts of cantatas and other choral works that change each year. The *Mass* is always sung on Saturday afternoon in two parts, with a long intermission that provides a welcome chance to take a stroll or sit beneath a shady tree and admire the grounds of the Lehigh campus, resplendent in spring blooms.

All of Bethlehem, in fact, is abloom during the Bach weekends, with the pinks and lilacs of azaleas softening the gray stone of historic buildings. The town bustles with activity, as local church ladies show off their best culinary skills serving lunches for music lovers, and the Moravian Book Shop on Main Street continues its longtime tradition of providing free Moravian sugar cake and coffee to all comers on Saturday morning. Many historic sites also have a special welcome mat out for visitors.

The sites are reminders that Bethlehem was one of early America's most interesting communities. A good plan for seeing the town is to start at the visitors center, located on the second floor of the restored Luckenbach Mill, where at 11 A.M. and 2 P.M. a film is shown that provides an introduction to early Bethlehem. You can also pick up a map that will guide you on a walking tour into the city's past. Two prime sites, the Moravian Museum and the Sun Inn, are closed on Sunday, so plan your time accordingly.

The Moravians, who settled the town, were a deeply religious Protestant sect determined to spread the Gospel, to the Indians as well as to their nonaffiliated neighbors. As the first of their New World colonies, Bethlehem was planned as an ideal community devoted to the church. Everyone was expected to work at the "general economy," a plan to make Bethlehem a center of trade and industry, with profits that would not only support the town but also fund missionary work.

Eventually 32 different crafts, trades, and industries were established along the banks of Monocacy Creek in the 1700s, producing goods of such high quality that buyers were attracted from miles around. Historic Bethlehem, a group devoted to preserving the town's unique past, has worked for three decades now to restore the industrial sites. So far the 1764 Spring House, the Luckenbach Grist Mill, and the 1761 Tannery have been completed, along with the 1762 Waterworks. The latter's huge wooden wheels turn once again to demonstrate how the first municipal-pumped water system in the colonies delivered water 95 feet uphill through wooden pipes to serve the town.

Another interesting building that has been restored is the once famous Sun Inn on Main Street, a lodging whose guest list included George Washington, John Adams, and General Lafayette. It is open for tours as well as for lunch and dinner in historic surroundings. Confetti Café and the Moravian Cook Shop on Main Street are convenient for a light lunch.

The Moravian church still thrives in Bethlehem. The early buildings erected by the first Moravian settlers have never needed restoration because they have been put to continual use since the 1700s. Many are now used by the Moravian Academy, a day school founded in 1856, and by Moravian College.

Residents in early Bethlehem lived in communal "choirs" divided according to age, sex, and marital status. A walking tour takes you past the Widows', Sisters', and Brethren's houses; the Bell House, where married couples lived; and the Gemein House, the oldest remaining structure in town. Even in God's Acres, the cemetery where the early settlers are buried, the plain stone markers divide them according to their earthly choirs.

Gemein House is now the site of the Moravian Museum, filled with mementos of the original settlement, and the splendid domed Central Moravian Church, built in 1803, still holds services. The first presentation of Bach's *Mass in B Minor* was given here.

Two other local museums are also of interest. The Kemmerer

Museum of Decorative Arts preserves the best furnishings of the early days, many of them owned by the museum founder, a lifetime collector of antiques. The 1810 Federal-style Goundie House was the home of a prominent Moravian brewer and includes period rooms as well as Historic Bethlehem's Shop, filled with quilts and colonial crafts.

When you've seen the sights, take a drive across the Lehigh River to get the full impact of the striking campus of Lehigh University, 700 acres and 70 buildings running uphill to the crest of South Mountain, where there are several observation points offering a commanding view of the Lehigh Valley. There are many fine residences in this area as well, running the architectural gamut from Greek Revival and Gothic Revival to Victorian. More Victorian mansions can be found back in town on East Market from New to Linden streets.

If you can't make it to Bethlehem in May, you may want to mark it down for the annual August Musicfest, when the Bach Choir usually gives a special performance, or go at Christmas, when crowds always descend for now-legendary candlelight tours. It is a special place whenever you choose to visit—but for those who love music, there's really nothing to match the rare duet of May in bloom and Bach in Bethlehem.

Area Code: 215

DRIVING DIRECTIONS Bethlehem is on Route 378 south, off Route 22. From D.C., take I-95 north to Philadelphia, connect with I-76 north, then I-176 west to Route 9 northbound, the Northeast extension of the Pennsylvania Turnpike. Get off onto US 22 east, then exit at Route 378 south to Bethlehem. Approximate distance from D.C., 201 miles.

ACCOMMODATIONS *Bethlehem Hotel,* 437 Main Street, 18018, 867-3711, centrally located, $$ ● *Econo Lodge Motel,* US 22, 18018, 867-8681, $ ● *The Bethlehem Inn,* 476 North New Street, 18018, 867-4985, 1845 B & B, $$ CP ● *Wydnor Hall,* Old Philadelphia Pike, RD 3, 18015, 867-6851, restored manor house south of town, $$$ CP.

DINING *Sun Inn,* 564 Main Street, 974-9451, $$–$$$ ● *Main Street Depot,* Main and Lehigh streets, 868-7123, restored train station, $$ ● *The Café,* 221 West Broad Street, 866-1686, combination bakery shop and Continental restaurant, $$–$$$ ● *Siam,* 81 West Broadway, 866-0448, change-of-pace Thai menu, $–$$ ● *Inn of the*

Falcon, 1740 Seidersville Road, 868-6505, Colonial country inn, $$–$$$ ● *Manor House Inn,* RD 3, Box 168, Central Valley (four miles from city limits), 865-8166, 1700s inn, French cuisine, $$–$$$.

SIGHTSEEING *Bach Choir of Bethlehem,* 423 Heckewelder Place, Bethlehem, PA 18018, 866-4382. Annual *Bach Festival,* two weekends in mid-May. General ticket sale opens March 1; phone or write for current dates and prices and *order early* ● *Eighteenth-Century Industrial Area,* walking entrance at Main Street and Ohio Road, driving entrance at South Main and Spring streets. Hours: July and August, Tuesday through Saturday 10 A.M. to 4 P.M.; Sunday noon to 4 P.M.; April to June, and September to December, Saturday and Sunday only. Adults, $3; children, $1.50. Information from Historic Bethlehem, 691-5300 ● *Moravian Museum,* 66 West Church Street, 867-0173. Hours: February to December, Tuesday to Saturday 1 P.M. to 4 P.M. Adults, $3; children, $1 ● *1810 Goundie House,* 501 Main Street, 691-5300. Hours: Monday to Friday noon to 4 P.M.; Saturday 10 A.M. to 4 P.M.; Sunday noon to 4 P.M. Free ● *Kemmerer Museum of Decorative Arts,* 427 North New Street, 868-6868. Hours: February to December, Tuesday to Friday 1 P.M. to 4 P.M.; Saturday 10 A.M. to 4 P.M.; Sunday 1 P.M. to 4 P.M. Donation ● *Sun Inn,* 564 Main Street, 974-9451. Hours: Tuesday to Friday 12:30 P.M. to 4 P.M.; Saturday 10 A.M. to 4 P.M. Tours: adults, $2; students, $1.50.

INFORMATION The Visitors Center, Bethlehem Chamber of Commerce, 459 Old York Road, Bethlehem, PA 18018, 868-1513. Hours: Monday to Friday 9 A.M. to 5 P.M.; Saturday 10 A.M. to 4 P.M. Orientation film admission, $1.50.

Having a Fling at Fair Hill

Highland Games are a Scottish tradition that has been around as long as anyone can remember. The bagpipes, nimble dancing, and unique sporting competitions that mark these events are loved by Scots no matter where they live—which is lucky for all of us, since the tradition is kept alive in the United States and everyone is invited to watch.

One lovely setting where this tradition thrives is Fair Hill, Maryland, which hosts the Colonial Highland Games. The twenty-fifth anniversary of the event was marked in 1987. The same grounds that host some of the top steeplechase racing events each year make an ideal backdrop for the gathering, with fields of tall grass waving in the wind, lending a faraway feeling to it all.

You can round out the weekend by visiting the nearby famous gardens of the Brandywine Valley, or by getting acquainted with the many attractions even closer in Wilmington, Delaware.

The only problem you face at Fair Hill is where to look first, for this daylong event boasts more attractions than a three-ring circus. Some of the more diverting are the athletic competitions.

According to legend, the Highland Games began as a kind of informal athletic test allowing kings and clan chiefs to pick the best men available for their forces. It still takes a mighty man to prevail. The main event, the Highland Heptathlon, is actually seven events that demand great strength and endurance. During the course of the action, participants lift and throw at least 1,000 pounds as they compete at weight, stone, and hammer tosses. The various missiles weigh anywhere from 16 to 56 pounds.

But all of the preliminaries pale before the incredible "tossing of the caber." A caber looks much like a telephone pole, measuring 16 feet in length and weighing over 150 pounds. Heaving the heavy pole is a feat to try even the halest, and some contestants find they can hardly *lift* the caber, much less toss it anywhere. Yet each year a few stout lads emerge who seem to have inherited the prowess of their ancestors and manage to give the king-size missile a prodigious toss that sets off wild cheering from the sidelines.

A far different but equally fascinating Fair Hill event is the championship sheepdog trials. One by one, each dog is given exactly 12 minutes to herd a flock of five sheep through and around a far-flung obstacle course of fences and into a pen. All that these carefully trained canine contestants have to guide them are the distant whistles of their masters, which they recognize as signals to go right, left, forward, or back. To see these wonderfully bright animals steering their charges around the course at top speed is nothing less than mesmerizing.

When you've had your fill of the flocks, seat yourself back in the bleachers to watch yet another kind of competition, a parade of fair lads and lassies clad in bright kilts, tunics, and plaid knee socks nimbly performing classic dances such as the Highland Fling, the Sailor's Hornpipe, and the Sword Dance while the judges rate their skill at executing the carefully prescribed steps of each dance. You'll appreciate their grace even more when you know that Highland dancing also originated as an athletic event, and dancers still must be in top physical shape to perform the vigorous dances. Until recently, dancing was used by Scottish regiments as a regular drill to develop stamina, agility, and endurance. The youngest contenders start in the morning, followed by big brothers and sisters and finally by the adults.

At the same time, off to the side of the field, pipers and drummers in full regalia are vying, first individually and then as bands, in the bagpipe competitions. The contestants, in colorful plaids, come from throughout the mid-Atlantic states.

There are even more diversions along the sidelines. Two teams of spinners and weavers are at work producing shawls that will be auctioned off to the highest bidder at 3 P.M. Mock warriors appear wearing shields and coats of mail, or armor, to reenact a sword fight, medieval style. Food booths tempt with Scottish specialties from scones to meat pies to fish and chips. A whole rainbow of tartan plaids are for sale, by the yard or as kilts or tams. Over at the Tea Barn beginning at noon, you can sit back and enjoy traditional Scottish music and learn Scottish dance steps from members of the Royal Scottish Country Dance Society.

But twice, during the midday ceremonies and after the awards are announced, everything else stops for the most colorful event of them all, the massed pipe bands parading the field in an unforgettable splash of color and sound.

Most of the real action begins at noon and continues all afternoon, so there is plenty of time on Saturday morning and Sunday for other diversions to fill out a trip to the games. Fair Hill is in the very northeastern corner of the state, just a few miles from the Delaware-Pennsylvania border. It's an easy drive to Longwood Gardens, the most outstanding floral attraction in the Northeast, or to Winterthur, the house-museum famed as the site of the foremost collection of early American antiques and furnishings. The annual two-month Winterthur in Spring event features 16 rooms not normally on display to visitors, in addition to the regular Two Centuries 18-room tour, and a tour of the 64-acre gardens, a woodland wonderland of rare azaleas, rhododendrons, and other prize plants. For more on these two exceptional sites, see ''Dropping in on the Du Ponts of Delaware,'' page 156.

Or you might choose to stay in Wilmington and take the opportunity to explore a pleasant small city that is often overlooked because of the many top attractions around it. With a zoo and train rides, the town has plenty to offer families.

Take a walk along the new Brandywine Gateway Park office complex and then on Market Street Mall to see the new vitality that is evident in downtown Wilmington as new buildings spring up and older structures are restored and turned into apartments, offices, and lively new restaurants. Pick up a handy printed walking-driving tour guide from the convention and visitors bureau to make your tour more meaningful.

Willingtown Square at the 500 block on the mall was a preservation effort that saved four of the city's early 1700s homes, moving them to this site. The Old Town Hall, headquarters for the historical society, has been turned into a small, worthwhile museum filled with historic mementos and fine early furnishings from the area. Kids love the old jail cell in the basement and the displays of old children's toys. One of the prize restorations on the mall is the Grand Opera House at Eighth Street. The state's most important Victorian landmark, it has been turned back to its early grandeur and now serves as Delaware's Center for the Performing Arts.

Walking farther on Market toward the Brandywine Creek brings you to a picturesque neighborhood known as Old Brandywine Village, once a prosperous milling center and now the site of many handsomely restored stone houses that were the homes of mill owners.

A lovely 80-acre park designed by Frederick Law Olmsted along the meandering Brandywine Creek is a welcome oasis of green in the midst of the city. Frequently the Fair Hill Gathering weekend coincides with the annual local Restaurant Festival held on a May Sunday in Brandywine Park, giving you the chance to sample some of the best of local eateries while you stroll. The park also has a zoo.

Not far away along tree-lined Kentmere Parkway is the Delaware Art Museum, boasting the country's largest collection of English Pre-Raphaelite art, as well as works by American artists from Thomas Eakins to Winslow Homer and Robert Indiana, and illustrations by the famous Brandywine School of artists, which included N. C. Wyeth, Frank Schoonover, and Howard Pyle. Don't overlook the excellent Museum Shop or, for that matter, the Eclectic Depot, the shop run by the historical society at its headquarters.

Besides Winterthur, Longwood, and the many other Du Pont properties detailed beginning on page 156, Wilmington offers the Rockwood Museum, a nineteenth-century country estate with a conservatory and a garden landscaped in the Romantic style, and some interesting landmarks on Church Street that recall the town's Swedish origins. Here you'll see the Hendrickson House Museum, a restored 1690 Swedish farmhouse, and the adjacent Old Swedes Church, a 1698 structure said to be the oldest church in the United States. The site of the Swedish landing in 1698, the first permanent settlement in Delaware, is marked at Fort Christina at the foot of Seventh Street.

It is interesting to see the activity at the busy Port of Wilmington at the bottom of Christina and Terminal avenues, the closest Delaware River port to the sea. Another pleasant local diversion is a nostalgic ride on the Wilmington and Western Steam Railroad, located on Route 41 in Greenbank Park.

Depending on the season, evening entertainment in Wilmington features drama, music, and dance at the Grand Opera House, action at the Brandywine Raceway, or drama by the Delaware Theater Company in the Hotel Du Pont. The hotel is worth a tour to appreciate its grand public rooms and fine art collection.

You'll find more than enough to do in and around Wilmington to fill out a weekend, an ideal complement to a Fair Hill fling.

Area Codes: Fair Hill, Maryland, 301; Wilmington, Delaware, 302

DRIVING DIRECTIONS   Fair Hill, Maryland, is 13 miles west of Wilmington, Delaware, at the intersection of routes 213 and 273. Take I-95 north toward Wilmington. From I-95, follow Route 273 west to Fair Hill; from Wilmington follow Route 2. To reach Longwood Gardens from Fair Hill, take Route 841 north and turn right on Route 1 to Kennett Square, Pennsylvania. For Winterthur, follow Route 2 east to Wilmington and turn left on Route 52 headed northwest. Continue on Route 52 to intersect with Route 1 at Kennett Square. Approximate distance from D.C., 106 miles.

PUBLIC TRANSPORTATION   Amtrak has excellent service to Wilmington's train station, bus transportation is available via Greyhound or Trailways, and there is a regular shuttle service to Wilmington from Philadelphia International Airport.

ACCOMMODATIONS   The closest lodgings to Fair Hill are in Newark, the attractive home of the University of Delaware. *Residence Inn by Marriott,* 240 Chapman Road (Route 273), Newark, 19713, 453-9200, all suites, $$$ • *Comfort Inn,* 1120 College Avenue, Newark, 19713, 368-8715, $ • *Sheraton Inn,* 260 Chapman Road, Newark, 19713, 738-3400, $$ • *Newark Holiday Inn– Wilmington Area,* 1203 Christina Road, 19713, 737-2700, $$ • *Hotel Du Pont,* Rodney Square, 11th and Market streets, Wilmington, 19801, 594-3125, $$$–$$$$, ask about excellent weekend package plans • *Radisson Wilmington,* 700 King Street, 19801, 655-0400, $$$, ask about weekend packages • *Christina House,* 707 King Street, Wilmington, 19801, 656-9300, all suites, $$$–$$$$ • *Marriott Wilmington Suites,* 422 Delaware Avenue, Wilmington, 19806, 654-8300, $$$$ • See also Brandywine Valley listings, page 199.

BED AND BREAKFAST   *Bed and Breakfast of Delaware,* 1804 Breen Lane, Wilmington, DE 19810, 475-0340.

DINING   *Fair Hill Inn,* routes 273 and 213, Fair Hill, MD, 398-4187, historic home, Continental fare, $$–$$$ • *Brandywine*

Room, Hotel Du Pont (see above), walnut paneling, a million dollars worth of Wyeths on the walls, $$$–$$$$ ● *Green Room, Hotel Du Pont* (see above), old-world elegance, $$$–$$$$ ● *Buckley's Tavern,* 5812 Kennett Pike, Centreville, DE (outside Wilmington), 656-9776, charm, roof terrace in spring, $$–$$$ ● *Bellevue in the Park,* 911 Philadelphia Pike, Wilmington, 798-7666, French and Continental in a restored Du Pont mansion, $$–$$$ ● *Harry's Savoy Grill,* 2020 Naamans Road, 475-3000, handsome traditional decor, $$$ ● *Columbus Inn,* 2216 Pennsylvania Avenue, Wilmington, 571-1492, colonial flavor in historic building, $$–$$$ ● *Tiffin,* 1208 North Market Street, 571-1133, contemporary decor, a local favorite, $$–$$$ ● *Christina House Bistro,* 707 King Street, Wilmington, 656-9300, informal, $–$$ ● *The Silk Purse,* 1307 North Street, Wilmington, 654-7666, fine dining, $$$–$$$$ ● *The Polo Club,* 3801 Kennett Pike, Greenville Center, 655-5266, grilled foods and pasta, dancing on Saturday night, $–$$.

SIGHTSEEING *Colonial Highland Gathering,* Fair Hill, MD, usually third Saturday in May, 9 A.M. to 5 P.M. For current date and admission fees, contact William Whisler, 2614 Darby Drive, Wilmington, DE 19808, 994-0134 ● *Old Town Hall,* 512 Market Street, Wilmington, 655-7161. Hours: Tuesday to Friday noon to 4 P.M.; Saturday 10 A.M. to 4 P.M. Donation ● *Delaware Art Museum,* 2301 Kentmere Parkway, Wilmington, 571-9590. Hours: Tuesday to Saturday 10 A.M. to 5 P.M.; Sunday noon to 5 P.M.; open Tuesday to 9 P.M. Free ● *Brandywine Zoo,* North Park Drive, Brandywine Park, Wilmington, 571-7788. Hours: October to March, daily 10 A.M. to 4 P.M. Adults, $2; ages 3–12, $1. Children under 3 free. ● *Fort Christina,* foot of 7th Street, 652-5629. Hours: Tuesday to Saturday noon to 4 P.M. Free ● *Old Swedes Church and Hendrickson House Museum,* 606 Church Street, 652-5629. Hours: Tuesday to Saturday noon to 4 P.M. Donation.

INFORMATION Greater Wilmington Convention & Visitors Bureau, 130 Market Street, Suite 505, Wilmington, DE 19801, 652-4088 ● Cecil County Office of Planning & Economic Development, County Office Building, Room 300, Elkton, MD 21911, 398-0200.

Down to the Sea at Solomons

Will success spoil Solomons Island? That's the question that worries the locals. The word is out about this miniature fishing village in southern Maryland, a quaint dot on Chesapeake Bay joined to the mainland by a bridge built on a bed of oyster shells, and the tourists and yachtsmen are coming faster every year.

But while things are changing and condos and motels are moving in fast, so far the spirit of Solomons is intact.

You can still come down on a fine day in May or June and feel a million miles away from the city, sniffing the salt air, watching the boats go by, and savoring a seafood dinner on an outdoor deck facing the water.

There's every good reason for a visit in late spring, in fact, because that's when the Calvert Marine Museum, the main sightseeing attraction in town, holds its annual Waterside Music Festival, a pleasant bring-your-own-blanket-and-wine affair. To add to the weekend's fun, there's the chance to scout for fossils, watch an archaeological dig in progress, or stroll beneath tall cypress trees in nearby Calvert County parks.

If you rent a catamaran at Sail Solomons or sign on for a charter or a fishing cruise at one of the many marinas, you'll need no further guidance as to how to spend your time in Solomons. And if you are a landlubber, there is just enough to do to keep things interesting when you tire of gazing out to sea.

The place to start is the Marine Museum, whose Drum Point Lighthouse has become Solomons's landmark. The 1883 structure, moved here in 1975 for restoration, is one of only three octagonal cottage-type lights remaining of the 45 that served Chesapeake Bay waters at the turn of the century. In the new museum building, galleries deal with three themes: boat building and maritime history; the plant and animal life of Chesapeake Bay and its Patuxent River arm; and the rich fossil deposits that lie at nearby Calvert Cliffs. Among the favorites are the boat-building gallery with its three-log, 28-foot Poquoson canoe, and the "Life of the Waterman" exhibit, showing the ways that fish, clams, oysters, and crabs are harvested. A film here features local watermen. The ship model and ship-carving shop has artisans at work, demonstrating their crafts.

At the Oyster House annex, half a mile south, there is more to be seen that tells the story of the fishing, clamming, crabbing, and oystering industries that once were Solomons' mainstay. Among the exhibits are re-created settings of a fisherman's shanty and a clam house.

And if all the talk of boats makes you want to get out to sea, you can take a cruise around the harbor and the Patuxent River on the museum's 60-foot 1899 bugeye, the *William B. Tennison,* the oldest licensed passenger vessel on Chesapeake Bay.

A complete tour of the rest of Solomons on land will take you about five minutes by car and fifteen on foot, that's how compact things are. A local sign tells you that back in 1680 Solomons was known as Bourne's. The island later took its name from one Isaac Solomon, who established a large oyster-packing operation here. It was also headquarters for several shipyards that developed to support the fishing fleet, known best for the bugeye sailing craft, like the *William B. Tennison,* that were built here in the nineteenth century. The deep, protected harbor has been a busy marine center ever since, though most of the industry today is pleasure boating.

A stroll around the island shows you marinas, the requisite white church, an old wooden pavilion, and the fine view from Sandy Point, where the Patuxent River and the bay converge. There's the old Bowen Inn with its 1926 taproom, the Lighthouse Properties building, whose owners still display wares from the general store that was here until 1912. Seafood restaurants are plentiful, and there are half a dozen little shops to explore, a try-your-luck potpourri with names like Island Trader, Grandmother's Store, and Cozy Cupboard offering crafts and antiques.

One modern brick-and-glass structure near the point seems out of place, but gives a hint of Solomons's possible future. It is the Chesapeake Biological Laboratory, a top marine scientific facility. Among other projects, it is working with the Calvert Marine Museum and the Maryland Historical Trust to study the vast marine and archaeological resources of the Patuxent and the bay. Some foresee Solomons developing as a rival of the well-known marine research complex in Woods Hole, Massachusetts.

If you while away a lazy Saturday in Solomons and want a change of scene on Sunday, you'll find much more to see and do nearby. Follow the graceful arching bridge over the Patuxent, and you can explore some of the history in neighboring St. Mary's County, namely Sotterley, an eighteenth-century plantation, and St. Mary's City, a re-creation of Maryland's earliest settlement.

Heading back toward Washington along Route 4 brings you to Calvert Cliffs State Park, covering 30 miles of shoreline on the western side of Chesapeake Bay. The high cliffs here, some dating back as much as 15 million years, were formed by winds and waves from ancient sea floors. The cliffs are famous for their Miocene fossils, and you may want to join the scouters looking for fossils along the open beach. No digging is allowed, but if your eagle eye spots a find, it's yours. In season, naturalists conduct guided fossil talks. There are also 13 miles of hiking trails.

A bit farther along Route 4, take a detour to Jefferson Patterson Park for another fascinating look at the past. The 512-acre park is the site of 52 identified archaelogical sites, some dating back to 7500 B.C. Digs are now in progress, and visitors are invited to watch the painstaking work of the archaeologists who sift and dig for ancient treasures. Some of their finds are on display in a visitors center.

Finally, Battle Creek Cypress Swamp Sanctuary is a 100-acre preserve for nature lovers who want to walk among the tall trees in the northernmost natural stand of bald cypress in America. The trees are unique, standing from 50 to 125 feet tall and having "knees" of roots as high as 4 feet. The park has been certified as a natural landmark. You can view the trees on your own or on a guided tour of the swamp along a one-fourth-mile elevated boardwalk.

Having left Solomons seafood behind, you might want to wind things up with a traditional Sunday dinner at either of two attractive Calvert County restaurants, the Penwick House in Dunkirk or the Old Field Inn in Prince Frederick. Both are located in lovely historic homes and are guaranteed to end the weekend on a gracious note.

Area Code: 301

DRIVING DIRECTIONS   Solomons is at the southern tip of routes 2 and 4. From D.C., follow Route 4 (the Pennsylvania Avenue extension) east to Route 4/2 south. Approximate distance from D.C., 67 miles. From Baltimore and points north, take Route 3/301 south to Route 4 south.

ACCOMMODATIONS   *Back Creek Inn,* Calvert and A streets, 20688, 326-2022, right on the water, but few rooms, so reserve early, $–$$ ● *Davis House,* Charles and Maltby streets, Solomons, 20688, 326-4811, a small Victorian charmer, $ CP ● *Comfort Inn,* P.O. Box 869, 20688, 326-6303, motel with pool, $$ ● *Holiday Inn by the Bay,* P.O. Box 97, 20688, 326-6311, $$.

DINING   All Solomons restaurants specialize in seafood and water views; reservations are recommended on weekends. *Pier 1,* routes 2 and 4, 326-3261, $–$$$ ● *The Dry Dock,* C Street, 326-4817, $$–$$$ ● *Lighthouse Inn,* Patuxent Avenue, 326-2444, $$–$$$ ● *Solomons Pier,* routes 2 and 4, 326-2424, $$–$$$ ● *Harbor View,* Main Street, Harbor Island Marina, 326-3202, $$–$$$ ● *The Old Field Inn,* Main Street, Prince Frederick, 535-1054, $$–$$$ ● *Penwick House,* Route 4 and Ferry Landing Road, Dunkirk, 257-7077, $$–$$$.

SIGHTSEEING   *Calvert Marine Museum,* routes 2 and 4, P.O. Box 97, 326-2042. Hours: May to September, Monday to Saturday

10 A.M. to 5 P.M.; Sunday noon to 5 P.M.; rest of year to 4:30 P.M. Free ● *Drum Point Lighthouse & J.C. Lore & Sons Oysterhouse.* Hours: May to October, Monday to Saturday 10 A.M. to 5 P.M.; Sunday noon to 5 P.M. Combined admission: adults, $1; children, $.50 ● *William B. Tennison Boat Cruises.* Hours: May to October, 1-hour cruise, Wednesday to Sunday 2 P.M. Adults, $3.50; children, $2.50; family rate, $12 ● *Waterside Music Festival,* late May. Contact Calvert Marine Museum for this year's schedule and rates ● *Calvert Cliffs State Park,* routes 2 and 4 south of Lusby, 326-4728, March to October. Hours: daily sunrise to sunset. Free ● *Jefferson Patterson Park and Museum,* Mackall Road (Route 265), 586-0050. Hours: mid-April to mid-October, Wednesday to Sunday 10 A.M. to 5 P.M. Free ● *Battle Creek Cypress Swamp Sanctuary,* Grays Road off Route 506, 535-5327. Hours: April to September, Tuesday to Saturday 10 A.M. to 5 P.M., Sunday 1 P.M. to 5 P.M.; October to March until 4:30 P.M. Free.

INFORMATION Calvert County Tourism, Courthouse, Prince Frederick, 20678, 535-4583 or 855-1880.

Tea and Serenity in Chestertown

People in Chestertown, Maryland, like to boast that *their* revolutionary "Tea Party" was far more daring than the one held in darkness by those publicity-grabbers in Boston.

It was broad daylight on May 23, 1774, when a band rowed out to the brigantine *Geddes,* moored in Chestertown harbor, and tossed the tea on board into the brink, an act that is re-created with great gusto every year on the Saturday before Memorial Day.

The whole town turns out for the fun—a morning colonial parade complete with fife and drum corps, demonstrations of colonial crafts from boat building to candle making, an art show, walking tours of the historic district, and all kinds of music and entertainment from puppet shows to choir concerts. There is a lot of prize Maryland Eastern Shore eating, from fried chicken to crab cakes.

They are celebrating a long-ago time when this small town was a major stop on the main land route between Philadelphia and the Virginia colony, not to mention one of Maryland's most prosperous ports, with a prime location just 20 miles upriver from Chesapeake Bay. In those days the 1746 customs house, still standing beside the

Chester River, was a bustling center for cargo from around the world.

As time passed, cities like Baltimore overshadowed Chestertown as a port, and the town did not grow or change for many years—which has turned out to be a very good thing for anyone today who loves strolling picturesque brick-paved lanes lined with prize eighteenth-century architecture.

The present riverfront is a treasury of fine homes dating back to the golden days of 1730–1775, many of them the gracious brick mansions of merchants and shipowners who grew wealthy along with the young town. The entire center of town has been declared a historic district. Bring the kids for the Tea Party fun, but come back to Chestertown when all is serene to experience a tranquil stroll into the past.

The local walking tour, available free in many of the shops on High Street, concentrates on Water Street and its eighteenth-century showplaces along the river. The old customs house next to the landing on Water Street was used as both business and residence, and like most of Chestertown's finest homes, it is notable for its Flemish bond brickwork with glazed headers (the shorter end of the bricks) forming patterns within the overall façade. Using headers meant more brick and extra expense, a kind of colonial conspicuous consumption particularly popular here.

The local showplace is Wide Hall, at 101 Water Street, a Georgian beauty built in 1770 by the town's wealthiest merchant, John Smythe, with a show-off exterior of all header bricks. Along with many of the riverfront houses, Wide Hall was later embellished with lovely gardens extending to the water's edge, and porches on the rear of the house for taking in the view.

The interiors of the houses are equally impressive. At River House, built by John Smythe's son, Richard, at 107 Water Street, the woodwork in an upstairs bedroom was so beautiful it was removed to the Winterthur Museum near Wilmington, Delaware, where it now adorns a chamber known as the Chestertown Room. All the fine homes are privately owned, but they do open once a year for the annual Candlelight Walking Tour held in the historic district in mid-September.

One home that does welcome visitors is the Geddes Piper House, a Philadelphia-style town house restored by the Historical Society of Kent County and filled with period furnishings to show what life was like in Chestertown in the eighteenth century. The Buck Bacchus Store Museum, restored to its 1700s appearance as a residence, is also open to the public. It displays household articles from the nineteenth and early twentieth centuries, when it also served as a general store.

Queen Street and Lawyers Row are other lanes worth exploring. The Nicholson House, at 111 Queen, home of a family of early naval heroes, is one of the few Federal-style houses in Chestertown. Picturesque Lawyers Row is a line of small Victorian buildings designed for law offices around 1840 and still used by local attorneys. There are many fine examples of later architecture such as these interspersed among the oldest buildings.

One other building of note is the Emmanuel Protestant Episcopal Church, where a 1780 convention voted to withdraw officially from the Church of England and take the Episcopal name, which was soon adopted everywhere in America.

Take a short drive to Washington College to see the only campus that George Washington personally sanctioned to use his name. Legend says that he even helped sell lottery tickets to finance the establishment of the college in 1782 as Maryland's first institution of higher learning. The original buildings were lost to a fire in 1827, but the redbrick nineteenth-century campus still merits a look.

Chestertown is not a shopping mecca, but on High Street you will find a few interesting browsing spots, many with art and gifts featuring the wild ducks and geese that abound on Chesapeake Bay.

Two of the inns on High Street are unusual enough to merit a stop for sightseeing. It would not be surprising if someone in colonial garb answered the door of the White Swan Tavern, so authentic is this restoration of an early 1700s lodging. New owners ordered an archaeological dig on the site to be sure the restoration was accurate. When the inn reopened in 1981, a display case was installed downstairs to show some of the dig's finds—clay pipes, wineglasses, stoneware mugs, and ale glasses, all used on this very spot centuries ago. The authentically furnished period rooms have enormous charm, but there are only five of them, so reserve early! The White Swan serves afternoon tea, a perfect way to visit if you can't get a room.

Across the street the Imperial Hotel re-creates a later period. The 1903 hotel will delight anyone who likes Victorian froufrou. The rooms are small for their tab, but beautifully furnished. You can also sample the ambience in the fancy dining rooms. Or you may choose among some very appealing inns in the countryside not far from town.

Chestertown's environs are flat, open areas leading to the bay, ideal territory for bikers. And bird-watchers will appreciate the many species to be spotted at the Eastern Neck National Wildlife Refuge or Remington Farms, both major resting places for migratory and wintering waterfowl. October to March is peak time for the birds, but the wildlife refuge offers nature trails that are pleasant strolls year-round, and rowboats are for rent just outside the entrance for fishing or crabbing in the bay. All it takes to try your hand at crabbing is a piece of string, a chicken neck, a pail, and lots of patience.

On the way to the refuge you'll pass Rock Hall, a tiny town with an interesting history of its own. Travelers once crossed the bay by packet from Annapolis to Rock Hall and boarded the stage here for Philadelphia and New York. You can see replicas of earlier days in the little town museum on Main Street. Rock Hall is also the place to charter a sailboat to get out on the bay. Just ask at any of the marinas.

For further exploring, take a drive through more of the picturesque villages that dot Maryland's Eastern Shore. To the south on Route 213 is Centreville, whose 1792 courthouse is the oldest in the state. To the north in Georgetown, you can dine in the former home of the legendary Mistress Kitty Knight, a heroine said to have saved the town from the British during the War of 1812, or tour an eighteenth-century tobacco plantation with formal boxwood gardens at Mt. Harmon Plantation, on the banks of the Sassafras River in Earleville.

Then again, you might be happy never leaving Chestertown at all, just meandering down to the landing to sit awhile watching the sailboats go by and admiring the gardens behind the houses on the river, then strolling back to the White Swan, just in time for your own afternoon tea party.

Area Code: 301

DRIVING DIRECTIONS   Chestertown is on Route 213. From D.C., follow Route 50/301 east across the Chesapeake Bay Bridge to Route 213 north. Approximate distance from D.C., 80 miles. From the north, take Route 301 south to Route 213 south.

ACCOMMODATIONS   *White Swan Tavern,* 231 High Street, Chestertown, 21620, 778-2300, $$$ CP ● *Imperial Hotel,* High Street, 21620, 778-5000, $$$ ● Some appealing lodgings are in the countryside outside town: *The Inn at Mitchell House,* P.O. Box 329, RD 2, Tolchester Estates, 21620, 778-6500, an informal, homey farmhouse on ten acres overlooking a pond, $$–$$$ CP ● *Great Oak Manor,* RD 2, P.O. Box 766, 21620, 778-5796, a 25-room mansion overlooking the bay that offers guests pool, golf, and tennis privileges at the nearby Great Oak Landing resort, $$$ CP ● *Brampton Hall,* RD 2, P.O. Box 107, 21620, 778-1860, a beautiful 1860s mansion on nicely landscaped grounds, 1 mile south of town, $$–$$$ CP.

BED AND BREAKFAST *Inns of Kent,* P.O. Box 609, Chester-town, MD 21620, listings of small B&B inns, 788-INNS; outside Maryland, 800-662-INNS.

DINING No visit to Chesapeake Bay is complete without a sampling of seafood. You'll find it in Chestertown. *Old Wharf Inn,* foot of Cannon Street, 778-3566, $–$$$$ ● In Rock Hall there are informal dockside eateries, such as *Waterman's Crabhouse,* Sharp Street Wharf, Rock Hall, 778-1803, $–$$ ● *Fin, Fur, and Feather Inn,* 424 Bayside Avenue, Rock Hall, 639-7454, fish and game specialties, $$–$$$ ● For more formal dining: *Imperial Hotel* (see above), $$$ ● *Great Oak Landing,* Handy Point Road, Chestertown, 778-2100, $$–$$$.

SIGHTSEEING *Geddes Piper House,* 101 Church Alley. Hours: May to October, Saturday and Sunday 1 P.M. to 4 P.M. Adults, $1; children, $.50 ● *Buck-Bacchus Store Museum,* High and Queen streets. Hours: May to October, Saturday 1 P.M. to 4 P.M. Admission: $1.50.

INFORMATION Kent County Chamber of Commerce, Inc., P.O. Box 146, 118 North Cross Street, Chestertown, MD 21620, 778-0416.

Show of Shows near Philadelphia

You don't have to be a horse lover to enjoy the festivities at the country's largest outdoor horse show, in Devon, Pennsylvania.

Nor need you be an art connoisseur to appreciate one of the world's outstanding private collections of Impressionist art, on display at the Barnes Foundation, a stunning show of 200 Renoirs, prize works by Matisse, Picasso, Van Gogh, and Rousseau, and more Cézannes than can be found in any one place outside the Louvre.

Put these two together just outside Philadelphia, add a dozen historic homes for touring, fine gardens for strolling, and posh shops for browsing, and you have all the makings for a show-stopper weekend, one that could pleasurably fill the three-day Memorial Day holiday.

The Devon event, billed as the Horse Show and Country Fair, began as a one-day fund-raiser, a genteel Main Line affair augmenting equestrian competition with a minivillage of quaint thatched-roof cottages where you could have tea served from silver teapots and buy country-fresh fruits and vegetables. It has grown to nine jam-packed days beginning Memorial Day weekend and has expanded to an 18-acre site.

But despite the addition of hoopla, midway rides, and booths where you can try your skill at winning a teddy bear, there is still an undeniable air of class about the whole thing. The vendors are housed in the same fairy-tale pastel-blue cottages built in 1919, unchanged except for "modernization" with wood shingled roofs. Along with crafts and horsey equipment and souvenirs, they offer boutiques from stores like Ralph Lauren, Bloomingdale's, and Strawbridge and Clothier, hardly the sort of thing you'd find at an ordinary country fair. You can still find tea sandwiches at some of the food stalls, and the pretty young girls vending "slurping lemon sticks," a Devon tradition, are obviously young socialites in the making. The entire fair is run by volunteers for the benefit of nearby Bryn Mawr Hospital, which over the years has gained more than $5 million from the event.

As for the horse show itself, almost 3,000 riders now compete for more than $100,000 worth of prizes before audiences numbering over 150,000. The action in the arena can be breath-stopping when the champs go through their paces, gracefully leaping high over the hurdles. This is a serious competition, the first chance to accumulate the points needed to qualify for the November National Horse Show Championship at Madison Square Garden, and the riders are top-notch.

But it is also fun to watch some of the junior events, featuring riders as young as four, five, and six, and the Family Class, where families compete as precision units. The Carriage Class brings out dozens of drivers in colorful period dress and high-stepping teams of pacers pulling fancy rigs.

Besides the competitions, there is plenty of exhilarating entertainment, from precision drill teams to acrobatic riders and marching bands.

It's a good idea to write ahead for the Devon schedule so you can pick the particular events you want to attend. This will also allow you to plan your visit to the Barnes Foundation, in Merion, Pennsylvania, about 20 minutes away.

This extraordinary art collection can be seen only three days a week, and reservations are well advised, since only 200 visitors are admitted on Fridays and Saturdays, and 100 on Sundays—and half of those are by prior appointment.

If the hours sound limited, they are actually a great improvement over the past, because for years the Albert Coombs Barnes collection of masterpieces was closed to the public. The story goes that Barnes was ahead of his time in recognizing the talent of many painters and he bought up canvases wholesale before the rest of the world caught on—50 Renoirs at a time, the first major purchases of Modigliani's work, and 60 Soutines at $50 per canvas. But the Philadelphia critics were not so astute, and when Barnes showed his acquisitions in a 1923 show at the Pennsylvania Academy of Art, the reviews were so vicious that Barnes withdrew from the art establishment. When he built his 24-room museum the next year, only handpicked art students and a few favored individuals were allowed to call. Barnes's will saw to it that his foundation remained almost inaccessible to the public until the State of Pennsylvania intervened in 1961, ten years after his death, and ruled that a tax-free educational institution had to allow the public inside to be educated.

The display of floor-to-ceiling and wall-to-wall paintings is all but overwhelming. Besides the most famous Impressionist works, the Barnes Foundation boasts outstanding Klees and Mirós, plus prize paintings by old masters such as El Greco, Daumier, Titian, and Tintoretto. Some say that the perverse Barnes deliberately hung his best paintings at the ceiling, so bring along a pair of binoculars if you want to decide for yourself.

Barnes was also interested in horticulture, and one of the pleasures of a spring visit is the 12-acre arboretum surrounding the foundation, filled with rare-specimen trees, shrubs, and flowers.

If you see the Barnes collection on Saturday morning, you will have Saturday afternoon left to discover some of the more beautiful and historic outlying sections of Philadelphia, the Chestnut Hill and Germantown neighborhoods, which visitors to the center of the city often miss.

Germantown's cobblestoned, tree-lined streets and centuries-old stone houses bear witness to a community that dates back to 1683, when William Penn deeded an area six miles northwest of Philadelphia to a group of German Quaker and Mennonite settlers. It was the site of a pitched battle between Continental and British forces in 1777, and after the Revolutionary War it was developed as a rural retreat for Philadelphia's elite. The arrival of one of America's first commuter railroads transformed Germantown into the city's first modern suburb, and by the 1850s, gingerbread Victorian homes had joined the original stone architecture. The area went downhill in this century and is only now reviving as a desirable place to live, but thanks to a group known as Historic Germantown, many of the finest historic homes have been beautifully maintained and are open to the public.

You could, in fact, easily spend a whole day touring homes here. Your choices may depend on the hours, since some houses are not open on Sunday, while others are open *only* on Sunday.

One must is Cliveden, a superb Georgian country house built in 1763 by Benjamin Chew, chief justice of Pennsylvania. It is now maintained by the National Trust for Historic Preservation and is filled with elegant Chippendale and Federal furnishings.

Wyck is one of the oldest houses in Philadelphia, dating back to 1690, and has been in the same family for nine generations. It is noted for its magnificent gardens of old roses. The Deshler-Morris House, also known for its gardens, is the fine home where George and Martha Washington lived in 1793 and 1794, when yellow fever epidemics drove the federal government out of Philadelphia. It is said that Loudoun, a gracious Greek Revival house on a hill, would have been the U.S. capitol had the government remained in Philadelphia. Built in 1801, the house was occupied by the same family until 1939.

Grumblethorpe and Stenton Mansion are two more eighteenth-century homes, and the Ebenezer Maxwell Mansion is a Victorian change of pace, showing the evolution of life in the neighborhood. Germantown's attractions also include the Mennonite Information Center, a complex featuring the home of the oldest Mennonite congregation in America and two homesteads, dating back to 1707 and 1768, as well as the Germantown Historical Society Museum Complex, comprising a visitors center and three 1700s homes.

When you've had your fill of touring, neighboring Chestnut Hill is the perfect antidote. Just driving the winding wooded roads and admiring the lovely stone houses of one of Philadelphia's prime residential areas is a treat. But Chestnut Hill also offers a chic shopping area along Germantown Avenue or the chance to get back to nature on a fine spring day at the Morris Arboretum, 100 acres of gorgeous greenery featuring more than 3,000 kinds of trees and shrubs. Some high points are the English landscaping, the rose gardens, and the azalea meadow.

The Chestnut Hill Hotel is an excellent stop for dinner, as well as a recommended home base for the weekend. Other suggestions are the pleasant hotels on City Line Avenue, near Merion. St. David's Inn, more motel than inn, is the closest lodging to Devon.

If time permits, there are more choice spring walks off Route 30 near Devon on the sylvan campuses of Bryn Mawr and Haverford, the latter a virtual arboretum. And if you are in the area on Memorial Day weekend, a drive into Philadelphia will bring you to the annual Jambalaya Jam, a festival of New Orleans jazz and good Cajun cooking held for three days on the waterfront at Penn's Landing. Besides top visiting groups (often including the famous Preservation Hall Jazz Band), Philadelphia's own Mummers bands are on hand to wind up the weekend with the most colorful show of them all.

Area Code: 215

DRIVING DIRECTIONS   Devon is at the intersection of US 30 and Route 252, west of Philadelphia. From D.C., take I-95 north. At Wilmington, take exit 8, Route 202 north to US 30 east. Approximate distance from D.C., 145 miles. From I-76 or I-276, the Pennsylvania Turnpike, take Route 252 south into Devon. For Merion, follow US 30 east to Route 1, City Line Avenue, and turn left at 54th Street, Old Lancaster Road. Watch immediately for Latch's Lane on the left. For Germantown and Chestnut Hill, return to Route 1 heading toward Philadelphia to Wissahickon Drive, then exit at Johnson Street and bear right to Germantown Avenue, the heart of Germantown. The avenue continues running north directly into Chestnut Hill.

PUBLIC TRANSPORTATION   Amtrak, Greyhound-Trailways, and many airlines service Philadelphia. It is possible to reach each suburb from the city via commuter railroads or trolley, but a car is necessary to go from suburb to suburb.

ACCOMMODATIONS   *Chestnut Hill Hotel,* 8229 Germantown Avenue, 19118, 242-5905, small hotel with attractive period furnishings, $$–$$$ • *St. David's Inn,* 591 East Lancaster Avenue (Route 30), St. David's, 19087, 688-5800, $$$ • *Guest Quarters Hotel,* 888 Chesterbrook Road, Wayne, 19087, 647-6700, all suites, $$$ CP • *Wayne Hotel,* 139 East Lancaster Avenue, Wayne, 19087, 687-5000, restored Victorian, $$$ • *Adams's Mark,* City Line Avenue and Monument Road, 19131, 581-5000, health club, indoor/outdoor pool, $$$$ • *Holiday Inn,* City Line Avenue at I-76, 19131, 477-0200, $$$.

BED AND BREAKFAST   *Bed and Breakfast of Philadelphia,* P.O. Box 252, Gradyville, PA 19039, 358-4747 or (800) 733-4747. • *Guesthouses,* RD 9, West Chester, PA 19380, 692-4575.

DINING   *Chautauqua,* Chestnut Hill Hotel (see above), original art on the walls, Continental menu, $$–$$$ • *Under the Blue Moon,* 8042 Germantown Avenue, 247-1100, batik and candlelight, Oriental dishes, $$ • *Roller's,* 8705 Germantown Avenue, 242-1771, cheerful, moderate, with interesting menu, $–$$ • *Flying Fish,* 8142 Germantown Avenue, 247-0707, seafood, $$–$$$ • *La Fourchette,* 110 North Wayne Avenue, Wayne, 687-8333, near Devon, French with an Oriental accent, $$–$$$ ● *Village Auberge,* Spread Eagle Village, 503 West Lancaster Avenue, Wayne, 687-2840, actually two restaurants, one for steak and seafood, another for fine French fare, $$$–$$$$ ● *Ristorante Primavera,* 384 Lancaster Avenue, Wayne, 254-0200, Italian, excellent pasta dishes, $–$$.

SIGHTSEEING   *Devon Horse Show,* P.O. Box 865, Devon, PA 19333, 964-0550, 9 days beginning Memorial Day weekend. Adults, $4; children, $1; additional charge for reserved seats in stands ● *Barnes Foundation,* 300 Latch's Lane, Merion, 667-0290. Hours: September to June, Friday and Saturday 9:30 A.M. to 4:30 P.M.; Sunday 1 P.M. to 4:30 P.M.; closed legal holidays. Reservations strongly advised. Admission: $1; no children under 12 admitted ● *Cliveden,* 6401 Germantown Avenue, 848-1777. Hours: April to December, Tuesday to Saturday 10 A.M. to 4 P.M.; Sunday 1 P.M. to 4 P.M. Adults, $3; students, $1.50 ● *Wyck,* 6026 Germantown Avenue, 848-1690. Hours: April to December, Tuesday, Thursday, and Saturday 1 P.M. to 4 P.M. Adults, $2; students, $1; children, $.75 ● *Deshler-Morris House,* 5442 Germantown Avenue, 596-1748. Hours: April to December, Tuesday to Sunday 1 P.M. to 4 P.M. Admission, $.50 ● *Loudoun,* 4650 Germantown Avenue, 248-0235. Hours: April to December, Sunday 1 P.M. to 4 P.M. Admission, $1.50 ● *Germantown Historical Society Museum Complex.* 5214 Germantown Avenue, 844-0514. Hours: Tuesday and Thursday 10 A.M. to 4 P.M.; Sunday 1 P.M. to 5 P.M. Adults, $2; children, $1.50 ● *Germantown Mennonite Church,* 6117 Germantown Avenue, 843-0943. Hours: Tuesday to Saturday 10 A.M. to noon, 1 P.M. to 4 P.M. Donation ● *Grumblethorpe,* 5267 Germantown Avenue, 843-4820. Hours: Saturday 1 P.M. to 4 P.M. Admission, $1 ● *Stenton,* 18th Street and Windrim Avenue, 329-7312. Hours: February to December, Tuesday to Saturday 1 P.M. to 4 P.M. Admission, $3 ● *Ebenezer Maxwell Mansion,* Greene and Tulpehocken streets, 438-1861. Hours: April to December, Wednesday to Sunday 1 P.M. to 4 P.M. Adults, $2; students, $1.

INFORMATION   Philadelphia Convention and Visitors Bureau, 1515 Market Street, Philadelphia, PA 19102, 636-1666.

Fireworks and Fun in Norfolk

It's no wonder they shoot off fireworks each June at Harborfest in Norfolk, Virginia. The rebirth of Norfolk's waterfront is good cause for celebration, since it has sparked the transformation of this old navy town into a lively magnet for tourists. An explosive weekend of free events to celebrate the change is a tradition now more than a decade old—and it is a fine time to get acquainted with this "City by the Sea," which turns out to have much to offer on land, as well.

The spark that ignited Norfolk was the Waterside, a waterfront marketplace by the same Rouse developers responsible for Baltimore's Harborplace. Theirs is a winning formula. Within the Waterside, an attractive and airy building modeled after the old ferry terminal it replaced, there are 120 shops and restaurants with something for everyone. Busiest of all is famous Phillips Seafood, where you can watch the boats come and go from the terrace while you feast on crab cakes, soft-shell crabs, oysters, clams, and other Chesapeake Bay delicacies.

But a lot of visitors don't want to be limited to one eating choice. They prefer visiting the indoor food stalls for a taste of this and that—fresh-shucked oysters, fresh-baked brownies, and food delicacies from around the globe from China to Mexico, not to mention a delicious old-fashioned Southern barbecue at Pierce's Pitt.

The Waterside began drawing the crowds to Norfolk in 1983, and the city and the marketplace merchants have kept them coming back with a regular program of weekend fun. An adjacent 6½-acre harborfront park hosts a series of locally sponsored "Festevents" from May to October—open-air concerts on Friday nights, dancing outdoors on Saturday nights, and games and dancing in the early evening on Sunday, all free except for the refreshments you buy.

For Harborfest, the waterfront is absolutely packed with action. There are tall ships to board, a sail parade to admire, entertainment and daredevil air stunts to watch, and music everywhere from pop to rock to the Virginia Symphony, performing on big outdoor stages throughout the area. The fireworks display on Saturday night is always a lollapaloosa, and if you get hungry, there's always plenty of succulent Chesapeake Bay seafood that is served up with the action.

The choicest lodging in town is the Omni International Hotel, which shares the waterfront, and it is entertaining just to stroll its walkway along the Elizabeth River. Norfolk is home port to the world's largest naval base, as well as a favorite destination for yachters, and there is almost always something to watch on the water.

Here's a town where you should not miss the harbor sightseeing tour aboard the paddle wheeler *Carrie B*. It offers a closeup look at the naval shipyard dating back to 1767—the nation's oldest dry dock—plus everything from nuclear subs and guided-missile ships to luxury liners. Longer cruises on the *American Rover* take you to Hampton Roads harbor. And there are evening dine-and-dance cruises that include entertainment on the *Spirit of Norfolk II*.

The tour of the huge naval base, where some 100,000 people work, has long been a favorite activity in Norfolk, especially on weekends, when there is open house aboard some of the ships. The base is home port for more than 120 ships of the Atlantic and Mediterranean fleets, including the nuclear-powered aircraft carrier U.S.S *Theodore Roosevelt*, 38 aircraft squadrons, and more than 65 shore-based military units.

It is a pleasant discovery for most visitors that this small city also has an unusually long list of interesting sights having nothing to do with the sea. A town trolley tour will give you the lay of the land, or you can follow the Norfolk tour signs by car.

Norfolk has a museum for every taste. The stately Chrysler Museum recently completed a $13 million renovation and expansion that added an enclosed, glass-roofed courtyard and enlarged galleries for its fine collections. Exhibits span the centuries and include many paintings by the masters, but this museum's unique claim to fame is one of the world's great glass collections, with extensive displays of Tiffany, Sandwich, and French Art glass.

Military buffs can relive the past at the Douglas MacArthur Memorial, a museum housed in the city's 1850 city hall. The galleries tell the story of a remarkable general whose life is also a chronicle of modern American history.

Among the historic houses in town, the Moses Myers House is outstanding, an impressive Georgian mansion built by one of America's first millionaires and still containing most of the owner's fine original furnishings.

Other interesting attractions include the 1739 St. Paul's Church, Norfolk's oldest building, and Hunter House, a Victorian mansion on a cobblestoned block in the historic Freemason neighborhood.

At Norfolk's Botanical Garden, flower lovers can tour 175 acres of camellias, laurel, roses, holly, tulips, and rhododendrons. You can see the sights on foot on meandering walkways, by trackless trams, or—best of all—aboard boats cruising the canals between the gardens.

Both flora and fauna can be seen at the Virginia Zoological Park, a 55-acre kingdom for 350 animals, plus the Botanical Conservatory, housing tropical and desert plants in a 1907 greenhouse.

For another pleasant outing, you can take the five-minute ride aboard the little paddle-wheel ferry from the Waterside across the river to Portsmouth to stroll streets lined with historic homes. The local information office near the dock will provide you with a free walking tour, or you can opt for the 45-minute trolley tour, which shows you more of the sights, including the Lightship Museum, the Virginia Sports Hall of Fame, and the Portsmouth Naval Hospital. If kids are along, don't miss a stop at the Children's Museum, a small and wonderfully creative place where children learn by doing such things as driving a bus or motorcycle, working in a post office, operating a telephone, or piloting a wooden boat. There's even a corner for trying on uniforms and playing firefighter or doctor for a while.

Back in Norfolk, antiquers should head for the shops around Bute, Freemason, and Botecourt, the cobbled streets in the city's old center. Art lovers will want to see the D'Art Center, where local artists are in residence. And to get a feel for the revitalization that is spreading from the Waterside inland, take a drive through the Ghent section, where the restoration of old homes has made this one of the city's most charming residential areas. Colley Avenue, nearby, features many fine restaurants.

Another lovely residential drive brings you to the Hermitage Foundation Museum, a Tudor mansion filled with the owner's Oriental art treasures. The ornate house may not be to everyone's taste, but the setting will be. Bring a picnic, and you're welcome to enjoy the 12-acre grounds bordering the Lafayette River.

Come night, you'll find that Norfolk is an arts-minded community, home of the Virginia Opera, Virginia Symphony, and Virginia Stage Company, and with its own chamber music and little theater groups. You'll also discover a wealth of good eating in local restaurants.

And should the weather be with you, it's a perfect chance to take the easy 15-minute drive to Virginia Beach before the summer crowds arrive.

How to fit it all into one weekend along with the Harborfest activities? You may well decide that Norfolk is a port that deserves a return call.

Area Code: 804

DRIVING DIRECTIONS   Norfolk is at the eastern tip of Route 64 and connects with Route 13 from the north via the Chesapeake Bay Bridge Tunnel. From D.C., take I-95 south to Richmond and follow Route 64 east. Approximate distance from D.C., 200 miles.

PUBLIC TRANSPORTATION   U.S. Air and several other airlines service the city, as do buses. Amtrak trains stop at nearby Newport News. City trolley service makes it easy to get around.

ACCOMMODATIONS *Omni International Hotel,* 777 Waterside Drive, 23510, 622-6664, pool, best location, $$–$$$$, less for weekend packages ● *Holiday Inn Downtown,* 700 Monticello Avenue, 23510, 627-5555, pool, $$–$$$ ● *Sheraton Inn,* 870 North Military Highway, 23502, 461-9192, pool, $$–$$$ ● *Econo Lodge,* 865 North Military Highway, 23502, 461-4865, $ ● *Old Dominion Inn,* 4111 Hampton Boulevard, 23508, 440-8277, $–$$.

BED AND BREAKFAST *Bed & Breakfast of Tidewater Virginia,* P.O. Box 3343, Norfolk, 23514, 627-9409 or 627-1983.

DINING *La Galleria,* 120 College Place, 623-3939, northern Italian, creative lighting, original art work, chance to watch bakers at work, $$–$$$ ● *Stripes,* 210 West York Street, 623-3871, elegant setting, award winner, $$–$$$ ● *Freemason Abbey,* 209 West Freemason Street, 622-3966, renovated church abbey, American cuisine, $–$$$ ● *Ship's Cabin,* 4110 East Ocean View Avenue, 583-4657, extensive wine list; try the Oysters Bingo, $$–$$$$ ● *Riverwalk Cafe, Omni International Hotel* (see above), $$–$$$ ● *Phillips Waterside,* 333 Waterside Drive, 627-6600; warning: mobbed on weekends, $–$$$ ● *Lockhart's Seafood,* 8440 Tidewater Drive, 588-0405, old family favorite for seafood, $–$$$ ● *Elliot's,* 1421 Colley Avenue, 625-0259, in charming Ghent area, $–$$ ● For lunch, try *Taste Unlimited,* 212 Main Street in the Selden Arcade, 625-2098, for salads and sandwiches ● *Doumar's,* 1919 Monticello Avenue, 627-4163, serves barbecue, sandwiches, and homemade ice creams; they claim, in fact, to have served the world's *first* ice cream cones.

SIGHTSEEING *Harborfest,* 120 West Main Street, Norfolk, 23510, 627-7809. Annual weekend festivities in early June; contact for current dates and full schedule ● *Norfolk Botanical Gardens,* Azalea Garden Road adjacent to Norfolk Airport, 441-5385. Hours: daily 8:30 A.M. to sunset. Adults, $2; under 6, free; boat and train rides additional ● *Chrysler Museum,* Olney Road at Mowbray Arch, 622-1211. Hours: Tuesday to Saturday 10 A.M. to 4 P.M.; Sunday 1 P.M. to 5 P.M. Free ● *Douglas MacArthur Memorial,* City Hall Avenue and Bank Street, 441-2965. Hours: Monday to Saturday 10 A.M. to 5 P.M.; Sunday 11 A.M. to 5 P.M. Free ● *Norfolk Naval Base,* 9809 Hampton Boulevard, guided tours leave from the Waterside or from naval base tour office, last 60 to 75 minutes. Hours: June to Labor Day, 9 A.M. to 2:30 P.M.; spring and fall, 9:30 A.M. to 2:30 P.M.; winter hours vary. For exact starting times of tours from the base, phone 444-7925; for the Waterside, Tidewater Regional Transit, 623-3222. Adults, $4; children, $2 from the Waterside; $1.50 from base • *Ship Open Houses,* Saturday and Sunday, 1 P.M. to 4:30 P.M. year round at naval base. Free • *Hampton Roads Naval Museum,* at the Norfolk Naval Base, 444-3827. Hours: Monday to Saturday 9 A.M. to 4 P.M.; Sunday 10 A.M. to 4 P.M. Free • *Hermitage Foundation Museum,* 7637 North Shore Road, 423-2052. Hours: Monday to Saturday 10 A.M. to 5 P.M.; Sunday from 1 P.M. Adults, $3; ages 6–18, $1 • *Historic Homes,* 622-1211: *Moses Myers House,* 323 East Freemason at Bank Street; *Willoughby-Baylor House,* 601 East Freemason Street; *Adam Thoroughgood House,* 1636 Parish Road, Virginia Beach; 460-0007. Hours: April to December, Tuesday to Saturday 10 A.M. to 5 P.M.; Sunday noon to 5 P.M.; January to March, daily noon to 5 P.M. except Sunday and Monday. Adults: 1 house, $2; students, $1. 2 houses, $3 and $2. All houses $4 and $3. Children under 6 free • *Hunter House,* 240 West Freemason Street, 623-9814. Hours: April to December, Wednesday to Saturday 10 A.M. to 4 P.M.; Sunday noon to 4 P.M. Admission, $2 • *St. Paul's Church,* 201 St. Paul's Boulevard, 627-4353. Hours: Tuesday to Saturday 10 A.M. to 4 P.M. Donation • *Virginia Zoological Park,* 3500 Granby Street, 441-2706. Hours: daily 10 A.M. to 5 P.M. Adults, $2; under 12, $1 • *Carrie B Harbor Tours,* the Waterside, 393-4735. Harbor tours (90 minutes), April 1 to October 31: adults, $9; children under 12, $4.50. Sunset tours (2½ hours): adults, $10; children under 12, $5. Check for current schedules • *American RoverSchooner Cruises,* the Waterside, 677-SAIL. 2- and 3-hour cruises, May to late October. Adults from $12; children from $7. Check current schedules • *Spirit of Norfolk,* Otter Berth, 627-7771. Lunch and dinner cruises, June to Labor Day. Call for current times and rates • *Norfolk Trolley Tours,* tickets for 1-hour tours from kiosk at the Waterside pickup point. Hours: early May to late September, daily 10 A.M. to 5 P.M.; on the hour in summer, noon to 4 P.M. in spring and fall. Adults, $1.50; children under 12, $.75.

INFORMATION Norfolk Convention and Visitors Bureau, 236 East Plume Street, Norfolk, VA 23510, (800) 368-3097. Self-service information booth also on second level at the Waterside.

SUMMER

Overleaf: **Canoeing at Delaware Water Gap, Pennsylvania.** *Photo courtesy of Pocono Mountains Vacation Bureau.*

The Washingtons and Lees of Westmoreland

You can't blame them if they like to name-drop in Westmoreland County, Virginia. This enclave between the Potomac and Rappahannock rivers at the top of Virginia's Northern Neck has produced more statesmen—George Washington, James Monroe, and Robert E. Lee, to drop a few names—than any other county in America.

History is impressive here, what with Stratford Hall, the magnificent ancestral home of the Lees, and Wakefield, the site of Washington's birthplace, to visit. But it isn't the only reason for a trip. There's swimming and boating on the Potomac at Westmoreland State Park, berries and fruits ripe for picking at Westmoreland Berry Farm, one of Virginia's top vineyards is nearby, and the seafood is fresh and sweet at Colonial Beach.

Without doubt Westmoreland's standout attraction is Stratford Hall, one of Virginia's most beautiful historic plantations, and worth a trip on its own. Allow plenty of time, for the house is only part of the pleasure of the visit.

Built high on a bluff above the Potomac in the 1730s by Thomas Lee, the acting governor of Virginia, Stratford spawned four generations of patriots who shaped the history of the nation. Richard Henry Lee, who introduced the motion for independence in the Continental Congress, and his brother Francis Lightfoot Lee, who also signed the document, were born here. Years later, in 1807, Ann Carter, wife of Revolutionary War hero "Light-Horse Harry" Lee, gave birth to Robert E. Lee in the big sunlit bedroom, the one with the canopy bed, on the upper floor. He slept in the cradle that remains in place at the window.

The H-shaped Georgian manor house was built of bricks made on the site and timber cut from virgin forest. The Great Hall in the center, 29 feet square with a tray ceiling 17 feet high, filled with elaborately carved walls and doors and exquisite antiques, is considered one of the most beautiful rooms in America. All of the rooms are of interest, but the 250-year-old kitchen, with a fireplace large enough to roast an ox, holds a special reward—cider and homemade ginger cookies are served to refresh hungry guests. From April through October, lunches also are available on the grounds at a log-cabin dining room on the edge of the woods.

Visitors can also walk the meadows where the Lees rode and follow a trail thick with wildflowers to the "cool, sweet spring" so fondly remembered by General Lee during the hardships of the Civil

War. A formal garden lined in boxwood invites a stroll along its oyster-shell paths, or you can visit the replicas of flourishing eighteenth-century vegetable and flower gardens. Eighteenth- and early-nineteenth-century coaches can be seen in the long Coach House and Stable. Down the "rolling road" where hogsheads of tobacco used to move downhill to the Potomac, the old plantation mill has been rebuilt on its original foundations. The huge waterwheel that once served several plantations is still turning, its wooden gears powering the millstone that continues to grind corn, wheat, oats, and barley. You can buy a take-home sampling from the Stratford Store.

Stratford Hall Plantation is still managed as a farm on 1,600 of its original acres, making it one of the oldest continuing agricultural operations in the country.

Just a few miles down the road, you can get a look at life as it was on a more modest colonial farm at the George Washington Birthplace National Monument, administered by the National Park Service.

George Washington was born here on his father's farm, located on Popes Creek off the Potomac River. He lived here for three and a half years, until the family moved to Ferry Farm near Fredericksburg. The original Popes Creek home was lost to a fire. The present Tidewater house and its acres were intended to re-create the sights, sounds, and smells of eighteenth-century plantation life—the kind of life that influenced the character and development of the nation's first president. A 14-minute film at the visitors center tells about early life at Popes Creek, and guided tours are available every half-hour explaining life in the house and kitchen.

In the fields, set off by split-rail fences, you can watch plowing, planting, hoeing, weeding, harvesting, and all the other day-to-day activities that take place on a farm during the growing season. There are demonstrations of plantation crafts such as woodworking, blacksmithing, and leather working, and of the female chores of spinning and weaving. And from May to September there are special events, including sheep shearing, garden tours, colonial music concerts, and archaeological walks, plus lots of other activities to keep things interesting.

When you've had enough history for one weekend, lighter diversions await. The 2,000-acre Ingleside Plantation, which is Virginia's largest plant nursery, also boasts a 20-acre vineyard within the grounds, and the only winery to win a gold medal at a recent statewide wine-tasting competition. The 30 varieties of grapes planted here are thriving under the watchful eye of Belgian wine specialist Jacques Recht, who was fulfilling a lifelong dream of sailing around the world when he and his wife cruised up Chesapeake Bay, never expecting he was to be recruited by the Ingleside owners as a pioneer in Virginia's growing wine industry. Visitors are welcome to tour the vineyard and winery and taste the wines. One pleasant way to get there is on a Rappahannock River cruise, which includes a stop at the winery for lunch.

Everyone is equally welcome at Westmoreland Berry Farm and Orchard along the Rappahannock River, where you are invited to come in your old clothes, pick up a basket, and head for the fields to pick your own fruit. Mid-May to mid-June means strawberries, summer brings raspberries and blackberries. Groves of apples, apricots, cherries, peaches, and plums are also being developed for future harvests.

When you're ready to simply relax, head for Westmoreland State Park and its 1,300 acres along the Potomac. The park facilities include camping sites, cabins, hiking trails, boat rentals, picnic grounds, and both the beach and a pool for swimming. Naturalists offer guided hikes and evening programs during the summer.

You'll also find a sandy strand of beach along the Potomac north a bit in the little town of Colonial Beach, as well as tasty dining.

Lodgings are in short supply in Westmoreland County. If the Inn at Montross is filled, you'll have to settle into Fredericksburg or go farther out on the Northern Neck around Irvington, each roughly 35 miles away.

Don't let that deter you, however. Even if you do nothing but visit Stratford Hall, you won't be sorry you made the trip.

Area Code: 804

DRIVING DIRECTIONS   Stratford Hall is on Route 3, reached via I-95 or Route 301 from north or south. From D.C., take I-95 south to Route 3 east. Approximate distance from D.C., 100 miles.

ACCOMMODATIONS *The Inn at Montross,* Courthouse Square, Montross, 22520, 493-9097, $$ CP. See also Northern Neck, page 114 and Fredericksburg, page 135.

DINING   *The Inn at Montross* (see above), $$–$$$ ● *Reno on the Potomac,* 301 Beach Terrace, Colonial Beach, 224-7055, candlelight dining on the water, $$–$$$ ● *Hunan Diner,* 422 Washington Avenue, Colonial Beach, 224-8754, wide Chinese menu, $.

SIGHTSEEING *Stratford Hall,* off Route 214, Stratford, 493-8038. Hours: daily 9 A.M. to 4:30 P.M. Adults, $4; children, $2 ● *George Washington Birthplace National Monument,* Route 204, off Route 3, 224-1732. Hours: daily 9 A.M. to 5 P.M. Free ● *Ingleside Vineyard,* Box 1038, Route 638 south of Route 3, Oak

Grove, 224-8687. Hours: Monday to Saturday 10 A.M. to 5 P.M.; Sunday 1 P.M. to 5 P.M., appointments appreciated ● *Westmoreland Berry Farm,* Route 637, Box 1121, Oak Grove, 224-9171. Hours: daily in season, 8 A.M. to 6 P.M. ● *Westmoreland State Park,* Route 347 off Route 3, 6 miles west of Montross, 493-8821. Daylight hours daily year-round; pool and restaurant open Memorial Day through Labor Day. Free except for boat rentals or special fees ● *Rappahannock River Cruises,* Warsaw, VA, 333-4646, daily cruises, from Tappahannock. Phone for current rates and schedules.

INFORMATION Westmoreland Travel Council, P.O. Box 996, Montross, VA 22520, 493-8440, 1021 East Cary Street, Richmond, VA 21219, 786-4484.

Combing the Beaches in Delaware

Undiscovered they're not. Worth discovering they are. There's good reason why Rehoboth and its neighboring towns on the Delaware shore have become known as "the nation's summer capital." Of all the beach areas along the mid-Atlantic, none offers so much variety as these bountiful shores.

Pick your own kind of atmosphere. You'll find seaside state parks incorporating miles and miles of unspoiled beach, your choice of relative quiet or a social scene, plenty of beachfront accommodations for sea lovers, places for families and scenes for singles, water and land sports galore, and even a bit of history to explore just in case the sun does not shine.

At the top of the Atlantic shore is Lewes, a fishermen's town with a surprising past. The center of Lewes is its busy dock, where anglers head out for mackerel, bass, and bluefish and compete in annual tournaments with prizes for hooking the biggest sea trout, sharks, tuna, and marlin.

But you needn't be a fisherman to enjoy the low-key ambience of Lewes or its location just one mile from 2,500-acre Cape Henlopen State Park, a beach- and nature-lover's delight situated at the junction where Delaware Bay opens into the Atlantic. The park is known for its "walking" sand dunes, which shift with the winds, and its 80-foot Great Dune, the tallest between Cape Hatteras and Cape Cod, as well as its nesting colonies of seabirds, nature trails, and unusual plants. There are also four miles of sandy Atlantic beachfront, plus bay shore for crabbing and fishing.

Little Lewes boasts of being the first town in the Delaware colony. It was a Dutch whaling outpost, known as Zwaanendael as early as 1631, and though the English supplanted the Dutch in 1664, the town remains proud of its earliest heritage. In celebration of the three-hundredth anniversary of the town's founding, a replica of the step-gabled town hall in Hoorn, Holland, was built honoring David Pietersen deVries, a Hoorn native who sponsored the first settlement. The building, called the Zwaanendael Museum, is unique in this country and has attracted visits from several members of the Dutch royal family. Inside, an exhibit known as "Lewes: A Good Harbor" tells the long history of Lewes.

The museum is the starting point for the Lewes Historic Walking Tour, a rather formal title for a handful of interesting sights. Among them are historic homes (the oldest dating back to 1685), two 1800s churches, and a small historic complex on Shipcarpenter Street that includes the Burton-Ingram House, now the local historical society, whose cellar walls are made of ships' ballast stones and brick. Rabbit's Ferry House, a restored one-room farmhouse, and the Thompson Country Store are also part of the tour.

It's just six miles from Lewes to Rehoboth Beach, the real center of shore activity. This busy little town is a far cry from the Methodist camp meeting that launched it as a seaside mecca where souls could be saved by baptism in the sea. In Hebrew, the name means "one more sinner."

Today Rehoboth boasts handsome residential sections that are summer retreats for numerous D.C. luminaries, and a thriving art colony revolving around the Rehoboth Art League, where exhibits and concerts are held. The league's attractive headquarters are in a complex of historic houses in Henlopen Acres, one of the town's most posh and pleasant neighborhoods.

Rehoboth has the finest homes and the most sophisticated restaurants on the shore, yet it is at heart an old-fashioned family resort. While socialites are entertaining one another at cocktail parties around Henlopen Acres, North Shores, and Silver Lake, children are playing on the sidewalks in the older section of town called the Pines, as their parents watch contentedly from big screened porches.

At one end of the mile-and-a-quarter boardwalk, a local landmark since 1884, lively bidding goes on at Saturday night auctions of Oriental rugs and antiques at the Stuart Kingston Galleries. The rest of the stretch, however, is a bustling lineup of pizza stands, T-shirt emporiums, penny arcades, and miniature golf games, a hangout heaven for young people. The entire boardwalk is lined with low-rise lodgings where you can almost fall out of bed onto the beach, a real plus for ocean lovers. This is definitely not the area to look for solitude, but it is fine for families. Teens love it, especially for the volleyball and other sports played on the lighted beach between Rehoboth and Olive avenues each night. For little ones, there's Funland, an amusement park in miniature with bumper cars and other gentle rides guaranteed to delight the small-fry.

Rehoboth runs south right into Dewey Beach, currently the young singles' favorite hangout. The beach is built up with low-rise motels and beach houses, but lacks Rehoboth's food stands and amusements, so though there may be plenty of people socializing on the beach, you don't have the ongoing bustle of a boardwalk. Only a narrow strip about two blocks long separates the Atlantic shore from Rehoboth Bay and the Lewes-Rehoboth Canal area here, both choice spots for clamming and crabbing. And, as in Lewes, both surf and deep-sea fishing here are prime.

Bethany Beach calls itself the Quiet Resort and is the best bet of all for a peaceful beach getaway by the sea. If you stay in a beachside motel near Bethany's quiet noncommercial boardwalk, you'll hardly need a car. You can walk out the door to the beach, walk only a block or so into town for meals and shops, walk to the center of the boardwalk to the concession stand for a hot dog or an ice cream cone.

Fenwick Island also bills itself as quiet, but on the route south from Bethany toward Fenwick begins the condominium buildup that culminates eventually in the maze of hotels and honky-tonks just down the road in Ocean City, Maryland. Fenwick Island does have its own unspoiled state park, and a lot of the coastal area south of Rehoboth has been preserved from any development as part of Delaware Seashore State Park, including a section south of Dewey Beach and just north of Indian River Inlet that is a favorite for surfers.

There's plenty of opportunity to bike, play tennis, rent a sailboat, or go fishing all along the coast. A few listings follow, but you can get more by looking at the current year's brochure put out by each town's tourist office. If you want to do some shopping, Rehoboth is the best bet. Preppy classics can be found at Penelope's Shop for Pappagallo, trendier clothes at boutiques like Crysti or South Moon Under. Check the little arcades off both sides of Rehoboth Avenue, where many interesting shops for clothes and gifts are tucked away. Interesting country gifts also can be found at Tulip Ltd., a little shop in Bethany Beach, and there are a few antique shops for browsing in Lewes. Both serious antiquers and spectators are welcome at the Rehoboth Saturday night auctions at Stuart Kingston Galleries on the boardwalk at Grenoble Place. For bargains, try Ocean Outlets, a group of discount stores on Route 1 near Rehoboth.

Don't come to the Delaware shore expecting solitude—there's too much going on here not to attract crowds. But do expect a relaxed atmosphere and enough variety to offer almost anyone a rewarding stay. And if you really long to get away, all you have to do is walk far enough from the parking lots at the state-run beaches and you'll find plenty of room for solitary communing, just you and the sun and the sea.

Area Code: 302

DRIVING DIRECTIONS Delaware beaches are along Route 1. From D.C., take Route 50/301 across the Chesapeake Bay Bridge to Route 404 east, which merges into Route 9. Follow Route 9 east into Lewes or turn south on Route 1 to Rehoboth, Dewey Beach, Bethany, or Fenwick Island. Approximate distance to Rehoboth from D.C., 125 miles. From northern points, take Route 113 south to Route 1 south.

ACCOMMODATIONS Many comfortable, almost interchangeable, motel-type choices on beach or bay. Write each town for full lists. A few possibilities: *Angler's,* Angler's Road at Market Street, Lewes, 19958, 645-2831, nothing fancy but overlooks canal and marina, $–$$ ● *Oceanus Motel,* 6 Second Street, Rehoboth, 19971, 227-9436, pool, $$–$$$ CP ● *Atlantic Sands,* Boardwalk and Baltimore Avenue, Rehoboth, 19971, 227-2511, pool, $$$–$$$$ ● *Atlantic View,* 2 Clayton Street North, Dewey Beach, 19971, 227-3878, pool, $$ ● *The Bay Resort,* Bellevue Street on the Bay, Dewey Beach, 19971, 227-6400, pool, $$$ ● *Sea Crest,* Oceanfront at Garfield Parkway, Bethany Beach, 19930, 539-7621, $$ ● *Bethany Arms,* P.O. Box 1600, Bethany Beach, 19930, 539-9603, $$–$$$ ● *Henlopen Hotel,* Lake Avenue at Boardwalk, 19971, 227-2551, the only high-rise hotel, nice views, $$$–$$$$ ● *Brighton Suites Hotel,* 34 Wilmington Avenue at 1st Street, Rehoboth, 19971, 227-5780 or (800) 227-5788, one block from beach, $$$–$$$$ ● For those who prefer inns: *Dinner Bell Inn,* 2 Christian Street, Rehoboth, 19971, 227-2561, $$$ ● *Corner Cupboard Inn,* 50 Park Avenue, Rehoboth, 19971, 227-8553, $$$.

BED AND BREAKFAST *Bed & Breakfast of Delaware,* 1804 Breen Lane, Wilmington, DE 19810, 475-0340.

DINING *Lighthouse Restaurant,* Fisherman's Wharf, Lewes, 645-6271, seafood with a view of the boats, $–$$$ ● *Fran O'Brien's Beach House Restaurant,* 59 Lake Avenue, Rehoboth, 227-6121, a longtime local favorite, $$–$$$$ ● *Garden Gourmet,*

Route 1 and Phillip Street, Rehoboth, 227-4747, elegant, $$ • *Blue Moon . . . a Restaurant,* 35 Baltimore Avenue, 227-6515, trendy, $$–$$$ • *Chez la Mer,* 2nd at Wilmington Avenue, Rehoboth, 227-6494, gourmet spot, $$–$$$ • *Obie's by the Sea,* Olive Avenue and Boardwalk, Rehoboth, 227-6261, casual, barbecue ribs and chicken, $–$$ • *Camel's Hump,* 21 Baltimore Avenue, 227-0947, excellent Middle Eastern fare, $$–$$$ • *Back Porch Café,* 21 Rehoboth Avenue, Rehoboth, 227-3674, popular, $$–$$$ • *Rusty Rudder,* Route 1, Dewey Beach, 227-3888, informal, popular outdoor deck, a singles meeting place, $–$$$ • *The Waterfront,* McKinley Street, Dewey Beach, 227-9292, outdoor barbecue, bay ribs, views, young crowd for later dancing, $–$$ • *Sydney's Side Street and Blues Place,* 22 1/2 Wilmington Avenue, Rehoboth, 227-1339, California cuisine, jazz and blues entertainment, $$–$$$ • Other spots for nightlife: *The Front Page,* 52 Baltimore Avenue, Rehoboth, 227-0948, varied entertainment • *Bottle and Cork,* Route 1, Dewey Beach, 227-8545, rock and roll, jammed on Saturdays • *Chuck's Country Crab,* Route 54, Fenwick Island, 436-5022, comedy, music, attracts a somewhat older crowd. (Note that some restaurants may be closed in winter.)

SIGHTSEEING Zwaanendael Museum, Savannah Road and Kings Highway, Lewes, 645-9418. Hours: Tuesday to Saturday 10 A.M. to 4:30 P.M.; Sunday 1:30 P.M. to 4:30 P.M. Free • *Restored Buildings of Lewes Historical Society,* 645-9673. Guided tours from Thompson Country Store, 3rd Street: July to September, Tuesday through Saturday 10 A.M. to 3 P.M.; April to June, Saturday and Sunday 1 P.M. to 3 P.M. Admission: adults, $3; under 12, free with adults. Summer special guided tours, 10:30 A.M., $3.50 • *Rehoboth Art League,* Henlopen Acres, 227-8408, classes and exhibits, call for schedules • *Rehoboth Jolly Trolley,* narrated tours, leave from Rehoboth Avenue at the boardwalk. Hours: May and September, weekends; in summer, daily. Schedule posted on the boardwalk.

SPORTS Biking: *Bob's Bike Rentals,* 30 Maryland Avenue, Rehoboth, 227-6807 • Boat Rentals: *Indian River Marina,* Rehoboth, 227-6594; *York Beach Mall,* South Bethany, 539-6679 • Fishing: *Angler's Fishing Center,* Lewes, 645-6080 • *Lewes Harbour Marina,* 645-9917, Fisherman's Wharf, Lewes, 645-8862 • *South Shore Marina,* Bethany Beach, 539-7384 • Tennis: In Lewes, Cape Henlopen State Park, 645-8983, and city-run courts at Cape Henlopen High School, Kings Highway, 645-7777. In Rehoboth, city courts located at Rehoboth Junior High School, State Road, and at Deauville Beach, Henlopen Avenue near the ocean, 227-3598. In Dewey Beach, Waterfront Sports Complex, McKinley Street,

227-8534. In Bethany, Bethany Club, Cedar Neck Road, 539-5111, or town courts at Lord Baltimore Elementary School, Route 26.

INFORMATION Lewes Chamber of Commerce, P.O. Box 1, Lewes, DE 19958, 645-8073 ● Rehoboth Beach–Dewey Beach Chamber of Commerce, P.O. Box 216, 73 Rehoboth Avenue, Rehoboth Beach, DE 19971, 227-2233; outside Delaware (800) 441-1329 ● Bethany-Fenwick Area Chamber of Commerce, P.O. Box 1450, Bethany Beach, DE 19930, 539-2100; outside Delaware (800) 962-SURF.

Back to the Beginning in St. Mary's

Southern Maryland is a world apart, the place where the state was born in 1634—and where the tranquillity of another era still pervades.

Tourists hurrying to the Eastern Shore seem to have forgotten this closer-to-home side of Chesapeake Bay, so there's blessedly little commercialism to intrude on the placid landscape. Take a drive, and you pass miles of lush green tobacco fields and weathered barns where the big broad leaves are hung to dry, old plantation houses still standing proud, and wooded groves hiding narrow sandy strands of beach along the bay.

This is the place for quiet pleasures—picnicking beside the water, hunting for wildflowers, or pushing off for a sail. For a change of pace, you can pull up beside the buggies at an Amish market, pay a call on an eighteenth-century plantation, or walk straight back into the seventeenth century at a unique living museum.

In summer, there are added incentives for the trip. From mid-June to mid-July the Maryland Shakespeare Festival and the Tidewater Music Festival at St. Mary's College add entertainment to fill a balmy night. Wait until August, and you can witness jousting, Maryland's state sport.

The main attraction for history-minded visitors is the chance to retrace the footsteps of some 200 English settlers who sailed to the edge of the world three and a half centuries ago with Leonard Calvert and planted Lord Baltimore's colony in the wilderness, the first

Catholic settlement in America. Only Jamestown and Plymouth have longer histories.

The settlers first landed on St. Clement's Island in the Potomac River, the spot marked today by a 40-foot cross facing out to sea. The island has been preserved in its natural state and can be reached by boat from the Potomac River Museum at Colton's Point, where a slide show fills you in on local lore. The museum itself is filled with exhibits that show the importance of the Potomac and its resources to the people who have lived here, from the earliest native American Indians to today's pleasure seekers.

For 60 years a tiny frontier village named for the Virgin Mary guided the affairs of this new colony called Maryland, and the 840-acre complex known as St. Mary's City gives you a vivid idea of what life was like in those earliest days.

The houses, barns, and tobacco fields of a settler named Godiah Spray have been re-created here to show the farm life that was the heart of early Maryland. The state house where Lord Baltimore established laws granting religious freedom has been reconstructed, along with Farthing's Ordinary, one of the state's earliest taverns. You can also board the *Maryland Dove,* a square-rigged replica of one of the two ships that arrived here in 1634, typical of those that traded on the Chesapeake Tobacco Coast.

This is more than a collection of buildings and a boat, however. St. Mary's City comes to life from mid-March to mid-October with living history performances that put you right in the middle of seventeenth-century life.

You can visit the Spray family on their plantation and watch the chores being done, sit in on trials for pig stealing or murder in the Old State House, and hear the latest gossip and a drinking song or two at the tavern. You may even be recruited to serve on a mock jury in the courtroom or join the hunt for a runaway indentured servant.

Also on the expansive grounds of St. Mary's City at Chancellor's Point are a nature center and a re-created longhouse, showing what the land and life here were like before the colonists arrived. At the nature center you can pick up a wildflower guide for the many miles of nature trails that offer tranquil bayside scenery hardly changed over the centuries. Guided wildflower walks are held monthly.

Archaeological sites and excavations in progress can also be seen at various points on the grounds, continually bringing more of the past back to light. An exhibit and slide show at the visitors center tells you more about the digs and shows you some of their finds.

The view alone is worth the trip to Sotterley Plantation near Hollywood, where you can see how well the early planters prospered. Home of an early governor of Maryland, the 1717 house commands a superb vista from a ridge overlooking the Patuxent River. It stands atop the old "rolling road," where hogsheads of tobacco once were rolled to waiting ships in the harbor. The low white house with tall chimneys is modest on the outside, but within it is a warm home filled with fine antiques and notable woodwork, especially the striking Chinese Chippendale staircase and the great shell-shaped alcoves of the drawing rooms. It has a special sense of life that is lacking in some historic homes because the present owner still arrives occasionally for a country weekend. A village comprising tenant houses, barns, a smokehouse, a tobacco shed, and other outbuildings reflects the self-sufficient community that constituted an early Maryland plantation.

Present-day diversions in St. Mary's County revolve around Point Lookout State Park, where there are beaches for sunning and swimming, boats for rent, hiking trails, fishing areas, and lots of big boulders where you can perch for a picnic lunch with an unbeatable bay view. If you want a more private strip of beach for strolling by the bay, you'll find it at Elms Beach off Route 235.

Point Lookout has its own special bit of Civil War history, told in a small museum. Back in 1862 it was the site of a Union hospital, later turned into a prison where more than 20,000 Confederates were confined in deplorable conditions. Many of their guards were blacks who were former slaves. More than 3,500 Southern soldiers died here.

Fishing and boating are other favorite pastimes in southern Maryland, and you'll find charter captains ready to take you out at many of the marinas in the area. Stop at the chamber of commerce for a list of names and numbers.

You can also board a boat at Point Lookout for a day cruise to Smith Island and a look at the unique life-style of the 750 hardy fisherfolk who populate this isolated isle. All are direct descendants of the original settlers, most of whom came here from Cornwall, England, in 1657. A big Chesapeake Bay seafood lunch on the island is part of the tour. Frances Kitching's crab cakes are a legend even on the mainland.

Shopping is not a major activity in these parts, but a few places worth a look are the restored Christmas Country Store and Old Mill in Great Mills and the Amish Farmers Market held every Wednesday and Saturday in Charlotte Hall on Route 5.

A pocket of neat Amish farms can be seen in the countryside near Charlotte Hall in a triangle formed by routes 488 and 6. You may want to stop off along Route 6 at Aunt Kate's, a little store located in a modest home. It is mainly a place where the Amish shop for grocery staples, but the back room holds a collection of handmade quilts and rugs at very good prices.

As for special events, the concerts presented by the annual Tidewater Music Festival are held from late June to mid-July at several outdoor and indoor locations around the area and offer a range of classical music from Brahms to Barber. Many of the concerts take place on the campus of St. Mary's College, adjacent to St. Mary's City. The college also cosponsors the Maryland Shakespeare Festival from mid-June to mid-August at the Riverfront Playhouse, an open-air theater in St. Mary's City.

Jousting, Maryland's colorful state sport, is shown off in two annual tournaments, one in Mechanicsville in mid-August, accompanied by parades and bands and country-fair fun, the other in Port Republic in nearby Calvert County a week later. The latter, held on the grounds of Christ Church, is the state's oldest tournament and features a bazaar and home-style dinner to fill out the day.

It's worth a return trip in the fall for the annual St. Mary's County Oyster Festival at the Leonardtown fairgrounds. This event includes the National Oyster Shucking Championship Contest and National Oyster Cook-Off, and features Chesapeake Bay oysters cooked up in just about every conceivable way. The Blessing of the Fleet in early October on St. Clement's Island is another colorful event. Check for this year's dates.

The fanciest of the restaurants in the area is probably the Olde Breton Inn on Breton Bay. For the most part, you will find fresh seafood at reasonable prices at no-frills marina cafes. A drive over to lively Solomons Island in Calvert County for dinner makes a nice change of pace.

As for lodgings, Patuxent Inn in Lexington Park is far and away the best of the scattered motels in the area. Better yet, live amid history at the guest cottage on the beautiful grounds of Sotterley Plantation, or visit one of the historic homes in the area offering bed-and-breakfast to guests, a live-in sampling of the placid lifestyle that still marks southern Maryland.

Area Code: 301

DRIVING DIRECTIONS   St. Mary's City is on Route 5. From D.C., follow Route 5 all the way. Approximate distance from D.C., 68 miles. From points north or south, take Route 301 and turn east on Route 5.

ACCOMMODATIONS   *Patuxent Inn,* Route 235, Lexington Park, 20653, 862-4100, $$ ● *Belvedere Motor Inn,* Lexington Park, 20653, 863-6666, $$ ● *Sotterley Mansion Guest Cottage,* c/o Lizette Day, P.O. Box 67, Hollywood, 20636, 373-5691, or at Sotterley, 373-2280, cottage with kitchen, accommodates up to four, $$$, $ on weeknights ● Bed-and-breakfast lodgings include *Potomac View Farm,* Tall Timbers, 20690, 994-0418, historic home on 100-acre farm, shared bath in main house, private cottage with bath and kitchen, $–$$$ CP ● *St. Michaels Manor,* Scotland, 20687, 872-4025, 1805 home on Long Neck Creek, $ CP ● *Old Kirk House,* Scotland, 20687, 872-4093, 1800 home on Biscoe Creek, $ CP.

DINING *Olde Breton Inn,* Society Hill Road, Leonardtown, 475-2699, $–$$ ● *Bay Cargo,* 1 St. Mary's Square, Lexington Park, 862-1870, $–$$ ● *Scheible's Crabpot Restaurant,* Scheible's Fishing Center, Ridge, 872-5185, $–$$ ● *Southridge Restaurant,* Route 5, Ridge, 872-5151, $–$$ ● *Evans Seafood,* Piney Point, 994-2299, $–$$. See also Solomons, page 46.

SIGHTSEEING *Historic St. Mary's City,* P.O. Box 39, Route 5, St. Mary's, 862-0990. Visitors center hours: daily 10 A.M. to 5 P.M. Free. Hours, exhibit buildings: Memorial Day to Labor Day, daily, 10 A.M. to 5 P.M.; late March to late May and September to late November, weekends only. Adults, $4; children, $2 ● *Tidewater Music Festival,* St. Mary's College, mid-June to mid-July, and *Maryland Shakespeare Festival,* mid-June to mid-August, Riverfront Playhouse, St. Mary's City, information for both at 862-0216. Call for current dates and rates ● *Potomac River Museum,* Colton's Point, 769-2222. Hours: Summer, Monday to Friday, 9 A.M. to 4 P.M.; Saturday and Sunday noon to 4 P.M. Rest of year, Wednesday to Sunday noon to 4 P.M. Donation ● *St. Clement's Island Boat Excursions,* check Potomac River Museum for current schedules and rates ● *Sotterley Plantation,* Hollywood, follow signs from intersection of routes 235 and 245 near Hollywood, 373-2280. Hours: June through September, daily 11 A.M. to 5 P.M. Adults, $4; children, $1 ● *Point Lookout State Park,* Star Route, Box 48, Scotland, 872-5688. Hours: daylight hours daily, $3 per Maryland car, $4 for out-of-state cars. Visitors center and Civil War Museum, Wednesday to Sunday, mid-June to Labor Day, weekends early June and September. Free ● *Smith Island Tours,* Capt. Alan Tyler, Rhodes Point, 425-2771, 6-hour cruise with lunch. Check current rates and schedule ● *St. Mary's County Oyster Festival,* P.O. Box 198, Hollywood, 373-5242, held at Leonardtown fairgrounds in October. Check for this year's dates and fees.

INFORMATION St. Mary's County Office of Tourism, Route 5, Box 1-B, Mechanicsville, MD 20659, 884-5555.

A Folklore Feast in Kutztown

It all began almost 40 years ago when three college professors joined forces to find a way to celebrate their Pennsylvania Dutch heritage over a Fourth of July weekend.

Today, the Kutztown Folk Festival has grown into a nine-day extravaganza that is one of the country's most colorful exhibits of folk arts—and food.

The people we call Pennsylvania Dutch actually are not Dutch at all, but descended from German immigrants of the late 1600s. *Deutsch* somehow became *Dutch* in the new land. Unlike the austere Amish sects to the south in Lancaster County, the settlers around Kutztown and Reading became known as the Fancy or Gay Dutch, famous for the brightly painted hex signs that adorn their barns "chust for nice." Their love of color, song, and dance gives this festival its lively flavor.

The grounds overflow each year with over 100 demonstrations of such traditional Pennsylvania German crafts as quilting, stenciling, wheat weaving, fraktur painting, basket making, wood carving, lace making, hex sign and tole painting, pewter molding, and tinsmithing.

Quilts are not only seen in the making; hundreds of finished handmade quilts entered in the annual Kutztown competition go on display and up for sale at very reasonable prices.

Because farm life is such a large part of the Pennsylvania Dutch tradition, many demonstrations show off typical farm activities, from threshing, shearing, and horseshoeing to butchering and making apple butter. And since cooking also has long been a specialty of these industrious folks, you can count on food galore: homemade sausage and scrapple, apple pandowdy, *Schnitz und Knepp* (dried apples and dumplings), and that famous molasses-flavored dish known as shoofly pie, to name just a few of the treats.

All of this is to the tune of music, folk songs, and polka bands. Free dance instruction allows everyone to join in the "hoedown" square dances and jigs.

Despite all the music and merriment and a certain amount of commercialism that has crept in as the event has grown, there is still an educational focus to the festival, which is sponsored by the nonprofit Pennsylvania Folklife Society and Ursinus College. Talks are held throughout the day for those who want to learn more about the customs of the Pennsylvania Dutch. One of the talks explains the difference between the Plain and Fancy sects; others explain the techniques of the crafts.

There's more than enough here to fill a happy day, plus plenty to fill out your stay in surrounding Berks County. For starters, drive north from Kutztown to Old Route 22, known as the Hex Highway, a prize route for viewing barns decorated with brilliant hex signs. If you write or call, the Berks County Visitors Information Association will send a map to guide you.

The little town of Kempton, north of Kutztown, offers several diversions—the small Pennsylvania Dutch Farm Museum, a ride on the W. K. & S. Steam Railroad, and Hawk Mountain Sanctuary, named for the birds of prey that can be sighted here in fall. The sanctuary provides 2,000 mountaintop acres for viewing protected birds and animals and lovely scenery. The Appalachian Trail crosses the crest of the Blue Ridge Mountains at the sanctuary's eastern edge, giving hikers unparalleled vistas of Pennsylvania Dutch farmlands.

A mile south of Kutztown on Nobel Street a giant flea market takes place every Saturday at Renninger's No. 2, and you'll find an authentic farmers' market at Renninger's on Fridays and Saturdays and nearby in Shillington on Thursdays and Fridays. Come early for the pick of the crop.

Any day is a good time to head south on Route 222 to scoop up bargains in Reading, a town that is "outlet city," boasting a host of major outlet centers, mostly old factory buildings converted to no-frills showrooms featuring merchandise from hundreds of top manufacturers. Corning, Manhattan, Polo–Ralph Lauren, Vassarette, Ship 'n Shore, Van Heusen, Evan-Picone, Bass, Quoddy, Mikasa, Vanity Fair, and Danskin are just a few of the brands with their own stores, and more labels of all kinds await in other outlets.

While you are in Reading, dine at Joe's, a restaurant famed among gourmets for dishes made with locally grown wild mushrooms, and drive to the top of Mt. Penn for the soaring view from the landmark known as the Pagoda.

More worthwhile sights nearby are the Daniel Boone Homestead, on Route 422 east of Reading, and Hopewell Village, a restored iron-making community dating back to 1771, located on Route 345 south of Birdsboro. French Creek State Park, adjoining Hopewell Village, offers 6,500 scenic acres in the Blue Ridge Mountains with areas for picnicking, swimming, hiking, and boating. And almost everyone marvels at the Blue Rocks, a natural wonder that is a fossil of the Ice Age, located northeast of Reading in the mountains of northern Berks County.

There are country inns in the area, and a host of motels near Reading, but you might want to make your headquarters for the weekend to the south in Ephrata, where you have three appealing choices. Doneckers is one part fine restaurant, one part posh store, and one part elegant inn in a series of restored local homes.

Smithton is a gracious 1763 home where every guest room has a fireplace and the four-poster beds are made up with handmade quilts and goose-down pillows. The inn even supplies nightshirts to put you in an old-fashioned mood. In summer you'll find fresh flowers in your room and breakfast served outdoors in the garden house. The Covered Bridge Inn is away from town near the bridge that inspired the name. On its grounds are a hammock for lazing, an herb garden, and lawns for badminton or croquet.

As for shops in Ephrata, Doneckers has recently added a major attraction in addition to its original store. The Artworks is a former factory transformed into four floors of some 60 shops and galleries for artists and craftspeople. Many artisans can be seen at work on their crafts. Photography, pottery, quilts, leather game boards, handmade kaleidoscopes, photography, paintings, and whimsical folk carvings are just a few of the offerings. Some other interesting stops in town include Martin's Chair Shop on East Farmersville Road, for handcrafted furniture, and the Self-Help Crafts Center on Route 272, which is run by the Mennonite Central Committee to help people in developing nations earn a living through the sale of their traditional crafts.

Both the Artworks and the Self-Help Crafts Center offer pleasant cafes for lunch. Doneckers is fine for dining locally, but if you are willing to take a drive into the countryside, you'll find excellent food at several inns in this area. Lancaster dining is also about twenty minutes away.

Ephrata boasts one of the more unusual historic attractions in this region. Ephrata Cloister is the restored community of a monastic sect founded in 1730. You'll have to duck your head to enter the low doorways (a reminder of humility) and go single file down the narrow halls (symbols of the straight and narrow path) to see where these dedicated people lived and the narrow wooden ledges where they slept, with eight-inch wooden blocks for pillows. There are eight surviving buildings, and they evoke an unusually vivid sense of the austere way of life practiced here. From the second Saturday in July through Labor Day weekend, the cloister presents Vorspiel, an outdoor musical drama depicting the everyday life of this spartan eighteenth-century communal society.

Rites a bit more festive are to be found nearby if you come to Kutztown over the Fourth of July. Hopewell Village celebrates the day with a living history pageant reenacting colonial camp life, and the summerlong jousting and medieval merriment of the Pennsylvania Renaissance Faire drama is in full swing at Mount Hope Estate and Winery in nearby Manheim.

But then again, no specific occasion or season is really needed to visit the gala Kutztown Folk Festival. Any day you pick is going to feel like a holiday.

Area Code: 215; Ephrata, 717

DRIVING DIRECTIONS Kutztown is on Route 222, off Route 78 or Route 9, the Pennsylvania Turnpike Extension. From D.C., take I-95 north to Wilmington. Exit here for Route 202 north, which turns into Route 322 north, connect to Route 100 north to Allentown, get onto Route 9 north briefly, and exit onto Route 222 west to Kutztown. Approximate distance from D.C., 190 miles.

ACCOMMODATIONS *Doneckers Guesthouses,* 301 and 318–324 North State Street, Ephrata, 17522, (717) 733-8696, $$–$$$$ CP ● *Smithton Inn,* 900 West Main Street, Ephrata, 17522, 733-6094, $$–$$$$ ● *Covered Bridge Inn,* 990 Rettew Mill Road, Ephrata, 17522, 733-1592, $–$$ CP ● *Sunday's Mill Farm,* RD 2, P.O. Box 419, Bernville, 19506, 488-7821, working farm with a fishing pond and creek, $ CP ● *Yellow House Hotel,* routes 662 and 562, Douglassville, 19518, 689-9410, historic inn, modest rooms, $ CP ● Glasbern B&B Inn, RD 1, P.O. Box 250, Fogelsville, 18051, 285-4723, rooms in restored barn; pool, whirlpool baths, fireplaces, $$–$$$ CP. Write for Reading motel listings.

BED AND BREAKFAST *Bed & Breakfast of Southeast Pennsylvania,* 146 West Philadelphia Avenue, Boyertown, PA 19512, 367-4688.

DINING *Joe's,* 450 South 7th Street, Reading, 373-6794, worth a special trip, $$$–$$$$ ● *Widow Finney's,* South 4th and Cherry streets, Reading, 378-1776, delightful restored log cabin; $$$ ● *Boyers Hotel,* Main Street, Boyers (southwest of Kutztown), 82-2900, country atmosphere, excellent value, $–$$ ● *Yellow House Hotel,* routes 562 and 662, Douglassville (south of Kutztown, west of Reading), 659-9410, historic inn, $–$$$ ● *Green Hills Inn,* Route 10, Green Hills, 777-9611 (south of Reading), excellent French, $–$$$ ● *Doneckers,* Ephrata (see above), Continental menu or light fare in cafe, $$–$$$.

SIGHTSEEING *Kutztown Folk Festival,* 461 Vine Lane, Kutztown, 683-8707, 9 days late June to early July, including Fourth of July. Hours: 9 A.M. to 5 P.M., activities to 7 P.M. Adults, $7; under 12, $3; parking, $2 ● *The Artworks at Doneckers,* 100 North State Street, 733-7900. Monday, Tuesday, Thursday 11:45 A.M. to 5 P.M.; Friday 11:45 A.M. to 9 P.M.; Saturday 10 A.M. to 5 P.M. Closed Wednesday and Sunday ● *Reading Outlet Stores:* listings available from Berks County. Most stores open Monday to Saturday 9:30 A.M. to 5:30 P.M.; Sunday noon to 5 P.M. Check individual listings ● *Ephrata Cloister,* 632 West Main Street,

Ephrata, 733-6600. Hours: Monday to Saturday 9 A.M. to 5 P.M.; Sunday noon to 5 P.M. Adults, $3; children, $1.50 ● *Vorspiel Performances,* late June through Labor Day, Saturdays. Adults, $7; children, $1.50 ● *Hopewell Village,* Route 345, south of Birdsboro, 582-8773. Hours: daily 9 A.M. to 5 P.M. Adults, $1; children, free ● *French Creek State Park,* Route 345 near Hopewell, 582-1514, daily daylight hours. Free except for boat rentals or swimming fees ● *Daniel Boone Homestead,* US 422, east of Reading, 582-4900. Hours: Tuesday to Saturday 9 A.M. to 5 P.M.; Sunday noon to 5 P.M. Adults, $1.50; children, $.50 ● *W. K. & S. Steam Railroad,* near Route 22, Kempton, 434-2158. Hours: July and August, daily; March to June and September to November, weekends. Adults, $3; children, $1.50. Check current schedules ● *Pennsylvania Dutch Farm Museum,* Kempton, 683-7130. Hours: May to October, weekends only. Adults, $1; children, free. *Hawk Mountain Sanctuary,* Route 2, Kempton, 756-6961. Daylight hours daily. Adults, $2; children, $1 ● *Pennsylvania Renaissance Faire,* Mount Hope Estate and Winery, RD 3, Manheim, (717) 665-7021. Hours: weekends, July 4 through Columbus Day. Adults, $10.50; ages 6–11, $3.

INFORMATION Berks County Visitors Information Association, Sheraton Berkshire Inn, Route 422 west, Paper Mill Road, Wyomissing (just outside Reading), PA 19610, 375-4085.

Sea Breezing at Spring Lake

Swans glide tranquilly across a mirror-smooth lake. Strollers take in the sea breeze from a pristine two-mile boardwalk, while old-timers rock gently on the porches of vintage Victorian hotels.

It's the New Jersey shore the way it used to be—and still is in Spring Lake, a perfect getaway for an old-fashioned weekend by the sea.

One of the towns along the posh oceanside stretch once known as the Gold Coast, Spring Lake seems determined to remain what it has been for a century—a gracious vacation oasis. Strict ordinances have deliberately held back the so-called progress that has afflicted so many shoreline communities in the form of video arcades, fast-food eateries, and newly built condominiums.

The heart of things remains the spring-fed lake for which the village was named and the shady green park that surrounds it, stretching for five blocks right through the center of town. Rimmed by weeping willows and spanned by a picturesque wooden footbridge, the lake is a haven for fishermen and boaters, a swimming pool for ducks and geese, and a frequent landing pad for sea gulls that shuttle back and forth between its tranquil waters and the ocean, just a shell's throw away.

The first to spot the unique attraction of a shore site with its own freshwater lake was a group of Philadelphia businessmen back in 1875. They formed the Spring Lake Beach Improvement Company, acquired the 285-acre property then known as Osborn Farm, and hired engineer Frederick Anspach to plan a whole new resort town. The centerpiece of the development was the ultra-elegant Monmouth House Hotel, completed in 1876 with 270 bedrooms, a dining room seating 1,000 guests, and large parlors overlooking the ocean.

A success from the start, it was quickly joined by more elaborate hotels and guest houses. Soon millionaires were building mammoth "summer cottages" in Spring Lake. A fire in 1900 slowed things temporarily, but the town rebuilt and remained a thriving part of the privileged people's shore.

Some of the hotels and many of the homes were transported here by wealthy businessmen directly from the 1876 Centennial Exposition in Philadelphia. Brochures from the town historical society point you to these and many other buildings remaining from the turn of the century.

The Monmouth House Hotel is gone, but you'll need no map to find many other sprawling wooden hotels of that earlier era. The huge Essex-Sussex, where the movie *Ragtime* was filmed, retains its prize spot across from the beach, while the Hewitt Wellington looks out at the lake as it has for decades. You can still dance sedately after dinner at the Warren, have a drink at the Shoreham or a meal at the Breakers just as Victorian vacationers did, and you'll find some of the hotels hardly changed with the passage of time. If the carpets are faded and there is no air-conditioning, it's because longtime summer guests seem to like it that way.

However, behind the unchanged façades, time marches on in Spring Lake. The Hewitt Wellington is now a condominium complex, with many of the newly elegant rooms available for weekend rentals. The Essex-Sussex is following this trend. Hotels like the Warren have been refurbished, and the Breakers has added air-conditioning, TV, and other modern comforts. And some of the old homes have become delightful bed-and-breakfast lodgings. Among the pleasantest is the Normandy Inn.

Spring Lake acquired its nickname, the Irish Riviera, for the many Irish families who were among the earliest to establish summer mansions here. The head of one prominent family, philanthropist Martin Maloney, built the town's showplace, St. Catherine's Church, in 1901 as a memorial to his daughter, who died at the age of 17. The ornate Romanesque architecture, marble altar, and frescoed ceilings, modeled after a Vatican chapel, are proudly shown off to visitors by the natives.

One remaining sign of the Irish influence is the Irish Center, a boutique on Third Avenue, the town's main shopping street, where you will find Irish fisherman sweaters, Donegal tweeds, Celtic jewelry, walking sticks, and a wide assortment of teas, cookies, and candies all imported from the Emerald Isle.

The three-block "downtown" of Spring Lake is more preppy than touristy, but it does make for a pleasant stroll and some interesting browsing for gifts, summer dresses, or colorful beach hats.

If you want a light lunch, Jeffrey's on Third Street will oblige, and the Sundae Times on Atlantic and First streets is guaranteed to satisfy your sweet tooth.

There's plenty to do by day in Spring Lake. Day passes can be bought for a modest fee at the beach, and some lodgings provide badges admitting their guests to the two town bathhouses, each with a saltwater pool. You can fish for the trout stocked in the local lake, play tennis in the park or golf at nearby facilities, jog along the boardwalk, or take a walk or ride a bike to look at the cupolas and gingerbread of the town's fine houses. Most of the inns will either lend you a bike or help you rent one. If your energy flags, hop the trolley that makes a regular loop from the train station along the lake and the park for 50 cents; all it takes is a "thumbs-up" signal and the driver will stop for you.

All of the blocks between Ocean and Third avenues have prize homes to be seen. Check out Coalbrook, Martin Maloney's 26-room carriage house at 105 Morris Avenue. On Monmouth Avenue, the Rolin House (circa 1888) at 207 and its neighbor at 214 are in the aptly named Spring Lake Beach Victorian style and are also worth a look (especially the latter, a gingerbread classic with carpenter Gothic shingles, floor-to-ceiling windows, and stained glass). Two survivors from the Centennial Exhibition are the Missouri State Building at 411 Ocean Road and the Portuguese Government Pavilion at 205 Atlantic Avenue.

One sight not to be missed is the beautifully planted lawn at Green Gables on Ocean Avenue between Washington and Madison streets. It contains two regulation-size croquet courts, which are used every Thursday by the members of the local croquet club, nattily attired in all-white. In September they are joined by players from all over at an annual invitational croquet tournament.

Evenings are quiet here. Along with dancing, the larger hotels offer some entertainment; there are summer productions at the theater located in the attractive local community house, and concerts are held in the park.

But mainly this is a town for an after-dinner stroll by the lake or the sea and quiet talk on the wide porch of your inn, pleasures of a more tranquil era in a town that remains a picture book from the past. The only swingers in Spring Lake are in the gliders on the front porch.

Area Code: 201

DRIVING DIRECTIONS Spring Lake is on the Jersey shore about midway between New York and Philadelphia, at exit 98 on the Garden State Parkway. From D.C., take I-95 north, across the Delaware Memorial Bridge to the New Jersey Turnpike. At exit 7A, follow I-195 east to Route 34 south; at the traffic circle, follow Route 524 east into town. Approximate distance from D.C., 206 miles.

PUBLIC TRANSPORTATION Connecting train service is available from Philadelphia. For information, call New Jersey Transit, 460-8444.

ACCOMMODATIONS Modernized hotels include *Hewitt Wellington,* 200 Monmouth Avenue, 07762, 974-1212, best and priciest in town, $$$$ • *The Breakers,* 1507 Ocean Avenue, 07762, 449-7700, outdoor pool $$$$ • *The Warren Hotel,* 901 Ocean Avenue, 07762, 449-8800 (open Memorial Day to mid-October), pool, tennis, putting green, $$$$ • Among the houses-turned-inns are *Normandy Inn,* 21 Tuttle Avenue, 07762, 449-7172, nicest of all, $$$ CP • *The Stone Post Inn,* 115 Washington Avenue, 07762, 449-1212, nice grounds, warm hostess, $$–$$$ CP • *Ashling Cottage,* 106 Sussex Avenue, 07762, 449-3553, charming rooms, $$$ CP • *The Lodge at Spring Lake,* 15 Mercer Avenue, 07762, 449-6002, modest outside, stylish inside, pool, dinners on request, many special weekends and dinners off-season, $$$–$$$$ CP • One pleasant motel deserves mention for its location on the park: *The Chateau,* 500 Warren Avenue, 07762, 974-2000, $$$; cooking units, $$$$. All require 2- or 3-night minimum reservations in season; all are less off-season.

DINING *The Old Mill,* Route 71, Spring Lake Heights, 449-1800, delightful ambience, but no reservations taken, so expect waiting lines, $$$ • *The Breakers* (see above), Italian, $$$ • *The Sandpiper,* Ocean and Atlantic avenues, 449-9707, Continental menu, $$$ ● *The Beach House,* Warren Hotel (see above), 449-9646, $$–$$$ ● *Whispers,* Hewitt Wellington (see above), $$$ ● *Champagne Porch,* 810 Highway 71, Spring Lake Heights, 449-5880, $–$$ ● *Eggiman's Tavern,* 2031 Highway 71, Spring Lake Heights, 449-2626, $–$$ ● Some nearby recommendations: *Evelyn's,* 507 Main Street, Belmar, 681-0236, no frills, good fresh fish, $$–$$$ ● *Peach Tree,* Route 35, Wall, 223-4844, good reports, $$–$$$ ● *Rod's Olde Irish Tavern,* 507 Washington Boulevard, Sea Girt, 449-2020, informal, $–$$ ● *Yankee Clipper,* Chicago and Ocean avenues, Sea Girt, 449-7200, ocean view, $$–$$$. Sea Girt pubs such as the Parker House are where younger vacationers go for nightlife.

INFORMATION   Greater Spring Lake Chamber of Commerce, P.O. Box 694, Spring Lake, NJ 07762, 449-0577 ● For complete list of lodgings, Spring Lake Hotel and Guest House Association, P.O. Box 134, Spring Lake, NJ 07762.

Reliving the Past at Gettysburg

The silent green countryside of Gettysburg, Pennsylvania, is a landscape peopled with ghosts.

Over 100 years after the Civil War battle was fought, it is still impossible to visit the site without feeling moved by the events that took place here long ago, when the nation's unity was saved by the bloodiest battle in its history.

During the annual Civil War Heritage Days, held the first week in July, when flags stand at attention in long rows on every main street in town, and a reenactment of the battle brings dust and smoke to the battlefield once again, the human drama and tragedy of battle become almost tangibly alive.

It was on July 1, 2, and 3, 1863, when soldiers from the North and South, Americans all, fought here in one of history's most memorable battles. Visiting Gettysburg means retracing the battle through its three-day course, and there are all manner of commercial enterprises ready to help you do this, the result of the large crowds that continue to be attracted to the site each year.

The best advice is to avoid them all—the Lincoln Train Museum, the Gettysburg Battle Theater, the wax museum Hall of Presidents, even the red-white-and-blue tour bus with its recorded narration by Raymond Massey accompanied by a "cast of thousands" re-creating the sounds of battle in "living stereo sound."

Instead, stick to the National Park Service offerings, where you get less sound and a more human side of a battle whose drama needs no embellishment.

As soon as you arrive in town, head for the Gettysburg National Military Park Visitor Center. Start with the Electric Map Orientation Program, a 30-minute overview of the battle's progress displayed on a giant relief map with colored lights tracing the course of the action.

If you are already knowledgeable about the battle, pick up one of the printed auto or bicycling guides for your own tour of the meticulously maintained and well-marked battlegrounds.

Otherwise, sign up fast for a licensed battlefield guide. These serious battle buffs have passed stringent written and oral exams to qualify for their posts. For a very reasonable fee, a guide will join you in your car for a private tour over the battleground and answer all your questions. In two hours, a knowledgeable guide can tell you more about the battle and the generals and men who decided its course than a dozen textbooks. Some of the guides are actually at work on their own books.

If you have a wait until a guide is available, you can whet your appetite at the Cyclorama Center, where you will see a film called *Gettysburg 1863*, and a sound-and-light program depicting the action of Pickett's Charge displayed against Paul Philloteaux's famous painting of the battle, a giant circular canvas 356 feet in circumference and 26 feet high.

You'll learn from the various exhibits that the first day of battle looked bad for the Union forces, who were chased through the streets of Gettysburg to the heights outside of town. That proved to be a major break for the Northerners, whose new lines turned out to be positions of strength, especially when Lee's generals were unable to coordinate their attack on the second day.

On July 3 General Robert E. Lee made the fateful decision to assault the center of the Union line on Cemetery Ridge in the battle that went down in history as Pickett's Charge. After a thunderous two-hour artillery bombardment that completely shrouded the field in smoke, the air cleared and Union defenders looked down on an unbelievable sight—15,000 Confederate soldiers shoulder to shoulder in a line a mile and a half wide, an ocean of an army sweeping forward, guns glinting in the sun, colors held high. The Confederates charged on, only to be mowed down by the murderous blasts of Union fire. In 50 minutes, 10,000 were dead or wounded, and the tide of the Civil War turned irreversibly to the North.

The human factors that contributed to the astounding battle are fascinating, even if you have never found much interest in battles or wars. Overconfident Confederate troops who had battered Union forces in the South were making their first foray into the North, where a third of their opponents were determined young Pennsylvania farm boys defending their home ground. The battle itself was never meant to happen; Lee was planning to fight in the cover of the mountains. It began only because a Southern regiment, in search of new shoes to replace those worn out in the long march north, bumped into a Union scouting party in Gettysburg. Reinforcements for this minor skirmish came willy-nilly, without any overall plan.

According to one guide, Lee's ill-fated charge, incomprehensible to us today, was the result of using traditional parade-ground tactics, which were ineffective against the high-power cannons that represented a new kind of warfare. And some of the South's mistakes were human errors. A major one can be attributed to the ego of General Sickels, who, overanxious to be a hero, rushed to be the first to lead an attack, thereby giving up a valuable Southern strategic position on the ridge.

The stories of brothers fighting brothers and of 12-year-old drummer boys lost in the fray are heartbreaking, and so are the neat rows of thousands of graves in the National Cemetery and the many state monuments to fallen heroes.

To add to your understanding of all these events and sites, free National Park Service ranger-guided walking tours are held at the National Cemetery and at the major action points, such as Pickett's Charge, the Valley of Death, Little Round Top, and the Devil's Den. Evening campfire programs take place at an amphitheater in the same woods where Confederate soldiers once camped.

During the weekends of Civil War Heritage Days, you can actually visit living history encampments where participants dressed in authentic Union and Confederate uniforms set up tent camps, realistic right down to campfire cooking and female "camp followers." Demonstrations show infantry and cavalry drills and artillery firing, and the well-informed mock soldiers answer any and all questions about the camp life of Civil War troops. During the week, lectures are held each night at Gettysburg College for those who want to learn more about the Civil War. The Fourth of July is marked in Gettysburg by fife-and-drum corps and brass band concerts, and the Fireman's Festival of rides, games, and entertainment.

The highlights of the week are on the Sunday afternoons before and after July 4, when reenactments of a specific battle take place. The earth shakes with the boom of cannon and rifle fire and the charging hooves of the cavalry, smoke clouds the battlefield, and you begin to understand in a new way the horrors of war and the terror that must have been in the hearts of the valiant young men who fought here, many of them only teenagers.

There's more history to be found on a walking tour in Gettysburg, a small town still a bit reminiscent of the way it looked in 1863. The printed tour available at the information center located in the old railway station on Carlisle Street shows you the routes where troops marched into town, where Lincoln lodged and worshiped when he came to give the Gettysburg Address, the school building that served as hospital for wounded from both sides, and the church-turned-hospital where holes had to be drilled in the floor to allow the heavy flow of blood from the wounded to drain through. One of the homes served for ten years following the war as an orphanage for the children whose fathers were lost in the war; another was a hotel whose liquor was "liberated" by Confederate troops; others still hold in their walls cannonballs fired over a century ago. One favorite local tale deals with Jennie Wade, a 20-year-old woman who was the only civilian casualty of the battle, struck down by a bullet in her own kitchen. Another story tells of the tavern where a cannonball literally cleared the table of its settings and landed safely in a mattress. Civil War buffs will also find lots of shops selling memorabilia in Gettysburg.

Just a few blocks from the heart of town is the campus of Gettysburg College and the office where the late President Dwight D. Eisenhower worked when he was president of the college. The lovely 495-acre Eisenhower Farm in the nearby countryside may be visited on National Park Service tours and is a vivid reminder of the spirits and personalities of the president and his wife, Mamie.

Tour or no, a drive out of town into the rolling Pennsylvania countryside is a happy ending to a Gettysburg visit. The 36-mile driving loop along Route 234 past covered bridges, farms, and the famous Adams County apple orchards is a consoling reminder that beauty transcends battles and that peace reigns supreme in the valley.

Area Code: 717

DRIVING DIRECTIONS   Gettysburg is on Route 15, roughly midway between Harrisburg, PA, and Frederick, MD. From D.C., take Route 170 north to Frederick, then Route 15 north into town. Approximate distance from D.C., 80 miles.

PUBLIC TRANSPORTATION   Nearest major Amtrak and bus stop is Harrisburg, 28 miles away.

ACCOMMODATIONS   *Doubleday Inn,* 104 Doubleday Avenue, Gettysburg, 17325, 334-9119, antique-filled Colonial on the battlefield, $$–$$$ CP ● *The Old Appleford Inn,* 218 Carlisle

Street, 17325, 337-1711, pleasant, modest, convenient bed-and-breakfast home, $$–$$$ CP ● *Sheraton Inn,* Business Route 15 south, Gettysburg, 17325, 334-8121, (800) 325-3535, $$$–$$$$ ● *TraveLodge,* 10 East Lincoln Avenue, 17325, 334-6235, $–$$ ● *Howard Johnson's Motor Lodge,* 301 Steinwehr Avenue, 17325, 334-1188, (800) 654-2000, $$.

DINING   Gettysburg is often mobbed, and restaurants are, too—try to dine early or late. *Dobbin House,* 89 Steinwehr Avenue, 334-2100, historic, charming, $$–$$$ ● *Spring House Tavern,* part of Dobbin House, easier to get into, light fare, $ ● *Farnsworth House,* 401 Baltimore Street, 334-8838, 1833 home, garden, $–$$ ● *Fairfield Inn,* Route 116, Main Street, Fairfield, 642-5410, country inn 8 miles west of town, $$.

SIGHTSEEING   *Gettysburg National Military Park,* Route 134, 334-1124. Visitors center hours: daily 8 A.M. to 6 P.M.. Free literature and tour guides ● *Electric Map Orientation Program:* Adults, $2; ages 15 and under, free ● *Cyclorama Sound and Light Program:* Adults, $1; ages 15 and under, free. Park Service ranger talks, free; private guides, $17 for 2 hours ● *Eisenhower National Historic Site* guided tours. Hours: 9 A.M. to 4 P.M. Adults, $2.25; children, $.70 ● *Gettysburg Tour Center,* 778 Baltimore Street, 334-6296, tickets for bus tours and package plans for all town attractions, $9.75 and up, depending on plan chosen ● *The Conflict,* 213 Steinwehr Avenue, 334-8003, a well-done multimedia, 6-projector film on the Civil War. Daily 10 A.M. to 9 P.M. Adults, $4; students, $3; under 6, free.

INFORMATION   Gettysburg Travel Council, Inc., 35 Carlisle Street, Gettysburg, PA 17325, 334-6274.

Communing with Nature at Chincoteague

There's absolutely nothing fancy about Chincoteague, Virginia's Eastern Shore beach retreat—and that's exactly why so many people fancy the place.

This low-key, laid-back little waterman's enclave offers no kitsch, no quaint, no frills. The condos and high-rises haven't made it here, nor will you find much in the way of nightlife or shopping or reason to dress for dinner.

What you *will* find is a causeway beckoning to 12 miles of exquisite unspoiled Assateague Island National Seashore beaches—beaches so wide that a short walk will bring space all to yourself even on the busiest summer day. Add the Chincoteague National Wildlife Refuge on Assateague, with the famous Chincoteague wild ponies and some of the most fascinating bird and animal life to be seen anywhere on the Atlantic seaboard, and you have a unique back-to-nature getaway.

Assateague is the northernmost of the sandy chain of barrier islands off the Eastern Shore. It stretches from just south of Ocean City, Maryland, to Chincoteague, with public entrances found only at either end. Though the island is only about 22 miles long, it is an hour-and-a-half drive between the two developed areas.

Maryland's beach area is a state park, while the National Park Service and the Department of the Interior maintain the larger Virginia section, which includes both lifeguard-protected beaches and a significant undisturbed portion of the coastal wetlands, 9,550 acres of preserve that is home to snow geese and mergansers, osprey and herons, ibis and egret, graceful deer and hundreds of other species of birds and animals.

They can be seen on the paved Wildlife Drive, which is limited to hikers and bikers until 3 P.M. each day, then is opened to cars until 7 P.M. There are also hiking trails leading to some of the best vantage points for spotting some 230 species of birds, and the daily morning Wildlife Safari ride offering a narrated 15-mile land tour through back roads normally forbidden to cars. There are many other National Park Service and Department of Interior programs all summer—guided walks, bike tours, and evening programs on birds and animals of the refuge, on the salt marsh and marine ecology, and on the Chincoteague ponies. Another regular feature are the narrated *Osprey* evening boat cruises, which head out through the channel and sail along the refuge shoreline. Many of the walks and talks are especially for children.

Almost universally, the sight that delights visitors most is that of the free-spirited wild ponies that roam the refuge. Youngsters seem particularly taken with the ponies, especially since a children's book and movie, *Misty of Chincoteague,* caught the fancy of children everywhere.

Legend says that the ponies are descendants of mustang horses that swam ashore from a wrecked Spanish galleon four centuries ago. Though their growth has been stunted by a sparse diet of marsh grasses and bayberry leaves, the shaggy, sturdy small horses nonetheless have managed to survive and thrive. At present there are two herds, a small one of about 40 horses in the Maryland part of the park and another of about 130 horses in the Virginia section, where a fence separates state and federal jurisdiction. The ponies travel in packs of from 2 to 20 horses, with the smaller horses often protected by a stallion.

The horses are bothered by mosquitoes and flies during the summer, but nature has provided them with help in the form of white cattle egrets, birds that feed on these insects. Camera shutters click furiously when the egrets perch on the ponies' backs to catch their prey. (Human visitors, not having such helpful guardians, are well advised to bring along insect repellent when they visit the refuge.)

A more remarkable sight drawing thousands of spectators is the pony swim and sale held annually the last Wednesday in July. The Chincoteague Volunteer Firemen round up the ponies and swim them across the channel to town, where excess young are sold at auction. The sale serves a dual purpose, keeping the herd down to a number that can be supported by the vegetation on Assateague and providing funds for community projects.

Having seen the beautiful ponies in the wild, it is almost painful to see them put through their paces for tourists at the Chincoteague Pony Farm, but if you have children along, you may be wheedled into paying the admission.

Back on Assateague, a long, thinning tail of shoreline hooking away from the ocean shelters the waters of Tom's Cove and is the setting for many water-related activities, including clamming and crabbing. Family fishing-boat trips are offered, and there are ''Blue Crab Specials,'' teaching the biology of blue crabs as well as the art of catching this Eastern Shore delicacy. Lessons in surf fishing are also given.

Assateague has seen a growing number of visitors since 1960, when a bridge was built connecting it to the mainland. Nevertheless, Chincoteague itself remains basically a town where most of the population of 3,700 continue to make their living from oysters, clams, and crabs, just as their families have done for generations. There is no sewage treatment plant, forestalling any thought of large development, and while some handsome vacation homes are being built, the town itself is basic, not beautiful. Most of the homes and buildings are modest frame structures.

Accommodations consist of campgrounds, trailer parks, cottages, a couple of inns, and lots of motels, making for a democratic mix, from RVs to BMWs, in local store parking lots. Among the motels, the picks are the Refuge and the Driftwood, the two located closest to Assateague, and the Island Motor Inn, which overlooks the bay and offers grounds for clamming and crabbing.

At dinner, you can opt for the Landmark, one of the newer restaurants geared to tourists and boasting the island's best sunset view, or join the mix of locals and visitors at Spinakers, or Pony Pines, or Don's, the last offering evening entertainment. In any case, you can count on a menu rich with delicious fresh clams and crabs and, in season, the special local pride, Chincoteague oysters. These famous salt oysters are cultivated on sand and rock public grounds that the oystermen seed and harvest much as landlubbers might tend a vegetable garden. The local Oyster Museum on Assateague Beach Road shows you how it is done, and also gives a close-up look at oysters, crabs, starfish, sea horses, and other denizens of the nearby deep.

A different kind of Chincoteague dining experience—gourmet food with a Spanish touch—can be found at the highly touted Channel Bass Inn, but if you go, be prepared for prices that are exorbitant and an atmosphere whose formality and tuxedoed waiters seem very out of place for this down-to-earth town.

Chincoteague has one other claim to fame, its wood carvers. The roster of the Chincoteague Decoy Carvers Association lists some 20 members who can be visited at their home studios, and fine decoys and bird carvings can be found in local shops, as well as at the Refuge Waterfowl Museum. The museum, containing an enormous private collection, is a must for anyone who is interested in shorebird art. The annual Easter Decoy Festival also brings many knowledgeable collectors to town.

Two other annual events are worth noting. One is the Oyster Festival, held over Columbus Day weekend in October, one of the months when the oysters ''r'' in peak season. The second is the annual Waterfowl Open House at the National Wildlife Refuge during Thanksgiving week, just in time for visitors to see thousands of migrating waterfowl in residence.

If you are in search of activity away from the beach, NASA maintains an experimental rocket program on nearby Wallops Island and offers a small museum as well as free tours to the launch sites during the summer months. Or you might take a drive across the peninsula to Onancock and board a boat for the remote otherworldly atmosphere of Tangier Island.

But if you get into the rhythm of things on Chincoteague, chances are you'll be happy right here, kicking off your shoes, slowing down your pace, and just enjoying unspoiled nature at its very best.

Area Code: 804

DRIVING DIRECTIONS   Chincoteague is off Route 13 at the northern end of Virginia's Eastern Shore. From D.C., follow Route 50/301 across the Chesapeake Bay Bridge, and take Route 50 to Salisbury. Turn south on Route 13, then turn off at Route 175 east into town. Approximate distance from D.C., 175 miles.

ACCOMMODATIONS *Refuge Motor Inn,* P.O. Box 378, Beach Road, 23336, 336-5511, $$–$$$ ● *Driftwood Motor Lodge,* P.O. Box 575, Beach Road, 23336, 336-6557, $$ ● *Island Motor Inn,* North Main Street, 23336, 336-3141, $$ ● *Chincoteague Motor Lodge,* Taylor Street, 23336, 336-6415, $$ ● For those who prefer a smaller inn atmosphere: *Year of the Horse Inn,* 600 South Main Street, 23336, 336-3221, $$–$$$ CP ● *Channel Bass Inn,* 100 Church Street, 23336, 336-6148, $$$$ CP ● *The Victorian Inn,* 105 Clark Street, 23336, 336-1161, $$–$$$ CP.

DINING *The Landmark Crabhouse,* North Main Street, Landmark Plaza, 336-5552, $–$$ ● *Beachway,* Maddox Boulevard, 336-5590, try their extraordinary crabmeat salad, $–$$$ ● *Spinnakers,* Maddox Boulevard, 336-5400, $-$$ ● *Pony Pines,* Church Street, 336-9746, $–$$$ ● *Don's,* North Main Street, 336-5715, $–$$ ● *Channel Bass Inn* (see above), $$$$.

SIGHTSEEING *Assateague National Seashore,* Route 2, P.O. Box 294, Berlin, MD 21811, (301) 641-1441, phone for current hours. Free except for Wildlife Safaris and other special guided tours and cruises. Check current schedules and rates ● *Chincoteague National Wildlife Refuge,* P.O. Box 62, Chincoteague, 23336, 336-6122, phone for current hours. $1 per person arriving on foot or by bike, $5 per car ● *Oyster Museum of Chincoteague,* Beach Road, 336-6117. Hours: May to mid-September, daily 11 A.M. to 4:45 P.M.; mid-September to November, weekends only. Adults, $1; children, $.25 ● *Refuge Waterfowl Museum,* Maddox Road, 336-5800. Hours: Memorial Day to Labor Day, daily 10 A.M. to 5 P.M.; rest of year, weekends only. Adults, $2.50; children, $1 ● *Chincoteague Miniature Pony Farm,* 201 Maddox Boulevard, 336-3066. Hours: mid-March to November, daily. Adults, $3.

INFORMATION Chincoteague Island Chamber of Commerce, P.O. Box 258, Chincoteague, VA 23336, 336-6161.

Taking the Waters in West Virginia

Never underestimate the power of a celebrity endorsement. Even in the 1700s, a few notable investors was all it took for the world to beat a path to the waters at Berkeley Springs, West Virginia, launching America's first successful health spa.

Of course, the list of names signing up to buy property at the mineral spring was quite impressive, beginning with George Washington himself and including three signers of the Declaration of Independence, four signers of the Constitution, seven members of the Continental Congress, and five Revolutionary War generals. Small wonder that people came from as far away as Europe to try out the benefits of the baths and that Berkeley Springs became one of early America's prime resorts.

Fickle fashion moved elsewhere, and things are a bit quieter now in the mountains of West Virginia, but you can still bathe in the beneficial waters and have your tensions massaged away in the bathhouse, now part of a small state park that is on the National Register of Historic Places. As a bonus, you can enjoy another of West Virginia's most popular state parks, plus one of its most delightful resorts, both located not far down the road.

The spring water that started it all comes from five main sources and many lesser ones, all within 100 yards along the base of a steep ridge rising above a narrow valley. The springs give off about 2,000 gallons of clear sparkling water per minute at the constant temperature of 74.3 degrees Fahrenheit.

Long before the first white men discovered them, these warm waters were already drawing Indians all the way from Canada and the Great Lakes to the Carolinas. It was the Indians, in fact, who introduced the colonists to the springs.

George Washington was a 16-year-old surveyor for Thomas, Lord Fairfax, in 1748 when he camped here while checking the western boundaries of the Fairfax property, an occasion he noted in his diary. Supposedly, he relaxed for a while in the small natural stone tub at the springs, a space that would never have been adequate for his grown-up six-foot frame.

Washington helped spread the fame of the health spa and in 1776 persuaded his friend Lord Fairfax to give his land holdings and 50 adjacent acres to the Colony of Virginia, which at that time included what is now West Virginia. The Virginia General Assembly borrowed the name of a famous resort in England and formed a town called Bath, which is still its official name. They created a board of trustees to govern the new town and began constructing bathhouses and other public buildings to take advantage of the natural springs. When some of the nearby property went up for sale, George and his friends were first in line. The Washingtons had their summer home here.

Today at the Berkeley Springs State Park there are two ways to soak up the benefits of the water—in a conventional bathtub or in one of 14 Roman baths, sunken pools lined with tile and marble holding 750 gallons of water each. Besides the baths, the park offers various forms of physiotherapy, such as infrared heat and massage, all at state-regulated rates far below those of the average health club. And there is now an outdoor swimming pool for more athletic summer visitors. Just be sure to make your reservations well in advance, since the schedule does tend to get filled. Two weeks ahead is none too soon to book.

The state park is in the center of the village, and right next door is the columned Country Inn. This is more hotel than inn, and bigger and busier than you might expect in a country town of 2,500, but lots of people seem to like it nevertheless.

When you emerge from the baths, the main diversions at Berkeley Springs are a few public tennis courts and the Old Factory Antique Mall, between Williams and Union streets. The only sightseeing is a small turreted stone structure known as Berkeley Castle. The most interesting thing about it is the guide's sad tale of the ill-fated May-September marriage that was the reason for its construction.

A far more exhilarating sight is the view from Prospect Peak off Route 9. Cited by no less an authority than *National Geographic* magazine as one of America's outstanding viewpoints, the overlook takes in the Potomac and Great Cacapon valleys and the states of West Virginia, Pennsylvania, and Maryland.

Having admired the view, unless you plan to spend a lot of time at the baths, it's better to seek accommodations out of town that take advantage of the scenic mountain surroundings and the out-of-doors.

One pleasant possibility is Cacapon State Park, one of West Virginia's superb state parks that are among the true travel bargains of the world. This long, narrow preserve of 6,115 acres extends across the state's eastern panhandle almost to the Maryland border, and encompasses Cacapon Mountain, whose bulk dominates the view everywhere on the broad plain below. A paved road and hiking and bridle trails lead 1,400 feet up to the summit.

There's plenty to do here—golfing at the 18-hole Robert Trent Jones championship course, tennis, fishing, boating, swimming, sunning, or strolling on a sandy lake beach, and hiking in the deep cool woods. The park staff also conduct guided hikes, marshmallow roasts, and other entertainment.

Rooms in the air-conditioned main lodge look down on the lush green golf course. The furnishings are basic motel, but you won't find a motel that touches these amenities for the price. Cabins are available here as well (by the week only, in season), and there are more rooms in the Old Inn, a building of rough-hewn logs that is reminiscent of the kind of rustic accommodations you might have had at summer camp. All of them go fast, and with good reason, so reserve way ahead.

The alternative to Cacapon Park is a uniquely attractive resort nearby called Coolfont, tucked in a valley in the woods with two small spring-fed lakes. The lodgings are hidden in the trees so as not to spoil the faraway feel of the landscape, and the modernistic Tree-top House Restaurant in the main lodge has been built high with big, wide windows overlooking the lakefront.

Classical music, art lessons, and low-key relaxation set the tone for this classy, small, health-oriented resort, where low-calorie meals are a daily option. Tennis, hiking, biking, boating, horseback riding, and swimming are standard activities, but there are many special weekend programs as well, including Massage and Stress Reduction Workshops, Smoke-Free Weekends for those who want to quit the habit, and low-calorie, high-exercise Health and Fitness Retreats. A new swim and fitness center, added weight-training equipment, and facilities for massages and facials add to the spa programs offered.

The yoga and the yogurt found at Coolfont are amenities that were not known in George Washington's day, but the hot tub would no doubt be right up George's alley.

Area Code: 304

DRIVING DIRECTIONS   Berkeley Springs is on Route 522 in the eastern panhandle of West Virginia. From D.C., take Route 7 west to Winchester, then Route 522 north. Approximate distance from D.C., 103 miles. For expressway driving, follow Route 270 north to Route 70 north to Hancock, Maryland, then take Route 522 south. Route 70 is the best route from points west and north.

PUBLIC TRANSPORTATION   Greyhound service to Hancock, Maryland, 6 miles from Berkeley Springs.

ACCOMMODATIONS   *The Country Inn,* 207 South Washington Street, Berkeley Springs, 25411, 258-2210, $–$$ ● *Cacapon Lodge,* Cacapon State Park, off Route 522 south of Berkeley Springs, 25411, 258-1022, $ ● *Coolfont Resort,* off Route 9 south of Berkeley Springs, 25411, 258-4500, from D.C. (800) 424-1232,

$$ • Two Victorian bed-and-breakfast homes in town are *The Manor Inn,* 415 Fairfax Street, Berkeley Springs, 25411, 258-1552, $$–$$$ CP, and *Highlawn Inn,* 304 Market Street, Berkeley Springs, 25411, 258-5700, $$–$$$ CP.

DINING   *Country Inn* (see above) • *Cacapon Lodge* (see above) • *Coolfont* (see above).

SIGHTSEEING   *Berkeley Springs State Park,* Berkeley Springs, 258-2711, warm spring baths, massages, swimming pool. Bathhouse open year-round. Hours: April to October, Saturday to Thursday 10 A.M. to 6 P.M.; Friday to 9 P.M.; November to March, Friday to 7 P.M. Reservations advised. Bath and massage rates from $8 to $20, depending on choice of treatments. Pool open Memorial Day to Labor Day. Adults, $2; children, $1.25. Best to check for current rates.

INFORMATION   Berkeley Springs Chamber of Commerce, 304 Fairfax Street, Berkeley Springs, WV 25411, 258-3738.

Riding the Rails to Paradise

"Wait for Daddy!"

The eager six-year-old outdistancing his dad wasn't the only one who couldn't wait to climb aboard. Everyone in the station seemed excited at the prospect of hopping on the cheerful yellow train whose steam engine was huffing and puffing in readiness for the ride from Strasburg to Paradise, Pennsylvania.

Riding the Strasburg Rail Road, the nation's oldest short line system, is a nostalgia trip for some, a new adventure for others, and a scenic treat for all, since the route runs right through the heart of Amish farm country and affords a rare close-up view of the Plain People at work. The 45-minute round-trip train ride to Paradise is the main attraction, but it is actually only one of the railroading stops in Strasburg, a town that is paradise for anyone who is entranced with history and the romance of trains. Pennsylvania's fine Railroad Museum, with one of the nation's most comprehensive collections of locomotives and rolling stock, the Toy Train Museum, and collectors' shops galore all are located in this railroading mecca, where you can even spend the night in a motel room that is a comfortable converted railroad caboose.

The lure of the trains brings many a camera-toting Lancaster

County tourist into town, yet Strasburg has managed to withstand most of the commercialism that has hit much of Pennsylvania Dutch country. It remains a small village of great appeal whose Main Street is a historic district.

You might want to make your first stop-off the Railroad Museum of Pennsylvania. You'll find some 20 classic locomotives and railroad cars here dating from 1831 to 1941, exhibited along four tracks in a setup reminiscent of train stations of yore. Among the displays are passenger cars, baggage and mail cars, and a Pullman combination sleeper and lounge-diner. Steps placed alongside some of the cars allow you to peek at the interiors and the engines, and an observation bridge gives you a view of the whole array.

The museum also contains displays of old signal lanterns, bells, dishes, timetables, and paintings, providing just enough background on American railroading history to whet your appetite for boarding the train at the Strasburg Rail Road 1892 Victorian station just across the road.

This train ride has been delighting the public ever since it became a tourist operation in 1958. It now attracts over 375,000 people each year, making this one of the few railroads to turn a profit on its passenger operations. Today the stock includes four steam locomotives and a dozen wooden coaches, all beautifully restored with green plush seats, polished wooden paneling, and oil lamps. Many passengers like to pay an extra quarter to ride on the open-sided observation car that was used in the movie *Hello, Dolly!*

With a *woo-woooo* of the whistle and a clanging of the bell that absolutely delight young passengers, the train departs on its sentimental journey past immaculate white farmhouses and green fields where straw-hatted Amish farmers and their families can be seen working in the fields with mule- and horse-drawn farm equipment, much the way their fathers and grandfathers used to do it 75–100 years ago.

Spinning windmills, black buggies on roadways in the distance, and neat rows of sober-colored clothing flapping on the line are further evidence of the way of life among these simple people, who seem to manage just fine without such modern contrivances as clothes dryers and refrigerators, telephones and cars. The Amish do not consider modern conveniences evil in themselves, but simply temptations to a worldly life.

Nor does lack of the latest technology diminish the productivity of these lush farms. There are some 14,000 Amish currently living in Lancaster County, each with a farm averaging around 80 acres— and worth about $6,500 per acre, according to the train conductor, who doubles as tour narrator. The fields outside the window are broadleaf tobacco, a lucrative crop that contributes $14 million annually to Pennsylvania's economy.

Paradise, unfortunately, has little to offer except a lumberyard and a sign warning of the end of the road. Still everyone applauds as the engine whistles past on a parallel track, on its way to be switched to the rear for the ride back to Strasburg. Many laugh as an Amtrak train roars by on an adjoining track. "You can connect here for Chicago," the good-natured narrator informs his passengers, "if you can run fast enough."

Back in the station, it's worth taking time for a quick tour of the private luxury coach owned by the president of the Reading Railroad during the heyday of train travel. It cost a whopping $100,000 back in 1916 and has separate sitting, dining, and sleeping quarters, all with cut-glass ceiling lamps, lace-curtained windows, and mahogany paneling inlaid with rosewood.

The gift shop in the station will provide you with train models, books on railroading, and caps and kerchiefs for young engineers. Collectors will find more treasures at the Strasburg Train Shop.

By now it's time for lunch, and there's no more appropriate setting than the dining car at the Red Caboose, one of the most unusual lodgings anywhere. The idea of converting old train cabooses into sleeping quarters has proven so popular that the owner recently applied for zoning changes to allow him to add eight more cars to the original twenty-five. Each has been renovated at a cost of some $15,000 to include one double bed at the back, four bunks up front, a bathtub and shower, and a television housed in a potbellied stove.

The Red Caboose is located just in front of the Toy Train Museum, which tends to fascinate nostalgic parents as much as the kids. The museum, which serves as national headquarters of the Train Collectors Association, houses antique toy trains that offer a miniature look at transportation progress over the years, plus a bundle of memories of holidays spent putting up toy train tracks around the Christmas tree. Three lavish working layouts include Standard Gauge, Lionel, and "0" gauge trains, with miniature trees, stations, homes, and churches making up realistic town settings.

Save a bit of energy for a stroll around Strasburg, which still has the look of an early Lancaster County village. It was settled in the early 1730s by a group of Swiss Mennonites who named their new home in honor of the cathedral city of Alsace. The present Main Street began as part of the Great Conestoga Road, the first westward trail from Philadelphia.

A dozen of the 29 oldest brick structures, dating back to the eighteenth and early nineteenth centuries, can be seen, including four of the oldest stone houses. And there are at least two dozen log houses still standing in the area along East and West Main and Miller and South Decatur streets, which has been proclaimed a National Historic District. The oldest of these is the Christopher Spech House, circa 1764. If you want to know more about the homes, pick up a printed "strolling tour" from the Strasburg Heritage Society head-quarters at 122 South Decatur Street.

During your walk, you'll surely want to take a break at the Strasburg Country Store and Creamery on the corner of Centre Square, restored in 1984 as an old-fashioned emporium with a pot-bellied stove, a player piano, and an 1890 soda fountain. Ice cream here is so rich it reminds you why the dish was named "cream" in the first place, and the scoops are served up in melt-in-your-mouth homemade sugar cones.

On the way out the door, you may well spy an Amish buggy sharing a red light with a group of cyclists or pulling up to the drive-in bank, the kind of contrast that makes Strasburg such a special place.

Adjoining the Creamery is the Strasburg Village Inn, the 1787 Thomas Crawford Tavern turned into an 11-room bed and breakfast with Colonial-style reproduction furnishings. Even more authentically restored is the Limestone Inn, a 1786 stone house that is one of the historic homes on Main Street. Also on Main is the Iron Horse Inn, a rustic restaurant that serves up good food amid railroad memorabilia.

If there's no room at the inns, Historic Strasburg Inn is a larger complex on Route 896 just outside town. It is neither historic nor a country inn, but it is a very pleasant motel complex, situated on expansive grounds that adjoin scenic farmlands, and it provides a pool and TV in the rooms to keep kids happy. If you're an antique car buff, the Gast Classic Motorcars Exhibit is right next door.

You might also consider staying at one of the nearby Mennonite farms, which could be an interesting experience for city children—or adults, for that matter. The Mennonite Information Center in Lancaster keeps a list of those accepting guests.

You may want to schedule some of the sights of Strasburg for Sunday in order to leave time on Saturday to visit one of the famous Amish farmers' markets offering bountiful fresh produce, home-baked goodies (including that sticky molasses confection known as shoofly pie), all kinds of relishes, and delicious homemade apple butter. Saturday markets can be found on Route 340 in Bird-in-Hand, farther north on Route 772 in Leola, or at the Southern Market at 102 Queen Street in Lancaster. Plan to get there early for the pick of the crop.

Since many of the shops along Route 340 in Bird-in-Hand and Intercourse are closed on Sunday, allow some shopping time on Saturday as well. Quilts are to be found at Fisher's Bakery, across from the Farmers Market in Bird-in-Hand, and at the Old Country Store in Intercourse, which features the handwork of some 200 Amish and Mennonite craftspeople. The People's Place in Intercourse is a cultural center offering films on Amish and Mennonite life, a book and crafts shop, a quilt museum, and an art gallery. You can pick up a handcrafted chair at Ebersol's Chair Shop in Intercourse and may find all kinds of unexpected prizes if you are lucky enough to be visiting on the day an auction is scheduled behind Zimmerman's store. And if you want to succumb to a buggy ride, Abe's, just west of Bird-in-Hand, will be glad to oblige.

On any day, a detour off Route 340 to any of the peaceful side roads leading south to Route 30 will give another perspective of the picture-book farm landscapes. Watch for the distinctive additions on some of the farms. Known as "gross dawdis," they are an Amish solution to the generation gap. When a farmer reaches retirement age, an annex to the main house is built, allowing him to enjoy the fruits of his labor and still be part of the family group without getting in the way of the younger generations.

Though most of the many Amish commercial attractions that abound in the area are more hokum than historic, you might want to visit either the Amish Farm and House or the Amish Homestead for the chance to see how a traditional Amish house looks inside.

One final recommendation for families is a visit to the Landis Valley Museum, a state-operated complex that presents all facets of Pennsylvania's rural heritage in a village of old buildings representing 150 years of architectural styles. The structures are filled with more than 100,000 objects and tools, and there are demonstrations to bring the traditional crafts and skills to life.

Like riding the rails, it's a look at life the way it used to be—and still is for some—in this picturesque corner of America.

Area Code: 717

DRIVING DIRECTIONS   Strasburg is at the intersection of routes 896 and 741, south of Lancaster. From D.C., take I-95 north to the Baltimore Beltway, I-695. Head northwest toward Towson and take exit 24, I-83 north to York, Pennsylvania, then Route 30 east through Lancaster, turning right on Route 896 to Strasburg. Approximate distance from D.C., 116 miles.

ACCOMMODATIONS   *Red Caboose Motel,* Route 741, Paradise Lane, Strasburg, 17579, 687-6646, $$ ● *Historic Strasburg Inn,* Route 896, Strasburg, 17579, 687-7691, children under 18 free in parents' room, $$$ ● *Strasburg Village Inn,* 1 West Main Street, Strasburg, 17579, 687-0900, $$–$$$ CP ● *Limestone Inn,* 33 East Main Street, Strasburg, 687-8392, $$ CP. For information on farm lodgings, contact Mennonite Information Center, 2209 Millstream Road, Lancaster, 17602, 299-0954.

DINING *Washington House* (see Historic Strasburg Inn above), $$–$$$ ● *Log Cabin,* 11 Lehoy Forest Drive, Leola, 626-1181, tops for decor and food, $$–$$$ ● *Groff's Farm,* Pinkerton Road, Mount Joy, 653-2048, out of the way but worth it for delicious Pennsylvania Dutch fare in a 1756 farmhouse (Chicken Stoltzfus here is famous), $$ ● Families may also enjoy sampling one of the more commercial Pennsylvania Dutch restaurants like *Willow Valley Inn,* US 222, 464-2711, less for gourmet fare than to taste regional specialties at reasonable prices, $–$$ ● *Iron Horse Inn, 135 East Main Street, Strasburg, 687-6362, $$.* (For more Pennsylvania Dutch area recommendations, see also page 83.)

SIGHTSEEING *Strasburg Railroad,* Route 741, Strasburg, 687-7522. Hours: May to late October, Monday to Friday 11 A.M. to 3 P.M.; Saturday 11 A.M. to 5 P.M.; Sunday noon to 5 P.M.; late March to mid-December weekends only. Phone for current operating hours. Adults, $5; children, $2.50 ● *Toy Train Museum,* Paradise Lane off Route 741, Strasburg, 687-8976. Hours: May to October, daily 10 A.M. to 5 P.M.; December to mid-March, by appointment; rest of year, weekends only. Adults, $2.25; ages 7–12, $.75; under 7, free ● *Railroad Museum of Pennsylvania,* Route 741, Strasburg, 687-8628. Hours: Tuesday to Friday 9 A.M. to 5 P.M.; Saturday 9 A.M. to 7 P.M.; Sunday 11 A.M. to 7 P.M. Adults, $3; children, $1.50 ● *Landis Valley Museum,* off Route 272, Landis Valley, 569-0401. Hours: May to October, Tuesday to Saturday 9 A.M. to 5 P.M.; Sunday noon to 5 P.M. Adults, $2; ages 6–18, $1; under 6, free ● *Amish Farm and House,* Route 30, east of Lancaster, 394-6185. Hours: daily 8:30 A.M. to 7 P.M.; spring and fall to 5 P.M.; winter to 4 P.M. Adults, $3.90; ages 6–11, $2; under 6, free ● *Gast Classic Motorcars Exhibit,* Route 986, Strasburg, 687-9500. Hours: daily 9 A.M. to 9 P.M. Adults, $4; children, $2.

INFORMATION Pennsylvania Dutch Visitors Bureau, 501 Greenfield Road, Lancaster, PA 17601, 299-8901, offers free maps, guides, introductory film on the area.

Landlubbing on
the Eastern Shore

The Bay Bridge spanning Chesapeake Bay to Maryland's Eastern
Shore is a four-and-a-half-mile crossing to another world, a landscape of shady villages whose homes date back 200 years, open
fields where corn and potatoes and onions grow, a seascape of 600
miles of bay and river waterfront filled with boats of every size and
shape and purpose, and a seafood lover's paradise where even gas
stations post signs in summer proclaiming "Crabs for Sale."

In colonial times, a planter aristocracy grew rich here from tobacco, while those who had no land became hard-working watermen, living off the bay's bounty of oysters, clams, and crabs. The
dichotomy between the two life-styles can still be seen three centuries later, especially in Talbot County, often referred to as the
"colonial capital" of the Eastern Shore.

Talbot, with its working fishing fleet, waterfront estates, picturesque homes and harbors, and posh shops, is a microcosm of the
Chesapeake mix, which is possibly why it has attracted so many of
the wealthy city folks who enjoy escaping here. They say that 200
bona fide millionaires live along the rivers and inlets of the county,
people with names like Houghton, Chrysler, and Du Pont, many of
them ensconced in some of the 100 or more remaining eighteenth-
century manor houses.

Their presence, along with the shops and restaurants serving
growing numbers of sailors and tourists, adds a new dimension, but
they haven't spoiled the original flavor that makes a visit to the
Eastern Shore unique. So, settle into one of Talbot County's choice
inns, get out the map, and prepare to sample the varied pleasures of
the Chesapeake.

St. Michaels, bordering the broad Miles River, is a good bet for
lodgings, as well as a good starting point for a landlubber's tour.
Once a shipbuilding center for bugeyes and Baltimore clippers, the
handsome harbor is now a popular port of call for weekenders, as
well as home to the Chesapeake Bay Maritime Museum.

This fine museum, where James Michener did much of the research for his book *Chesapeake,* is a place to get a real feel for the
role the water has played in Chesapeake history. You'll see the
largest floating fleet of historic bay boats in existence—the skipjacks and bugeyes and log canoes of days gone by. One highly
visible exhibit is the Hooper Strait Lighthouse, one of the last three
remaining Chesapeake cottage-type lighthouses, where you can
climb up for the view, examine the magnifying lenses that sent the

light miles out to sea, see the lighthouse keeper's potbellied stove and iron bed, and even read a bit of his diary. Other exhibits include the Point Lookout Bell Tower, a one-ton fog bell once found at the mouth of the Potomac; a waterfowl building featuring decoys; a boat-building shop; a building with exhibits tracing the history of the bay; and maritime displays of all kinds, including ships' bells, ship models, marine paintings, and black-and-white photos.

If you want to venture out to sea, board the 65-foot cruise boat *Patriot,* berthed at the museum, for an hour-and-a-half 11-mile cruise on the Miles. It's a good way to see watermen working crab-laden trotlines, as well as some of the hidden mansions along the water. You can also rent your own sailboat or pedal boat at the Town Dock Marina and other marinas around the harbor.

Pick up a copy of the St. Michaels walking tour either at the Maritime Museum or at one of the local shops to see some of the landmarks of the town, the oldest in Talbot County. People here still like to tell about how the British were outwitted during the Revolutionary War when the lights in town were blacked out and lanterns were posted in the fields to misdirect the cannon fire. Most of the oldest sites are clustered between Talbot Street and the water. Among them is St. Mary's Square, where you can tour the St. Mary's Museum, a restored and furnished colonial home, and see other historic homes and churches dating from the late seventeenth to early nineteenth centuries.

You'll need no guide to the shops on Talbot Street—or to the seafood restaurants along the mast-filled harbor. Busiest is the Crab Claw, where they serve up 100 bushels of steamed crabs on a busy summer day.

A ten-mile drive straight out Route 33 and across the Knapps Narrows drawbridge to Tilghman's Island makes for a complete change of scene. Tilghman is a no-frills home port to the last working skipjack fleet, as well as to scores of sports fishermen. The skipjacks are broad-beamed sailboats used for dredging oysters. The sails remain because state conservation law forbids oystering in power boats for fear they might take up too many of the shellfish, depleting the next year's crop. If you wander down to Dagwood Harbor in summer, you'll likely see the fishermen there repairing their craft in preparation for the colder months ahead. You may well find someone who is willing to be hired out for a little cruise, including an explanation of the oyster fisherman's art.

Harrison's Chesapeake House on Tilghman is the center for fishing charters and also the place for delicious, generous family-style seafood dinners with a water view. Their food ranks among the area's best.

Take the road back past St. Michaels and watch for the turnoff to the south leading to the scenic countryside through Royal Oak to Bellevue. And keep your eye out for a bit of antiquing along the way.

In Bellevue, you can board the Tred-Avon Ferry, America's oldest operating ferryboat. History has it that it was started up in 1683, the first keeper subsidized by the Talbot County Court to the tune of 2,500 pounds of tobacco annually. Now the ferry takes just six cars at a time across the water to the serene, shady, brick-paved lanes of Oxford, a town of old homes, white picket fences, and enormous charm.

This village of 862 people, surprisingly once Maryland's largest port, is now a sailor's and stroller's delight. It is a glorious sight in August, when as many as 300 sailboats, colorful spinnakers unfurled, take part in the annual Oxford Regatta.

Just opposite the harbor is one of Talbot County's most appealing lodgings, the Robert Morris Inn, built about 1710 by the father of Robert Morris, Jr., the man who was known as the "financier of the American Revolution." The dining room here is renowned. You'll also find no more delightful spot for a steamed crab feast than the outside deck of the Pier Street restaurant, overlooking the Tred-Avon River in Oxford.

As for seeing Oxford sights, all it takes is a stroll along those herringbone brick lanes. The Custom House on the water is a replica of the original, but the home called Byeberry, facing the town creek, has been standing since 1695; Jena, the white clapboard house off Oxford Road, dates from 1700; and nearby Plimhimmon is flanked by stately Osage orange and ginkgo trees and a willow oak estimated to be 350 years old. Stop at the little local museum if you want some accurate town history.

Oxford and Easton are 12 miles and many light-years apart. Compared to Oxford, this county seat (population 8,300) seems positively citified, its gift shops and shopping centers bearing witness to the influence of the newcomers who have come to Talbot County.

However, Easton has managed to retain much of its own charm and history. You'll get a delightful lesson at the historical society complex on South Washington—an 1810 Federal town house and a 1700s Quaker cabinetmaker's cottage flanking a lovely English garden. The society conducts town walking tours, or you can pick up a map at the museum or at local shops and do your own thing in the historic district along Washington, Harrison, and intersecting streets, such as Goldsborough, Dover, and West. Two principal sights are the 1791 Talbot County Court House and the 1682 Third Haven Meeting House, said to be the nation's oldest frame building devoted to religious worship. At the corner of Dover and Harrison you'll find the Tidewater Inn, the stately pride of the Eastern Shore, and headquarters for the wonderful Easton Wildfowl Festival each November. There are also many handsome homes in town.

Chesapeake means "great shellfish bay," and as you'll discover, feasting on seafood, which means mainly crab in summer, is one of the greatest pleasures here, whether you hammer away at Old Bay–spiced steamed crabs served on newspapers or sit down to a Crab Imperial dinner. Our quest for the best crab cake, conducted over three visits to the Eastern Shore, produced a clear winner. Although Chesapeake House was close, our choice was out of Talbot County, down the coast in Crisfield, a working fisherman's town where the ferries leave for Tangier and Smith islands. The atmosphere is short on charm, but the crab cakes at the Captain's Galley can't be beat.

One final nonculinary recommendation: On the way to or from a Chesapeake weekend, detour for the bit of history at Wye Oak. The Wye Oak, Maryland's state tree, is 400 years old and, with a circumference of 37 feet, is the largest white oak in the country. It is carefully tended by the state on a protected site by the road, where tourists pause to gaze and take snapshots, turning their cameras this way and that trying to fit the enormous tree into their picture.

Just beyond is the Old Wye Church, a 1721 jewel whose restoration was financed by Arthur Houghton, a Steuben Glass executive who is a member of the vestry and one of those Talbot County millionaires. The actual work was done by the same architects responsible for Williamsburg's Bruton Parish. The arrangement of the window-high pews is authenticated from a drawing in the vestry records dating back to 1723. The patterned green brocade box pews, the arched windows, and the bargello chair seats and petit-point kneeling cushions at the altar rail, the handiwork of local women, are lovely to see and worth the detour.

It's something of a tradition when you are in this neighborhood to ring the back doorbell at the frame house of Ruth Orrell, right next door to the church, and pick up a batch of her noted homemade Maryland beaten biscuits. Or, if you prefer, you can go down to the Old Wye Gristmill on the river, where they've been grinding grain since 1680, and pick up flour for some baking of your own. They'll gladly supply the recipes.

Area Code: 301

DRIVING DIRECTIONS   Easton is on Route 50, about 26 miles south of the Chesapeake Bay Bridge. From D.C., take Route 301/50 across the bridge, then follow Route 50 south to Easton. Approximate distance from D.C., 73 miles. A bypass off Route 50 leads to Route 33 west to St. Michaels, and Route 333 heads west to Oxford; each is about 12 miles from Easton.

ACCOMMODATIONS *Robert Morris Inn,* P.O. Box 70, Oxford, 21654, 226-5111, historic charmer, great range in rooms, $$–$$$$ ● *Robert Morris Lodge,* same owners as the Robert Morris Inn, pleasant site on the river, $$–$$$$ ● *Inn at Perry Cabin,* St. Michaels, 21663, 745-5178, 6 well-furnished rooms, scenic, part of very busy restaurant and bar, $$$–$$$$ ● *Victoriana Inn,* 205 Cherry Street, St. Michaels, 21663, 745-3368, delightful lawn with a harbor view, $$$–$$$$ CP ● *Two Swan Inn,* foot of Carpenter Street, St. Michaels, 21663, 745-2929, 1720 home on the water, $$–$$$ CP ● *Kemp House Inn,* 412 Talbot Street, P.O. Box 638, St. Michaels, 21663, 745-2243, attractive small bed-and-breakfast home, $–$$$ CP ● *Harrison's Chesapeake House,* P.O. Box B, Coopertown Road, Tilghman, 21671, 886-2141, rooms in main house with bath down the hall, motel with private bath adjoining, headquarters for fishermen, $–$$$ ● *Wade's Point Inn,* McDaniel (just outside St. Michaels), 21647, 745-2500, airy bed-and-breakfast home with perfect spot on the water, $$–$$$ CP ● *Tilghman Inn,* Knapps Narrows, Tilghman, 21671, 886-2141, small, modern with water views, pool, tennis court, $$–$$$ ● *Tidewater Inn,* Dover and Harrison streets, Easton, 21601, 822-1300, totally elegant, $$–$$$$.

DINING *Robert Morris Inn* (see above) $$–$$$ ● *Pier Street,* Pier Street Marina, Oxford, 226-5171, $–$$ ● *Bay 100,* Route 33 at Knapps Narrows, Tilghman, 886-2622, $$–$$$ ● *Inn at Perry Cabin* (see above), $$–$$$ ● *Crab Claw,* Navy Point, St. Michaels, 745-2900, informal, on the water, $–$$$ ● *Harrison's Chesapeake House* (see above), $$ ● *The Bridge,* Route 33 and Knapps Narrows, Tilghman, 886-2520, house specialties are crab cakes and fried chicken, $–$$ ● *Captain's Galley,* at the dock, Crisfield, 968-1636, $–$$.

BED AND BREAKFAST *The Traveller in Maryland,* P.O. Box 2277, Annapolis 21404, 269-6232 in Maryland; (301) 261-2233 toll free in D.C.

SIGHTSEEING *Chesapeake Bay Maritime Museum,* Navy Point, St. Michaels, 745-2916. Hours: April to September, daily 10 A.M. to 5 P.M.; October to December, 4 P.M.; closed rest of year. Admission, $4 ● *Patriot* boat cruises from the maritime museum, 745-3100. May to October. Adults, $6; children, $3 ● *Historical Society of Talbot County,* 25 South Washington Street, Easton, 822-0773. Hours: Tuesday to Saturday 10 A.M. to 4 P.M.; Sunday 1 P.M.

to 4 P.M. In January and February, closed Sunday. Adults, $4; students, $2; children, $.50 • *Tred-Avon Ferry,* 226-5408. Hours: May 1 to Labor Day, Monday to Friday 7 A.M. to 9 P.M.; Saturday and Sunday 9 A.M. to 9 P.M. Boats run every 15–20 minutes from Oxford to Bellevue and back. $3.75 per car, $.25 per passenger.

INFORMATION   Talbot County Chamber of Commerce, 7 Federal Street, P.O. Box 1366, Easton, MD 21601, 822-4606.

Sights and Sails on the Northern Neck

Surrounded by water, steeped in history, and serene as a perfect summer day, Virginia's Northern Neck is an escape to tranquillity.

The twentieth century seems light-years away from the tip of this narrow picturesque peninsula bound by the Potomac and Rappahannock rivers and Chesapeake Bay. Life here is a blend of country living and saltwater tang, with fragments of the past still present on every byway. Places like Christ Church near Irvington, built in 1732, the year George Washington was born, are well worth seeing and are on a scale small enough not to tax the energy level on a hot summer day.

If you have the time and energy, there is plenty more to see and do nearby. Yorktown is only 35 minutes away, and it is less than an hour to all the sights of Williamsburg. Or you can literally sail away to the past on a boat in Reedville bound for Tangier Island, an enclave so remote from the rest of the world that many of its residents still speak with an Elizabethan accent.

Or you can be easily tempted to forget about history and just head for the water that beckons everywhere, settling into a resort and spending your time doing absolutely nothing but having fun in the sun.

One compromise plan might be to devote Saturday to relaxing and leave some of Sunday for sightseeing. Another is to mark this down for a long weekend, with time for all the many pleasures the area holds.

Two ideal places to sample resort life, Northern Neck–style, are the Tides Inn in Irvington, one of Virginia's landmarks, and Windmill Point, a more modest complex with a perfect location right at land's end.

Lots of people who can afford the tab happily spend a whole

vacation at the Tides with never a thought of leaving at all. This gracious and handsome family-run resort is surrounded by water, water everywhere, and its special claim to fame is a fleet of yachts that regularly take guests out on the Rappahannock and the bay, and up Carter's Creek for luncheon picnics or to watch the sunset over the bay with cocktail in hand. Besides the boats, the Tides offers 45 holes of golf, tennis, sailing, paddleboats, and a giant saltwater pool overlooking the water. Young and old alike enjoy it here, but note that this is not a resort for swingers. Evening entertainment means sedate dancing, maybe a mock horse-race game in the parlor, and milk and crackers set out about 10 P.M.

Golfers and families often opt for the less formal and slightly less expensive Tides Lodge, which offers equal recreational facilities, its own restaurants, and accommodations in modern lodges instead of a grand hotel.

Although Windmill Point rooms are motel variety, the spectacular location, where the Rappahannock meets the bay, makes the place something quite special. Besides its own pool and busy marina, it shares the golf course and tennis facilities of an adjoining condominium complex and offers windsurfing and boats for hire. Ask for a room on the river, and you'll open your door to a delightful little sand beach running along the Rappahannock.

If you don't want to pay resort prices, there are a couple of appealing bed-and-breakfast inns in and around Irvington, and you won't be completely without recreation. The Inn at Levelfields offers an important summer bonus—its own swimming pool—and there are public golf courses and tennis courts around Irvington.

It will take only a little while away to fit in a visit to the area's prime attraction, historic Christ Church, widely considered to be Virginia's finest example of Colonial church architecture.

Robert "King" Carter, who funded its construction, played a major role in state and American history as patriarch of one of Virginia's most important families. His descendants numbered eight governors of Virginia, three signers of the Declaration of Independence, two U.S. presidents, and General Robert E. Lee. Carter's generosity in replacing an earlier wooden church here stemmed partly from his desire to retain the church on the site of his parents' grave, which remains there today. The tombs of the benefactor and two of his wives are outside the church, Carter's being among the largest and most ornate of his day.

The church itself is in the form of a Latin Cross, with three-foot-thick walls made of brick fired in the Carter kilns. Exterior bricks are alternated lengthwise and endwise in the Flemish bond pattern that was popular in colonial America. The rare original three-decker walnut pulpit still stands, the original marble baptismal font remains, and the 25 pews are the only original high-backed pews left in Virginia. A reception center on the grounds offers a narrated slide show about the church and a small museum.

There are other rewarding excursions nearby. One will take you to Lancaster Green, which is surrounded by an original 1797 clerk's office, an 1819 jail, and an 1863 courthouse. The Mary Ball Washington Museum and Library on the green honors George Washington's mother, who was born in Lancaster County, and Washington family memorabilia is displayed. Epping Forest, site of the 1690 home where Mary Ball was born, is on Route 3 near Lively. And on Route 622 you'll find St. Mary's White Chapel, the 1669 church where young Mary Ball worshiped and where many of the tombstones in the churchyard bear her family name.

You'll have to allow a full day for the boat trip from the fishing town of Reedville to Tangier Island, the place that is called "the soft-shell crab capital of the world." Ninety-five percent of the nation's soft-shell crabs come from here, and you'll see them swimming in long tanks at the docks, where they are kept until they have shed their shells and are ready to market.

If you think of this trip as a visit to the quaint past, you will be disappointed. The crab farms on pilings at the harbor, the fishing boats and shanties along the shore, and the narrow carless lanes of the island are picturesque, but there is nothing quaint or cute about Tangier. The homes are modest and plain, the yards surrounded by plain chain-link fences to keep out motorbikes.

The appeal of the island is the look it affords at a way of life little changed for centuries. Unfortunately, it is a life-style hardly seen by the crowds who file off the boat, get in line for the big family-style noonday meal at Hilda Crockett's, and see nothing beyond the tour conducted by island ladies via golf cart, dodging teenagers careening about on bikes as they go.

To get the feel of the place you have to walk away from the crowds, maybe forgo the quantity of food at Crockett's for the fresh quality at one of the little hole-in-the-wall cafes or, better yet, picnic by the water after stopping at one of the homes whose signs offer crab cakes and fresh bread for sale.

Then stroll away from the one and only main road to the eerie beauty of the marshes or to the life along the side lanes, narrow unpaved paths without road signs or house numbers, where groups of youngsters call to each other in accents from another age.

Tangier was discovered and named by Captain John Smith back in 1608, but it remained the hunting and fishing grounds of the Pocomoke Indians until 1666. History has lost the first name of the Mr. West who bought the island from the Indians that year for two overcoats. West, in turn, sold to John Crockett, who in 1686 moved here from Cornwall with his family. Almost all of today's 900 residents are descendants of Crockett, whose four sons and daughters married mainlanders and proceeded to bring them back to populate Tangier, where they lived off the rich oyster and crab grounds surrounding the island. They added the names Parks, Thomas, and Pruitt, which account for most of the families today. Long isolated from the rest of the world, the people on Tangier still retain accents similar to the Cornish John Crockett spoke all those years ago, but now punctuated with local slang.

Tangier's present residents are fishermen, crabbers, and oystermen, like all the generations who came before them, and they still work hard wresting a living from the sea, rising at dawn and boarding their wooden boats to defy the elements. Although some things are changing on Tangier, what with the advent of motorbikes and cable TV, some other things have not changed at all. There is still no doctor on the island, and residents continue to bury their dead in their own gardens in concrete boxes set above ground to keep water from seeping in at high tide. And as yet, there is no crime on Tangier, no need to lock the door by day or night.

The lifeblood of the island, the livelihood that binds everyone together, and the ever-present dependence on the weather and the sea also have not altered with the centuries. Understanding the power of nature has made these islanders churchgoing and God-fearing people who worship as well as work together.

Rustic, hard-working, honest Tangier shows us an interdependence among neighbors and a sense of caring and community that our mechanized modern world cannot match.

Area Code: 804

DRIVING DIRECTIONS   Irvington is on Route 3, near the tip of Virginia's Northern Neck. From D.C., take I-95 south to Route 3 east. Approximate distance from D.C., 135 miles.

ACCOMMODATIONS   *The Tides Inn,* Irvington, 22480, 438-5000 or (800) 552-2461 in Virginia, (800) 843-3746 out of state, $$$$ MAP ● *Windmill Point Marine Resort,* Windmill Point, 22578, 435-1166, or (800) 552-3743 in Virginia, $$$ ● *The Inn at Levelfields,* P.O. Box 216, Lancaster, 22503, 435-6887, $$$ CP ● *The King Carter Inn,* Irvington, 22480, 438-6053, $-$$ CP ● *Greenvale Manor,* Route 354, P.O. Box 174, Mollusk, 22517, 462-5995, $$ CP.

DINING   *The Tides Inn* (see above) $$$$ ● *The Tides Lodge,* $$–$$$ ● *Windmill Point* (see above), $$–$$$ ● *The Inn at Levelfields* (see above), $$.

SIGHTSEEING *Historic Christ Church,* off Route 3, Irvington, 438-6855. Hours: daily 9 A.M. to 5 P.M.; reception center, April to Thanksgiving, Monday to Friday 10 A.M. to 4 P.M.; Saturday 1 P.M. to 4 P.M.; Sunday 2 P.M. to 5 P.M. Free • *Tangier Island Cruises,* leave Reedville May to mid-October, daily 10 A.M. to 3:45 P.M.; Tangier and Chesapeake Cruises, Inc., Warsaw, 22572, 333-4656, reservations required, check for current rates • Cruises also available to Smith Island, Maryland, May to September, via *Island & Bay Cruises, Inc.,* Route 1, P.O. Box 289-R, Reedville, 22539, 453-3430.

INFORMATION Northern Neck Travel Council, P.O. Drawer H, Callao, VA 22435, 529-7500; or Virginia Division of Tourism, 1021 East Cary Street, Richmond, VA 23219, 786-4484.

Fiddling Around at Hibernia

Promenade on down to Hibernia Park near Coatesville, Pennsylvania, and get ready for a toe-tapping, hand-clapping, old-fashioned winging for the whole family.

The annual Chester County Old Fiddlers' Picnic is not only a jubilee of fiddling, banjo strumming, and guitar twanging entertainment, but the chance to "all join hands" for a real down-home hoedown with square dancing open to all.

There are hayrides, tours of the Hibernia Ironmaster's Mansion, clog dancers showing off their steps, crafts booths featuring the work of some two dozen artisans, and lots of barbecue and other good country fare on hand when you need refueling.

It's a daylong event that has attracted national attention since it began in the 1920s, and offers a perfect opportunity to get acquainted with northern Chester County, a back-roads world of stone houses, picture-book farms, and parklands perfect for summer outdoor pleasures.

The Fiddlers' Picnic runs from 10 A.M. until 8 P.M. in the shady groves of Hibernia Park. The lineup of fiddlers and other musicians ranges from old-timers to teenagers, many of them playing tunes that have been passed down from their fathers and grandfathers. As fascinating as the official contests onstage is the "jamming" that goes on among the tall trees nearby, where older masters teach the young fiddlers some of the tricks of the trade or marvel at the latest comer who can show them a trick or two.

If you take time out to stroll the quiet paths of the 800-acre park or fish on the banks of historic Brandywine Creek, you'll find it hard to imagine that this was once the site of a bustling iron-producing industry. Tour Hibernia Mansion, a late-eighteenth-century home that was built when the first forge was constructed nearby. From ironmaster's home it was remodeled at the beginning of this century into a gentleman's estate when embellishments such as a ballroom were added. The house has been restored to its full glory, ballroom and all, and contains many of the original furnishings of the last wealthy owners, the Swayne family of Philadelphia.

If the day is hot and you want a change of pace, follow the Brandywine a few miles south to Northbrook and try cooling off by tubing, a floating journey downriver in a giant inner tube that is becoming increasingly popular in the area. If you prefer staying dry, Northbrook Canoe, the tube-trip people, will also be glad to rent you a canoe for an hour—or a day, if you're a serious paddler.

At day's end, it's worth a drive to see the imaginative productions and talented players at the People's Light and Theatre Company in Malvern.

On Sunday you'll have your choice of activities in many directions. Not far away is Hopewell Village, a restored iron-making village, where a self-guided tour will give you an idea of what life was like in this region in the eighteenth century. Historic Yellow Springs, a onetime colonial health resort and spa, retains its old stone farmhouse and ruins of the only Revolutionary War hospital commissioned and built by the Continental Congress. It also offers an attractive inn for dining.

For families, Springton Manor Farm offers tours of a working farm and a petting zoo to please the kids, a manor house tour and Victorian gardens for the grown-ups.

As you drive around, do detour to the back roads to see the real beauty of the area. Near Lyndell you can check out one of the 15 picturesque covered bridges in the county.

If it's too nice a day to think about anything but being outdoors, head for French Creek State Park, adjoining Hopewell Village. You'll find 6,000 acres of woodland with over 50 miles of hiking and nature trails, and two lakes and a pool. Or drive south to Marsh Creek State Park, which offers a 535-acre lake and an Olympic-size swimming pool. Both parks have picnic facilities.

Or you might want to try out your legs on part of the 120-mile Horseshoe Trail, a scenic route that crosses all the way from Hopewell to Valley Forge.

To the more populated south in Chester County, different kinds of diversions await. The Brandywine River Museum in Chadds Ford, the hometown of the Wyeth family, is dedicated to this preeminent family in American art, featuring work by three generations of Wyeths: N. C., Andrew, and Jamie. The rustic setting—a restored gristmill still with its original big beams and plaster walls and newly added glass walls looking out over the Brandywine River—is just right for the area.

Also in Chadds Ford, the 1729 John Chad House, the restored home of a ferryman and innkeeper, is a step back to colonial times, as is a visit to historical Brandywine Battlefield State Park, 50 acres marking an important Revolutionary War battle and including the restored homes that served as quarters for Washington and Lafayette.

Just down the road in Kennett Square, Longwood Gardens is not only in peak bloom but is putting on its fantastic summer Festival of Fountains, with illuminated fountain displays, outdoor concerts, and unforgettable fireworks displays. And this is one garden you can enjoy even in the rain. The four-acre conservatory is a wonder no matter what the weather.

Few destinations can match Chester County's mix of art and history and the great outdoors. Add Longwood's beauty and a toe-tapping fiddler's beat, and you have a weekend guaranteed to please.

Area Code: 215

DRIVING DIRECTIONS   Hibernia Park is off Route 30, north of Coatesville, Pennsylvania. From D.C., take I-95 north. After the Susquehanna River Bridge, watch for Route 272 and follow it west to Route 1 at Nottingham. Continue north on Route 1 to Kennett Square, then north on Route 82 to Knoll Road. Turn left on Knoll and follow signs to Hibernia. Approximate distance from D.C., 120 miles.

ACCOMMODATIONS *Coventry Forge Inn Guest House,* Route 23, Coventryville, mailing address, RD 2, Pottstown, 19464, 469-6222, guest house across the road from a superb country restaurant, $$ CP ● *Waynebrook Inn,* routes 10 and 322, Honey Brook, 19344, 273-2444, historic inn completely modernized inside, $$ CP ● *Duck Hill Farm,* Little Washington–Lyndell Road, Downington, 19335, 942-3029, just a couple of rooms in a farm setting, pool, $$$$ AP ● *Holiday Inn,* P.O. Box 1100, Route 100, Lionville, 19353, 363-1100, $$ ● *Fairway Farm B&B,* Vaughn Road, Pottstown, 19464, 327-1351, German hosts and decor, pool and tennis and trumpet museum on the grounds, $$ CP ● If you prefer to stay in the central part of the county, try *Duling-Kurtz House,* 146 South Whitford Road (off Route 30), Exton, 19341, 524-1830, $$–$$$ CP.

BED AND BREAKFAST *Bed and Breakfast of Chester County,* P.O. Box 825, Kennett Square, PA 19348, 444-1367 ● *Guest Houses,* RD 9, West Chester, PA 19380, 692-4575.

DINING *Coventry Forge Inn* (see above), $$$–$$$$, Saturday prix fixe, $$$$ ● *Waynebrook Inn* (see above), $$–$$$ ● *The Inn at Historic Yellow Springs,* Art School Road (off Route 113), Chester Springs, 827-7477, $$–$$$ ● *Vickers,* Welsh Pool Road and Gorden Drive, Lionville, 363-6336, $$–$$$$ ● *The Peddler Inn,* Route 322, Honey Brook, 273-2422, $$–$$$$ ● *Country House at Kimberton,* Kimberton and Hares Hill roads, Kimberton, 933-8148, $$–$$$ ● *Durling-Kurtz House* (see above), complete dinners, $$$–$$$$ ● *Stottsville Inn,* Route 372 at Strasburg Road, Pomeroy, 857-1133, $$–$$$. See also page 199.

SIGHTSEEING *Chester County Old Fiddlers' Picnic,* 10 A.M. to 8 P.M., usually second Sunday in August, Hibernia Park, $3 per car. Bring your own chair or blanket; plenty of food for sale, but picnics are welcome. Contact Tourist Center or County Parks Department, 344-6415, for current information ● *French Creek State Park,* RR 1, P.O. Box 448, Route 345, Elverson, 582-1514. Daylight hours daily. Free except for swimming fees or boat rental ● *Marsh Creek State Park,* Lyndell Road off Route 100, between Eagle and Lyndell, 458-8515. Daylight hours daily. Free except for swimming fees or boat rentals ● *Springton Manor Farm,* P.O. Box 117, off Springton Road, Glenmoore, 942-2450. Hours: farm tours, Memorial Day to Labor Day, daily 10 A.M. to 4 P.M.; rest of year, weekends only. Adults, $2; ages 2–12, $1.50; family, $7 ● *Brandywine River Museum,* Route 1, Chadds Ford, 388-7601. Hours: daily 9:30 A.M. to 4:30 P.M. Adults, $3; children, $1.50 ● *Brandywine Battlefield Park,* routes 1 and 202, Chadds Ford. Summer, daily 9 A.M. to 8 P.M.; rest of year, Tuesday to Saturday 9 A.M. to 5 P.M.; Sunday noon to 5 P.M. Adults, $1; children, $.50 ● *John Chad House,* Route 100 off US 1, Chadds Ford, 388-7376. Hours: June to August, Saturday and Sunday 10 A.M. to 5 P.M. Adults, $1; children, $.50 ● *Longwood Gardens,* Route 1, P.O. Box 501, Kennett Square, 388-6741. Hours: April to October, daily 9 A.M. to 6 P.M.; until 5 P.M. rest of year. Adults, $8; children, $2 ● *Festival of Fountains,* illuminated fountain displays, Tuesday, Thursday, and Saturday, 9:15 P.M., usually preceded by garden concerts 7 P.M. to 8 P.M.; mid-June through August, advance tickets required. Check for current dates. Adults, $10; children, $3. Fireworks displays held on four weekend evenings, mid-June through August.

INFORMATION   Brandywine Valley Tourist Information Center at Longwood Gardens, Route 1, Kennett Square, PA 19348, (800) 228-9933.

Appalachian Arts at Augusta

Augusta was the name given to West Virginia in the early days, when it was still part of the state of Virginia and the first homesteaders were making their way west into the Appalachian Mountains to carve a new life out of the wilderness.

Today Augusta means a series of workshops where people of all walks of life come with the common goal of learning and preserving the Appalachian arts of those early settlers, and a gala weekend festival where these arts are celebrated.

It is the perfect opportunity to appreciate anew the skills and talents nurtured long ago in West Virginia's hill country—and to find renewal in the unchanged beauty of the mountains themselves.

Ingenuity was a necessity in this rugged highland region. The crafts of the mountain people were born of practical need, for they had no choice but to make everything for themselves. You might say their music was a necessity, as well, because it brought them joy, a precious commodity where life is hard. Music also was a means of worship and a way to pass on treasured stories and traditions from one generation to the next.

Three Elkins-area women, fearful that these time-honored folkways would be forgotten in the fast-paced modern world, began the first Augusta workshops back in 1972 and have seen them grow beyond their fondest dreams. Now sponsored by Davis & Elkins College, which is set among the hilltops overlooking town, Augusta attracts over 1,500 participants to this town of 9,000 each year. Even more arrive to share the grand finale weekend.

The Augusta Heritage Arts Workshops are held for five weeks, beginning in mid-July, at the college. Participants come from every state in the union to study with an 80-year-old musician or a young fifth-generation basket maker; to master bagpipes and blacksmithing, bluegrass and stained glass; to get the hang of white oak basketry, wood carving, lace making, folk painting, making a quilt, or building a guitar.

Some come hoping to pick up old-time musical savvy, the fine points of playing the autoharp or finger-style guitar, or of building a banjo or a dulcimer from scratch. They want to share the dances and tunes and storytelling that are long-treasured traditions in the mountains.

All of these crafts and arts, the music and dance and more are on display for the final Augusta Festival weekend in mid-August, a showcase of the talents of Augusta's instructors. The weekend features many crafts demonstrations and entertainment of every kind—clogging and folk dancing; singing and storytelling; dances celebrating the heritage brought to the hills by Scottish, Irish, and English settlers; and lively musical "jams." Workshops for the kids and homemade Appalachian food fill out a full round of festivities.

The scenery adds greatly to the pleasures of a visit. Nestled in a valley on the northwestern slope of the Appalachians, Elkins is surrounded by the ridges of Cheat and Rich mountains and some of the greatest wilderness country on the East Coast. It is headquarters for the Monongahela National Forest, nearly a million acres of West Virginia woodlands. Its region, the Potomac Highlands, boasts 603 miles of native brook trout streams, 24 prime white-water rafting rivers, and 110 mountain peaks over 4,000 feet high, keeping things nice and cool even in midsummer.

The best of the easily accessible outdoors is 35 miles east of Elkins in the Canaan Valley, which according to legend got its name in 1753 from settlers who were so moved by its beauty they cried out, "Behold, the land of Canaan." Now known as "kuh-nayn" (accent on the last syllable), the Canaan Valley State Park sits 3,000 feet above sea level surrounded by peaks rising to well over 4,100 feet. Canaan is one of the state's superbly developed, moderately priced resort parks, with a pleasant lodge, an 18-hole golf course, tennis courts, and swimming facilities. It also offers acres of lush, verdant forests and clear mountain streams for fine fishing and canoeing.

On the way from Elkins to Canaan, watch for the Old Mill on Route 32 in Harmon. The 1877 water-powered gristmill still turns, and the grinding of grain is demonstrated each Saturday at 3:30 P.M. Upstairs is a shop with a large selection of crafts by West Virginia artisans, and there are daily weaving demonstrations on an 1830s loom and occasional spinning demonstrations. On Saturday afternoons there often is a state artist, craftsperson, or musician in residence showing off his or her talents.

From Canaan Valley continue ten miles north on Route 32 to Davis for spectacular scenery at Blackwater Falls State Park, where the Blackwater River takes a dramatic plunge to boulders 60 feet below, then continues turbulently winding down Blackwater Canyon in a series of falls and cascades that descend another 1,350 feet in ten miles. Blackwater Park offers a lodge with scenic views, horseback riding, swimming, and unlimited nature walks in the cool of the Monongahela Forest. For hikers, the Allegheny Trail begins here, continuing 150 miles south to Greenbrier County.

Most unusual of all the natural wonders in the vicinity is the Dolly Sods Wilderness Area. Situated in a high wild section of the Allegheny Plateau, which rises 4,000 feet above sea level, this spot has been described as a bit of Canada gone astray, with a starkly beautiful terrain reminiscent of Arctic tundra. Winds are so fierce in winter that limbs do not grow on the windward side of trees, leaving stately spruce standing like tall masts with their sails blasted to one side. The diversity of unusual plants attracts many naturalists.

Dolly Sods is also rich in wildlife—deer, beavers, black bears, foxes, raccoons, bobcats, and snowshoe hares are a few of its denizens. It is a mecca for hikers, berry pickers, and photographers, and provides magnificent vistas of the eastern ridges. The tower near Red Creek Campground gives a full 360-degree mountain panorama.

Also within easy reach of Elkins is the Spruce Knob–Seneca Rocks National Recreation Area and Visitor Center. It serves majestic Spruce Knob, West Virginia's highest point at 4,860 feet, and Seneca Rocks, an outcropping of 1,000-foot-high cliffs of Tuscarora sandstone that is a challenge to even the most venturesome rock climbers. Many are happiest watching the action from the base, picnicking along the bank of the North Fork River, and viewing the climbers through telescopes at the visitors center operated by the U.S. Forest Service. The center also has films and programs on nature topics conducted by naturalists.

A visit to Augusta and its surroundings will leave you with fresh appreciation for the simple mountain people whose highly personal arts and crafts have special appeal in our mass-produced age—and for the mountains that inspired them.

Area Code: 304

DRIVING DIRECTIONS   Elkins is at the intersection of routes 33 and 219. From D.C., take I-66 west to Route 81 south. At Harrisonburg, Virginia, turn west on Route 33 to Elkins. Approximate distance from D.C., 200 miles.

PUBLIC TRANSPORTATION   United Express offers direct flights from Washington, D.C., to Elkins airport.

ACCOMMODATIONS   *Best Western Motel of Elkins,* Route 33, 26241, 636-7711, $ ● *Elkins Motor Lodge,* Harrison Avenue,

26241, 636-1400, $ ● *Wayside Inn Bed and Breakfast,* Sycamore and Buffalo streets, Elkins, 26241, 636-1618, $ ● *Cheat River Lodge,* Route 1, P.O. Box 116, Elkins, 26241, 636-2301, lodge and log homes along the river; lodge, $; 2- and 3-bedroom houses, $$$ ● *Cheat Mountain Club,* P.O. Box 28, Durbin, 26264, 456-4627, private hunting lodge gone public, on trout stream in the forest, excellent food, $$$ MAP ● *Smoke Hole Lodge,* P.O. Box 953, Petersburg, 26847, remote rustic lodge reached via 4-wheel drive (yours or theirs), no electricity or phone, hearty meals, escapists love it, $$$ MAP. See also Canaan Valley, page 219.

DINING *The Starr Cafe* at Augusta Books, 224 Davis Avenue, Elkins, 636-7273, light fare as well as full entrées, great home baking, $–$$ ● *Cheat River Inn,* Route 33, Elkins, 636-6265, simple decor, excellent trout, $ ● *1863 Tavern Restaurant* at Elkins Motor Lodge (see above), $–$$$. See also Canaan Valley, page 219.

SIGHTSEEING *Augusta Heritage Arts Workshop and Augusta Festival,* Augusta Heritage Center, Davis & Elkins College, Elkins, WV 26241, 636-1903. Five weeks of workshops, mid-July to mid-August; weekend Augusta Festival, mid-August. Contact for current schedules and rates ● *The Old Mill,* Route 32, north of Harmon. Hours: Memorial Day to Labor Day, Monday through Saturday 10 A.M. to 5 P.M.; Labor Day to Columbus Day, Monday to Friday 1 P.M. to 5 P.M. Saturday 10 A.M. to 5 P.M. Free ● *Dolly Sods Wilderness and Scenic Area,* Route 19 off Route 32, four miles north of Harmon. Information from Forest Supervisor, Monongahela National Forest, Sycamore Street, Elkins, WV 26241, 636-1800 ● *Spruce Knob–Seneca Rocks National Recreation Area and Visitor Center,* Seneca Rocks, 567-2827. Hours: Memorial Day to Labor Day, daily 9 A.M. to 5 P.M.; rest of year, Wednesday to Sunday 9 A.M. to 4 P.M. ● *Canaan Valley Resort State Park, Blackwater Falls State Park,* and all West Virginia state park and forest information available toll-free, (800) CALL-WVA.

INFORMATION Potomac Highlands Convention and Visitors Bureau, P.O. Box 1459, Elkins, WV 26241, 636-8400 ● Elkins Area Chamber of Commerce, P.O. Box 1169, Elkins, WV 26241, 636-2717 ● West Virginia State Travel Information, (800) CALL-WVA.

Feasting and Festing near Annapolis

Zounds and huzzah! The jugglers, jesters, jousters, and knights and ladies are on hand and the fun is fast-paced and fanciful at the Maryland Renaissance Festival, an event that goes full tilt for six weekends each year in late August and September in Crownsville, just outside Annapolis.

Pick the weekend after Labor Day for your lighthearted look at the sixteenth century, and you can follow with a favorite twentieth-century diversion—feasting on crabs and oysters and clams at the Maryland Seafood Festival, a delicious celebration of the bounty of Chesapeake Bay held each year at Sandy Point Park, on the far side of Annapolis in the shadow of the Bay Bridge.

Put the two together with the chance to see the town known as America's sailing capital while the picturesque harbor is still at its bustling best, and you have a winning late-summer combination.

With a superb setting on a river opening to Chesapeake Bay and a heaping helping of history and charm, Annapolis is a fascinating port of call. A good plan might be to use Saturday for sightseeing and seafood and save Sunday for the Renaissance Festival.

Well over a century before anyone dreamed of establishing a national naval academy, Annapolis was already the state capital and a thriving port. More than 300 eighteenth-century buildings remain in the town to attest to its prosperous past, some of them open for fascinating touring.

But most of all the history of Annapolis is tied to the sea, a connection you can't miss, since the town dock and its narrow waterway extend the harbor almost into the heart of the city. Part of the fun of an Annapolis visit is boarding one of the boats for a cruise on the bay.

The dock is also a fine starting point for getting a sense of bygone days with a walking tour past the picturesque homes and enticing shops. The historic area of the town is compact, and it is easy to navigate on foot. A guide called "Rambling Through Annapolis," available from the chamber of commerce information desk or in local shops, will fill you in on local lore.

If you are a first-time visitor, you may prefer to start with one of the excellent walking tours available from Historic Annapolis, Inc., or Three Centuries Tours, the latter providing a guide in colonial garb. On your own, you will find on-site tours offered if you want to learn more when you visit the two major attractions of the city, the Maryland State House and the U.S. Naval Academy.

A logical starting point is the Victualing Warehouse Museum on

Main Street, just off Market Space, the picturesque square at the end of the dock where seafood to go is a local institution. A scale model here shows you the waterfront as it was from 1751 to 1791, when Annapolis was the principal seaport of Upper Chesapeake Bay. Other exhibits tell more about the early trade and commerce of the area.

Cornhill is one of the many narrow streets radiating out from Market Space that are lined with historic homes, some of them tippy with age. Different-colored plaques are used to tell you which of the town's three centuries each home represents. Among the smaller houses are the local showplaces, four fine mansions belonging to signers of the Declaration of Independence.

Follow Cornhill Street to its end, and you'll find yourself gazing at the statehouse that is the country's oldest capitol in continuous legislative use. It served as the nation's capitol in 1783 and 1784. Inside you'll see the Old Senate Chamber, where Congress received George Washington's resignation as commander in chief and where the Treaty of Paris was ratified, officially ending the Revolutionary War.

From here, follow State Circle around to Maryland Avenue to discover some of the shops and art galleries that make Annapolis a browsing and antiquing mecca. Military buffs will want to check out the Ship and Soldier Shop at 55 Maryland Avenue for its military and naval miniatures, and the Annapolis Country Store at number 53 is a good spot for small souvenirs such as pottery, potpourri, wicker, and old-fashioned painted porcelain soap dishes.

Two notable homes open for touring on Maryland Avenue are the Chase-Lloyd House, known for its grand-columned main hall, and the Hammond-Harwood House, considered one of the finest Georgian homes in the country. Follow Maryland to Prince George Street and make a right turn for the William Paca House, built in 1763 by one of the Declaration signers, who was also an early governor of the state. The dignified brick home and its exquisite gardens are the city's finest.

Veer left past the Paca House onto East Street and then right on Prince George to reach the magnificent waterfront campus of the U.S. Naval Academy. The museum and chapel are high points on the campus tour, but a stroll amid the quadrangles to see the midshipmen in their spiffy uniforms is enough to give you a feeling of the proud tradition that has been carried on here since 1845. Take a walk along the seawall for an incomparable view of the sailboats tacking to and fro across the Severn River and into Chesapeake Bay.

By now you'll no doubt be ready to get out to sea yourself. You can choose anything from a 40-minute cruise of the harbor area and bay on the *Harbor Queen* to a day's outing aboard the *Annapolitan*

II across Chesapeake Bay to picturesque St. Michaels on the Eastern Shore. If you get the urge to go farther out to sea, you can also plan to return for an overnight or two-to-five-day cruise on the *Mystic Clipper,* the tall ship that docks in Annapolis in April, May, September, and October.

Normally, by now you probably would be ready to sample one of the excellent restaurants in town, but instead save your appetite for the day's delicious end at the Maryland Seafood Festival. As soon as you pay your admission here (proceeds to local charities), you will be confronted with a giant menu offering just about every kind of seafood dish yet concocted. There are crab cakes, crab fluff, crab balls stuffed with shrimp, and fried crabs, hard or soft. Oysters come raw, steamed, fried, or in a loaf. Mussels in wine sauce, seafood gumbo, clam chowder, spicy crab soup—the list goes on and on, and prices are reasonable. You pick your favorites, buy tickets, and head for the tent that specializes in each type of shellfish. Then find a spot at a picnic table, and the feast is on. While you are resting between courses, you can wander over to enjoy the entertainment that goes on nonstop, everything from Mandy the Clown to the U.S. Army Stage Band. There are face painters and fortune-tellers around as well, but truly the big attraction here is the food—and it could hardly be improved upon.

Come Sunday, drive west on Route 50 and north on Route 178 to Crownsville, turn left through the hospital complex, and follow the signs back to the sixteenth century at the Maryland Renaissance Festival. This is one of only a dozen locations in the nation where you can see this kind of revelry, a combination medieval-style street fair and daylong nonstop entertainment by scores of performers in Elizabethan costumes. There's something for every taste, from good-natured mock adventures in Queen Elizabeth's court to mud wrestling. Over the course of the day dancers cavort, falcons soar over a trainer's watchful eye, archers practice their sport, and knights of old match wits and swordsmanship in the Living Chess Game.

In the center of it all is a mock village of thatched booths where more than 80 artisans and merchants offer anything from flower garlands bedecked with flowing ribbons to tarot card readings of your future. All the booths have a medieval theme. You can buy a spear or a shield, have your face painted in medieval designs, pick up a pair of Robin Hood boots or a tankard of ale, buy a candle or a piece of blown glass in the shape of a dragon, a castle, or a unicorn.

Strolling troubadours, jesters, and storytellers keep everyone amused, and if you should tire of just watching, you can try your mettle at fencing, jousting, or darts, or in such contests as Fight the Knight or Duelling Buckets. To add to the atmosphere, dozens of costumed actors stroll about impersonating typical townspeople, right down to the local lady of ill repute, who wears a sign reading "Rent-a-Wench."

All of it is a lot of fun, but nothing compares with the grand finale, when trumpet blares and timpani introduce a jousting duel between two knights in full armor. It's a rousing send-off that makes a return to the twentieth century seem very tame, indeed.

Area Code: 301

DRIVING DIRECTIONS   Annapolis is on Chesapeake Bay, off Route 50/301. From D.C., take Route 50 east and exit at either Route 450 or Route 70 for town. Approximate distance from D.C., 33 miles.

PUBLIC TRANSPORTATION   Limousine service from nearby Baltimore-Washington International Airport, $12; nearby Amtrak station has free shuttle to the airport for connections.

ACCOMMODATIONS   *Maryland Inn,* Church Circle and Main, 21401, 263-2641, 1776 landmark, $$$ CP ● *Historic Inns of Annapolis,* 16 Church Circle, 21401, 263-2641, historic preservations by same owners as Maryland Inn include *Governor Calvert House, Robert Johnson House, Reynolds Tavern, State House Inn,* all $$–$$$ CP ● *Hilton Inn,* Compromise and St. Mary's streets, 21401, 268-7555, prize location, $$$$ ● *Gibson's Lodgings,* 110-114 Prince George Street, 21401, 268-5555, charming small guest house in historic district, $$–$$$ CP ● *Annapolis Holiday Inn,* 210 Holiday Court, 21401, 224-3150, $$ ● *Thr-rift Inn,* 2542 Riva Road, 21401, 224-2800, $ ● Upscale newcomers include *Loews Annapolis Hotel,* 126 West Street, 21401, 263-7777 or (800) 333-3333, $$$ ● *Courtyard by Marriott,* 2559 Riva Road, 21401, 266-1555, $$$–$$$$ ● *Annapolis Ramada Hotel,* 175 Jennifer Road, 21401, 266-3131 or (800) 351-9209, $$$–$$$$.

BED AND BREAKFAST   *Traveller in Maryland, Inc.,* P.O. Box 2277, Annapolis, MD 21404, 269-6232; in D.C area, (301) 261-2233 ● *Amanda's Bed & Breakfast Reservation Service,* 1428 Park Avenue, Baltimore, MD 21217, (301) 225-0001 ● *Annapolis Association of Licensed Bed & Breakfast Owners,* P.O. Box 7444, Annapolis, MD 21404, offers a brochure listing local hosts.

DINING   *Treaty of Paris,* in Maryland Inn (see above), charming, reserve, $$–$$$ ● *Middleton Tavern,* 2 Market Place, 263-3323, historic 1750 tavern, attractive but overpriced, $$$–$$$$ ● *Har-*

bour House, 87 Prince George Street, 268-0771, old warehouse, outdoor dining, $$–$$$ ● *Reynolds Tavern,* 7 Church Circle, 263-6599, 1737 colonial tavern, contemporary menu, $–$$$ ● *Cafe Normandie,* 195 Main Street, 263-3382, French cafe, $–$$ ● *Griffins,* 22 Market Space, City Dock, 268-2576, informal, seafood, $–$$ ● *Corinthian,* Loews Annapolis Hotel (see above), fine American cuisine, $$–$$$ ● Fran O'Brien's, 113 Main Street, 268-6288, old-timer in town, $$–$$$ ● *Carrol's Creek Cafe,* 410 Severn Avenue, Eastport, 263-8102 (a few minutes' drive across the Eastport bridge), waterfront setting, fish specialties, $–$$$ ● *Fred's Restaurant,* 2348 Solomons Island Road, 224-2386, Italian and seafood, tops for crab cakes, $–$$$ ● *McGarvey's,* 8 Market Space, 263-5700, pub fare, $$.

SIGHTSEEING *Maryland Renaissance Festival,* Route 178, Crownsville, MD, 266-7304. Six weekends, late August through September, 10:30 A.M. to 6 P.M. Adults, $9.95; ages 12–15, $8; ages 5–12, $3.95 ● *Maryland Seafood Festival,* 152 Main Street, Annapolis, 268-7682. Held second weekend in September, Friday to Sunday noon to 8:30 P.M. at Sandy Point State Park, Route 50/301, just before the Chesapeake Bay Bridge ● *Maryland State House,* State Circle, 974-3400. Hours: daily 9 A.M. to 5 P.M.; 20-minute tours, hourly 10 A.M. to 4 P.M.; orientation slide shows, hourly 9:30 A.M. to 4:30 P.M. Free ● *U.S. Naval Academy,* King George Street, Annapolis, 267-3363. Grounds open daily 9 A.M. to 5 P.M. Free ● *U.S. Naval Academy Museum,* Monday to Saturday 9 A.M. to 4:45 P.M.; Sunday 11 A.M. to 4:45 P.M. Free. Walking tours from visitor information center in Ricketts Hall at Gate 1, daily March through Thanksgiving, 9:30 A.M. to 4 P.M. Check current fee ● *William Paca House,* 186 Prince George Street, 263-5553. Hours: Tuesday to Saturday 10 A.M. to 4 P.M.; Sunday noon to 4 P.M. Adults, $3.50; ages 6–10, $2.50 ● *Chesapeake Marine Tours,* Slip 20, City Dock, 268-7600, 40- and 90-minute evening and daylong cruises, daily Memorial Day through September, weekends spring and fall. Check for current schedules and fees ● *Walking Tours: Historic Annapolis,* Old Treasury Building, State Circle, 267-8149 ● *Three Centuries Tours,* 48 Maryland Avenue, 263-5401. Call for current schedules and rates; reservations necessary.

INFORMATION Tourism Council of Annapolis and Anne Arundel Co., 6 Dock Street, Annapolis, MD 21401, 268-TOUR.

FALL

Who's Who in Colonial Fredericksburg

Everyone who was anyone in early America seems to have played a role in the history of Fredericksburg, Virginia.

For starters, there were the Washingtons. George Washington, who once said, "All that I am I owe to my mother," showed his filial gratitude by buying a home for his widowed mother in Fredericksburg, near the mansion where his sister, Betty Washington Lewis, lived in style in one of the loveliest homes in colonial America.

George, himself a local boy who made good, said his last farewell to Mary Ball Washington in her Fredericksburg home and rode off with his mother's blessing to be inaugurated as the first president of the United States.

The Washington family homes are among more than 350 original buildings remaining in the 40-block historic district to tell of the illustrious past of this settlement along the Rappahannock River.

Come and follow the footsteps of the Founding Fathers, who plotted the American Revolution here in a tavern built by Washington's brother, Charles, and visit the office where James Monroe practiced law before he became president of the United States. Stand on the spot marking where Thomas Jefferson declared religious freedom a legal right in Virginia, then walk the silent battlegrounds where blue and gray troops decided the fate of the Civil War a century later, keeping the young states of America united.

The spirit of the past even seems to have rubbed off on present-day Fredericksburg, inspiring a new generation of artisans who recreate handicrafts of the colonial era. Dropping in on the local pewter-, silver-, and coppersmiths adds to the fun of a visit—as does dining and living in historic quarters and visiting the many antique shops that have burgeoned in the historic district.

Begin at the visitors center on Caroline Street for a free film that will fill you in on local lore. Then you'll be ready to see the sights for yourself. You'll learn that George Washington grew up on Ferry Farm, right across the Rappahannock River, where Mrs. Washington was still living when her concerned son moved her into town. It was here that the famous legends of chopping down the cherry tree and tossing a coin over the Rappahannock were born.

The law offices of James Monroe were located just a few blocks from Mrs. Washington's home. Another monument marks the spot where Thomas Jefferson met with a committee in 1777 to draft the Virginia Statute for Religious Freedom, which later was incorporated into the U.S. Constitution as the First Amendment to the Bill of Rights. Jefferson considered this statute one of his most important achievements.

All of these are among the 29 historic stops marked on the free walking and driving tour available at the center. You might begin with a visit to the house of the mother of the Father of Our Country. Mary Ball Washington spent her last 17 years in this cozy home, which is still filled with her favorite possessions. When General Lafayette stopped by to pay his respects to his commander's mother, he found her at work in her beloved garden, which is restored much as she left it, planted with boxwoods along a brick walkway to separate the vegetables from a lush English-style flower garden.

Mrs. Washington is buried on the estate of her daughter, at a favorite spot where she often came to meditate and pray. A marker has been installed in her honor.

Betty Washington's showplace home, Kenmore, stands on Washington Avenue, just a couple of blocks from her mother's house. The impressive brick residence built in 1752 by Betty and her husband, wealthy planter Fielding Lewis, originally was the main house of an 863-acre plantation. The house is known for the exquisite decorative plasterwork carving on the ceilings and cornices that make it one of the most elaborate homes of colonial times. Two rooms are included in the book collection *100 Most Beautiful Rooms in America*.

Betty married well, but not because she was a beauty. Her portrait shows a striking resemblance, nose and all, to brother George, 16 months her senior.

If you take a walk along Washington Avenue, you'll see the fine Victorian homes that went up later in Fredericksburg, after the Kenmore land was subdivided.

Over at the Rising Sun Tavern, built around 1760 by Washington's youngest brother, Charles, the period furnishings remain and you can almost hear the echoes of the history makers who dined and plotted in this "hot-bed of sedition"—men like Washington, Jefferson, Patrick Henry, and the Lees of Virginia. Have a spot of spiced tea, take a look at the stand-up desk said to have belonged to Thomas Jefferson, and listen to the tavern's story, told by a costumed hostess.

Another fascinating stop on the tour is the Hugh Mercer Apothecary Shop. Once again you are stepping back 200 years, this time to learn about the medicines and surgical treatments Dr. Mercer might have prescribed for your ailments, such things as leeches, lancets, and crab claws. Mercer, a personal friend of George Washington's, practiced medicine here for 15 years, with Mary Washington as one of his many noted patients. He left to join the revolutionary cause and gave his life at the Battle of Princeton.

The tavern, shop, and Mary Washington House are all maintained by the Association for the Preservation of Virginia Antiquities (APVA). Their fourth property, Saint James's House, was owned by another Mercer named James, the Washingtons' attorney, and sits on land that George Washington had bought from his brother-in-law, Fielding Lewis. The beautifully furnished eighteenth-century gentleman's home is open only by appointment and for special events, including the annual mid-September Quilt and Loom Show held at the APVA properties. The juried show is a special treat for quilt lovers.

The annual Christmas candlelight tour on the first Sunday in December is another special time for a visit to Fredericksburg.

The last major in-town site is the James Monroe Law Office–Museum and Memorial Library. A onetime governor of Virginia, Monroe held many high offices, including minister to France, and his office contains some of the furniture in rich mahogany with inlaid brass that he brought back with him from Europe. The Louis XVI desk is where he signed his annual message to Congress in 1823, including the section that became known as the Monroe Doctrine, declaring the United States as protector of all the Americas from foreign aggression. Besides the unusually fine furnishings, there are displays of some of the costumes worn by the Monroes at the Court of Napoleon and the exquisite gems owned by Mrs. Monroe.

The walking-driving tour will point out other places of interest, including historic churches, the campus of Mary Washington College, and, on the other side of the river, the charming eighteenth-century home called Belmont, where painter Gari Melchers lived and worked. His studio and gardens remain on a lovely site overlooking the Rappahannock.

It is something of a miracle that so many of these early buildings survive, because Fredericksburg, located exactly midway between Union headquarters in Washington and the Confederate capital in Richmond, was a highly sought prize that changed hands seven times during the Civil War and was the scene of four bloody battles. The first, in 1862, was the most one-sided battle of the war, resulting in a smashing victory for Lee's forces, ensconced on Marye's Heights, high above the Rappahannock. Another victory came the following year at nearby Chancellorsville, but at a terrible cost. It was here that "Stonewall" Jackson, the brilliant Confederate general who was Lee's most trusted subordinate, was mortally wounded by an unwitting shot from his own troops. A shrine to Jackson stands about 15 miles south of Fredericksburg.

The Wilderness Campaigns outside town were followed by the Battle at Spotsylvania Court House in 1864, the most intense hand-to-hand combat of the war. It was one of Lee's last successful stands, but one whose heavy Confederate losses led to the eventual end of the war.

The Fredericksburg National Cemetery contains the graves of over 15,000 Union soldiers, and the Confederate Cemetery holds many more, including those of five rebel generals, evidence of the terrible toll taken here on both sides.

The Fredericksburg/Spotsylvania National Military Park offers films describing the battle action and maps of a self-guided tour of the battle sites in the park. A second visitors center, with its own audiovisual program, is open at the Chancellorsville Battlefield, about ten miles west of Fredericksburg.

One other interesting site relating to both the Civil and the Revolutionary wars is the Old Stone Warehouse on Sophia Street in town along the river. Once a colonial tobacco warehouse, it now contains a museum of Civil War and colonial artifacts. An archaeological dig in the basement is open to public view, and the gift shop offers some excavated souvenirs of both the Civil War and the colonial periods. (Note that the museum is open only on Sunday afternoon.)

A new attraction in town is the Fredericksburg Area Museum and Cultural Center, housed in the early-nineteenth-century Town Hall/Market House. It interprets Fredericksburg history through the centuries.

Sophia Street is where some of Fredericksburg's 70-plus antique shops begin. More are one block away on Caroline Street. The largest selection under one roof can be found at the Antique Court of Shoppes, with two locations, 1001 Caroline and 106 William streets.

Art is part of the Fredericksburg scene as well, at the Gallery De May and Premier Gallery, both on Caroline Street.

The most delightful shopping, however, is at the workshops of the Fredericksburg craftspeople. The Copper Shop along the river at 701 Sophia is headquarters for a father-son team of artisans, Alan Green II and Alan III. Their graceful hand-forged Fredericksburg lamps, contemporary versions of traditional colonial designs, hang in all 50 states and in 44 foreign lands, and their made-to-order weather vanes, in shapes from cigar-store Indian to rock guitar, are true collector's items.

Handsome handcrafted bowls, plates, and candlesticks can be found at Cardinal Pewter, 309 Princess Elizabeth Street, while tinsmith James Glynn fashions handsome lighting fixtures and other period pieces at 107 Hanover Street. Ralph Gooch, the Fredericksburg pewtersmith, has his workshop and small salesroom behind his home at 309 Princess. Gooch's burnished goblets, plates, mugs, and bowls are shaped at the wheel into designs that are a beautiful blending of function and art. Many people collect the Christmas ornaments he makes in a different historic design each year.

The craftspeople are a living continuation of the colonial spirit, bringing the Fredericksburg of the past gracefully into the present.

Area Code: 703

DRIVING DIRECTIONS Fredericksburg is at the intersection of routes 1 and 3, just off I-95. From D.C., follow I-95 south to Fredericksburg exits. Approximate distance from D.C., 50 miles.

PUBLIC TRANSPORTATION The Amtrak station is right in the heart of town. No car necessary in town; bus tours available to Civil War sites.

ACCOMMODATIONS *Kenmore Inn,* 1200 Princess Anne Street, 22401, 371-7622, 1700s home-turned-inn, convenient, $$$ CP ● *The Richard Johnston Inn,* 711 Caroline Street, 22401, 899-7606, charming and convenient, fireplaces, outdoor patio, the "summer kitchen" with brick floors and walk-in fireplace is special, $$-$$$ ● *Fredericksburg Colonial Inn,* 1707 Princess Anne Street, 22401, 371-5666, small motel-style rooms, but with nice old-fashioned furnishings, $ ● *Sheration-Fredericksburg Resort and Conference Center,* I-95 and Route 3, 22404, 786-8321, $$$ ● *Ramada Inn,* I-95 and Route 3, 22404, 786-8361, $-$$.

DINING *Kenmore Inn* (see above), $$-$$$ ● *Chimneys,* 623 Caroline Street, 371-9229, charming 1729 home, $$ ● *La Petite Auberge,* 311 William Street, 371-2727, French, $-$$$ ● *Ristorante Renato,* 422 William Street, 371-8228, good Italian, $-$$$ ● *Sophia Street Station,* 503 Sophia Street, 371-3355, overlooking the Rappahannock River, $-$$ ● *Old Mudd Tavern,* off I-95, Thornburg (south of Fredericksburg), 582-5250, $$-$$$ ● *Sammy T's,* 801 Caroline Street, 371-2088, good for a light lunch, $.

SIGHTSEEING Discount block tickets available for first 6 sites. *Mary Washington House,* 1200 Charles Street, 373-1569. Hours: March 1 to November 30, daily 9 A.M. to 5 P.M.; December to February 10 A.M. to 4 P.M. Adults, $2.50; students, $.50 ● *Kenmore,* 1201 Washington Avenue, 272-2881. Hours: March 1 to November 30, daily 9 A.M. to 5 P.M.; December to February 10 A.M.

to 4 P.M. Adults, $4; children, $2 ● *Rising Sun Tavern*, 1306 Caroline Street, 373-1569. Hours: March 1 to November 30, 9 A.M. to 5 P.M.; December to February 10 A.M. to 4 P.M. Adults, $2.50; children, $.50 ● *Hugh Mercer Apothecary Shop*, 1020 Caroline Street, 373-1569. Hours: March to November 9 A.M. to 5 P.M.; December to February 10 A.M. to 4 P.M. Adults, $2.50; children, $.50 ● *James Monroe Law Office–Museum and Memorial Library*, 908 Charles Street, 899-4559. Hours: daily 9 A.M. to 5 P.M. Adults, $2.50; children, $.50 ● *Belmont*, off Route 17 east toward Falmouth, 373-3634. Hours: April 1 to September 30, Monday to Saturday 10 A.M. to 5 P.M.; Sunday 1 P.M. to 5 P.M.; rest of year to 4 P.M. Adults, $3; children, $1 ● *Fredericksburg Area Museum & Cultural Center*, Princess Anne and William streets, 371-3037. Hours: Monday to Saturday 9 A.M. to 4 P.M.; Sunday 1 P.M. to 4 P.M. Adults, $2; children, $1 ● *Old Stone Warehouse*, Sophia and William streets, 373-1674. Hours: Sunday 1 P.M. to 4 P.M. Free ● *Fredericksburg/Spotsylvania National Military Park Visitor Center*, Lafayette Boulevard (US 1) and Sunken Road, 373-4461. Hours: 8:30 A.M. to 5 P.M. Free ● *Chancellorsville Battlefield Visitor Center*, off Route 3, west of I-95, 786-2880. Hours: 9 A.M. to 5 P.M. Free.

INFORMATION Fredericksburg Visitor Center, 706 Caroline Street, Fredericksburg, VA 22401, 373-1776 or (800) 678-4748, free orientation film.

Sweet Season in Hershey

Kids are sweet on Hershey, Pennsylvania. But then so are their parents and grandparents and uncles and aunts.

It's hard not to love a chocolate-covered town where even the streetlights are shaped like chocolate kisses, where the main downtown intersection is at Chocolate and Cocoa, and all the street signs have Hershey Bar lettering.

But you will please more than your sweet tooth in the place known as Chocolate Town, U.S.A. In Hershey there are magnificent gardens with 8,000 rosebushes featuring 250 varieties of blooms, a fine zoo, a museum of American life, a super-duper amusement park, tennis courts, and five golf courses, all waiting after your chocolate tour is over.

There are few destinations with so many ways to please the whole family—and no better time for a weekend visit than early autumn. The days are a bit cooler then, and crowds of vacationing families have gone home, but Hersheypark remains open on weekends, and the roses are still in bloom.

Milton Hershey, who made a fortune on candy bars, would be pleased if he could see what has happened in his town. Hershey never planned all these attractions with tourists in mind. Having made his first million on caramel candies in Lancaster, in 1904 the former farm boy came back to his hometown, known then as Derry Church, to build a chocolate factory in a cornfield. Hershey never had children of his own, so he adopted his workers, dedicating himself to making their town a pleasant place to live. The first parks, gardens, museum, and zoo were strictly for their benefit.

But from the start people wanted to see how this new confection called milk chocolate was made, and the factory began offering tours to meet the demand. Savoring the sweet smells, the free samples, and the atmosphere of this unusually pleasant little town, visitors sent their friends. In 1928 the count was 10,000; by 1970 it was pushing a million, and the factory could no longer accommodate the crowds.

Chocolate World was built in 1973 to take the place of the old tour, and it is now almost everyone's first stop in Hershey. The free ten-minute trip in a Disneylike automated car whisks you off on a make-believe journey to the chocolate plantations of Ghana, and as you travel, you watch the story of chocolate unfold from bean to candy bar. There's no longer the chocolate smell or free samples that were so luscious in the real factory, but well over a million and a half tourists took the ride last year anyway.

Opposite Chocolate World is Hersheypark, once the place where factory employees came to picnic, play ball, go boating, and be entertained at the pavilion. Hershey kept improving the facilities, adding a swimming pool and convention hall that doubled in season as an ice-skating rink.

Some of the major structures in town, including the lavish Hershey Hotel, went up during the Depression as part of Hershey's campaign to provide jobs.

Hershey Zoo was actually Hershey's own private animal collection, one of the country's largest, housed at the park for all to see. And for the kids he bought a carousel and, as a twentieth birthday present to the town, a roller coaster.

Once again the crowds grew, and the evolution into an amusement park seemed only natural; planning for Hersheypark began in

1971. Unless you have a total aversion to theme parks, it's hard not to like this clean and pretty one on 87 treed and landscaped acres where you stroll through a mock English town called Tudor Square, a Pennsylvania Dutch community known as Der Deitschplatz, and an eighteenth-century German village labeled Rhine Land. All come complete with appropriately costumed denizens, music, shops, and restaurants. Sure it's corny and commercial, but the happy crowds don't seem to care.

The 1919 carousel at the park now has a lot of company, including three roller coasters. The scariest of them is the SooperDooper-Looper, which literally turns you upside down. Recently added were new water rides, including Canyon River Rapids, simulating a white-water rafting trip, and Frontier Chute-Out, a quadruple-flume water-slide ride.

There are a couple of dozen other choices, a total of 45 rides, from "scream machines" to gentle go-rounds for the tots.

You can get a view of the whole park from the kiss-shaped windows of the 330-foot Kissing Tower or take the monorail for a scenic ride with an audio accompaniment.

There is also continuous live entertainment at four theaters scattered through the park, and the adjoining arena hosts not only the Ice Capades and hockey games but big-name entertainers. At the Starlight Arcade, where the sidewalks are replicas of those at Hollywood's Mann's Chinese Theater (formerly Grauman's), you'll find handprints of such stars as the Osmonds, Kenny Rogers, Sha Na Na, Barry Manilow, Loretta Lynn, John Denver, and the Harlem Globetrotters, all of whom have performed in Hershey.

Almost everyone's favorite souvenir of the park is a photo taken with the life-size candy-bar characters who greet visitors. Don't forget your camera.

Mr. Hershey's zoo, too, has come a long way. It now represents the major natural regions of North America—waters, deserts, woodlands, plains, and forests—and is stocked with plants and animals indigenous to each zone in replicas of their native habitats. You'll see alligators in the swamps; pumas, bison, and eagles in Big Sky Country; bears and timber wolves in the forest; wild turkeys, bobcats, otters, and raccoons at home in the woodlands. A highlight is the Grassy Waters replica of the Florida Everglades, which features a live oak tree some 20 feet in diameter.

There's more than enough to fill a Saturday here, and more still to come for Sunday. All ages can appreciate the beauty of the Hershey Gardens. From its start in 1936 when Hershey ordered that "a nice rose garden" be planted near his new hotel, the garden has grown to 23 acres. In addition to roses, there are six themed gardens, including a Japanese garden and displays of evergreens, shrubs, and ornamental grasses. September marks the beginning of a spectacular display of chrysanthemums. The gardens are an attraction too beautiful to miss.

Even the Hershey Museum proves to be more than you might expect. It's less overwhelming than a lot of museums and, for that very reason, makes its points unusually well. In addition to some fascinating collections of Indian artifacts, Pennsylvania Dutch crafts, and early clocks, you get a compact tour through the changing life-styles of America in terms of decoration and fashion, including the effect of inventions like the sewing machine. The Pennsylvania German collection is one of the largest in existence, and another favorite section is the collection of music boxes and phonographs that can be turned on by pressing buttons. Try to time your visit to coincide with the noon performance of the Apostolic Clock, with moving carved figurines depicting the Last Supper. There is also an exhibit telling about the town's unusual founder, Milton Hershey.

One other Hershey institution has nothing to do with tourists. The Milton Hershey School was founded in 1909 by Milton and Catherine Hershey to provide a free home as well as an educational center for orphan boys. Now coed, the school tries to create an atmosphere of family life for its residents with 92 homes spread across 10,000 acres of campus. Each house provides room for 12–16 children and house parents. The educational program, which extends through high school, includes time for work on community projects and the opportunity to learn a trade or prepare for college, according to each student's abilities and inclinations.

Founders Hall, a striking domed limestone building constructed as a tribute to the Hersheys, serves as church, theater, and concert hall for the school. A film about the school is shown here regularly. Some of the profits from the Hershey enterprises are used to supplement the endowment Milton Hershey left to the school.

Where to stay in Hershey? The natural choices are the excellent Hershey-run establishments, either the grand Hershey Hotel or the attractive motel-style Hershey Lodge. Both offer pools, tennis, golf, and many other activities, and with package plans, including all of the admissions, they may well fit into your budget. If not, there are some less-expensive motel choices in town and nearby.

The only problem with Hershey is fitting it all into one weekend. You may just decide to take it in installments. That way you can come back to see the tulips bloom in the spring.

Area Code: 717

DRIVING DIRECTIONS Hershey is on Route 422, about 10 miles east of Harrisburg, close to routes I-81, I-78, and I-76. From

D.C., take I-95 north, exit at I-695, the Baltimore Beltway, then take I-83 north to Harrisburg and Route 322 east to Route 422 into Hershey. Approximate distance from D.C., 110 miles.

PUBLIC TRANSPORTATION Amtrak and Capitol Trailways buses to Harrisburg and air service to Harrisburg Airport, 15 minutes away. Hershey accommodations provide complimentary limousine service from Harrisburg.

ACCOMMODATIONS *Hershey Resorts,* Hershey 17033, 533-2171 or toll-free (800) 533-3131 ● *Hotel Hershey,* $$$$ ● *Hershey Lodge,* $$$. Check for much lower package rates that may include meals and admission to the Hershey attractions. Children's rates also available ● *Hershey "Colonial" Motel,* 43 West Areba Avenue, 17033, 533-7054, $ ● *Bruwin Motel,* 150 East Governor, 17033, 533-2591, $ ● *Palmyra Motel,* Route 3, Palmyra, 17078, 838-1324, $–$$ ● *Union Canal House,* 107 South Hanover Street, Union Deposit, 17033, 566-0054, B&B in an historic building, $$.

BED AND BREAKFAST *Hershey Bed and Breakfast,* P.O. Box 208, Hershey, PA 17033, 533-2928.

DINING First choices, once again, are the Hershey properties: *Hershey Lodge,* with three choices, the *Tack Room,* $$$; the *Hearth,* $$$; and the *Copper Kettle,* for family dining, $ ● *Hershey Hotel,* elegant dining room, jackets requested, $$$$. Other recommendations: *Lucy's Cafe,* 267 West Chocolate Avenue, 534-1045, Italian, $–$$ ● *Spinner's Restaurant,* 845 East Chocolate Avenue, 533-9050, wide variety, $$–$$$ ● *Union Canal House* (see above), basic menu, steaks and seafood, $–$$.

SIGHTSEEING For all Hershey attractions, phone 800-HERSHEY. *Hersheypark:* Hours: mid-May to Labor Day, selected September weekends. Opening time, 10:30 A.M., closing varies with season, phone for current operating hours. Age 9 to adults, $19.95; ages 4 to 8, $16.95. *Hershey Museum of American Life:* Hours: daily 10 A.M. to 5 P.M.; Memorial Day to Labor Day to 6 P.M. Adults, $3.50; ages 4–18, $1.25. *ZOOAMERICA:* Hours: June to August, daily 10 A.M. to 8 P.M.; rest of year to 5 P.M. Adults, $3.50; ages 3–12, $2.25. *Hershey Gardens:* Hours: April through October, daily 9 A.M. to 5 P.M. Adults, $3.50; ages 4–18, $1. *Chocolate World:* Hours: daily 9 A.M. to 4:45 P.M. except winter Sundays, noon to 4:45 P.M. Free. Check for current package rates for savings.

INFORMATION *HERSHEY,* Information and Reservations, 300 Park Boulevard, Hershey, PA 17033, 800-HERSHEY.

Currents of History at Harpers Ferry

In Harpers Ferry, West Virginia, the date is 1860, not long after the day that John Brown and his band marched into town to free the slaves and inscribe the town indelibly in American history.

Then, as now, Harpers Ferry was a beauty spot, set at a bend where two mighty rivers meet, after carving steep gorges in the surrounding wild, wooded Appalachian Mountains. It is a picture still worthy of Thomas Jefferson's 1780s description as "one of the most stupendous scenes in nature."

The town was all but destroyed by bloody Civil War battles and a series of floods afterward, but since the National Park Service took over in 1960, Harpers Ferry has come back to life as a historical park, reconstructed to look the way it was at its most important moment in history and populated with costumed guides who spin fascinating tales of the momentous events that took place here long ago.

It's a living history lesson in a setting that is at its most spectacular bathed in autumn color, and a chance to get out and walk amid the mountain scenery as well. You can continue tracing history at Antietam, the fabled battlefield just across the river in Maryland, where part of the Harpers Ferry saga continued to a tragic conclusion.

Everything at Harpers Ferry seems to have stood still for the last century—the dresses in the window of the general store have bustles, the smithy is hard at work at his open hearth, and you must visit the combination telegraph, ticket, and post office when you want to communicate with the outside world. All the tradespeople are in period dress.

If you come for Election Day, held here in mid-October, you'll find yourself in the thick of the 1860 election, with the chance to cast your presidential ballot for Stephen Douglas, John C. Breckenridge, or John Bell. There will be debates, speeches, harangues, and demonstrations typical of nineteenth-century American elections, trying to sway your vote. If you favor a Republican candidate, one Abraham Lincoln, you're out of luck. He had no elector in what was then Jefferson County, Virginia, and thus was not an option.

Start your visit with a stop at the visitors center to get the lay of the land and a schedule of talks, then join the group sitting in the shade of an ancient tree where a guide in period dress is explaining the events that once shook this peaceful scene.

The rivers were Harpers Ferry's beginning and ending. The town's story really started in 1748, when the powerful waters of the Potomac and the Shenandoah tempted Robert Harper to stake out a claim here. A millwright and architect, Harper gained a patent on 125 acres of land from Lord Fairfax, bought a cabin, a canoe, and a corn patch, and built himself a mill powered by the rushing water. The town was named for the ferry service Harper took over from an earlier settler.

The rivers' strong currents were also the attraction that inspired George Washington in 1790 to choose Harpers Ferry as the site for the National Armory and Arsenal, which grew into one of the largest factories in early America. It occupied 20 brick workshops and offices along the river and employed 400 people. The town prospered also as a center of commerce with cotton and flour mills, sawmills, an iron foundry, inns, and a number of shops. It was an important stop for the Baltimore and Ohio Railroad and the Chesapeake and Ohio Canal.

All of that began to change when abolitionist John Brown fixed on Harpers Ferry and its armory as the starting point on his crusade to free the slaves.

Brown and his 22-man "army of liberation" came across the B & O Railroad bridge over the river in the dark of night on October 16, 1859, and occupied the armory before the startled townspeople realized what had happened. His wild dream was that thousands of slaves would join him and follow him north into Pennsylvania. Instead, the alarm went out and the raiders were forced to barricade themselves in the army fire engine and guard house. They were captured when reinforcement troops commanded by Colonel Robert E. Lee and Lieutenant Jeb Stuart stormed the building on October 18, breaking down the door with a ladder. Two of the ten men killed were Brown's sons.

John Brown was tried and hanged at nearby Charles Town in December, but on the day of his execution he wrote a last message that proved prophetic. It read "I, John Brown, am now quite certain that the crimes of this guilty land will not be purged away but with blood." Sixteen months later his words came true when the Civil War began.

In April 1861, when Virginia seceded from the Union (West Virginia remained part of Virginia until 1863), Federal troops set fire to the arsenal, but townspeople extinguished the flames and the cache of machinery and weapons was sent to Richmond to outfit the Confederate army.

Even without the arms, Harpers Ferry's railroad and river supply lines made it the central point of access to the Shenandoah Valley, and both sides wanted it badly. It changed hands eight times, the biggest battle occurring in September 1862, when Confederate troops under General "Stonewall" Jackson seized the town and captured the 12,700-man Union garrison, the largest Union surrender in the Civil War.

By the end of the war the town was devastated, and many residents had fled. Those who did come back hoping to start anew had their hopes dashed by a series of disastrous floods in the late 1800s. For years after, the ruined town stood almost desolate.

There's much to see today in the historic park—the shops, the small brick engine house where John Brown hid, the John Brown Museum, the Civil War Museum, and the Master Armorer's House, with exhibits on the history of gunmaking, including the first handmade flintlock rifles made for the U.S. Army in Harpers Ferry in 1803.

When you've retraced the fateful history of the town, climb the old stone steps to the oldest surviving building, the house Robert Harper built the year he died. It has been refurbished to represent a tenant's dwelling of the 1850s, complete with quilts, cooking pots, and washstand.

Thomas Jefferson was a guest here while Harper House served as an inn from 1782 to 1803. Up the hill at Jefferson Rock you can share the view that inspired him to write, "The passage of the Patowmac [sic] through the Blue Ridge is . . . worth a voyage across the Atlantic." Behind the rock is the graveyard where Robert Harper and his wife are buried.

On High Street leading up the hill from the park, a dozen or so shops hope to tempt visitors with gifts or souvenirs or snacks of ice cream or fudge. The best of the lot is the bookstore run by the Harpers Ferry Historic Association, stocked with over 500 titles on the Civil War, regional history, and Americana. A couple of attractive little restaurants also offer refreshments with a view. Farther up the hill in Bolivar, another cluster of antique shops and crafts stores awaits.

If you want to enjoy more views and a hike in the autumn woods, there are several hiking trails within the park, the Appalachian Trail is nearby, and the C & O Canal Towpath is just across the river. Rafting on the river is another popular pastime. Ask for further information at the park visitors center.

There are a few small bed-and-breakfast homes in town, but Harpers Ferry's best-known lodging, the Hilltop House, is showing its 100 years. Better choices are the growing number of inns in neighboring towns. In Charles Town, the site of a popular Thoroughbred racetrack, the Carriage House, a grand early 1800s home on Main Street, gets the nod for convenience, but even nicer are two choices out in the countryside. The Cottonwood Inn is a warm, comfortable farmhouse with a book-lined living room and a hammock out back, while Hillbrook is country elegant, a showplace done with taste and charm. Owner Gretchen Carroll is also known for her multicourse gourmet dinners.

Possibilities in Martinsburg include the Dunn Country Inn, a nineteenth-century stone farmhouse filled with interesting antiques collected by the well-traveled owners, and Boydville, an 1812 landmark mansion in town. Martinsburg's chief lure is its Blue Ridge Outlet Center, onetime woolen mills that now boast some 40 top manufacturers' outlets from Levi Strauss to Ralph Lauren. The smaller Martinsburg Factory Stores complex adds Liz Claiborne, Reebok, and half a dozen other top names to the list.

Two more top choices are in Shepherdstown, a quaint village that boasts of being the oldest in West Virginia. The six-room Thomas Shepherd Inn is cozy, and the Bavarian Inn, a resort perched on a cliff, offers perfect views of the Potomac. Shepherdstown's tippy buildings are blooming with interesting shops, and the town also offers the area's best dining, with excellent German specialties at the Bavarian Inn and a trendy menu at the Yellow Brick Bank. For lunch, the lush garden at the Mecklenburg Inn is hard to beat.

In Shepherdstown, you'll be just across the bridge from Sharpsburg and the Antietam battlefield. Following his victory at Harpers Ferry in 1862, "Stonewall" Jackson moved on to join General Lee's forces at Antietam Creek near Sharpsburg, where the Confederate force making its first attempt to carry the war into the north was brutally mowed down by Union fire in the bloodiest battle of the war. Twenty-three thousand men were killed or wounded here. It is a moving story told vividly by the film in the National Park Service headquarters and equally well in Union General Joseph Hooker's written report of the encounter: "In the time I am writing, every stalk of corn in the northern and greater part of the field was cut as closely as could have been done with a knife and the slain lay in rows precisely as they had stood in their ranks a few moments before." The battle was critical because British aid to the Confederacy depended on the outcome.

Follow the markers of the battle, and you will find that corn waves peacefully again in the silent fields once soaked in blood, and two nice country inns stand on ground where part of the battle was fought—happy contrasts to the sad events that took place here a century ago.

Area Code: 304 for West Virginia; 301 for Maryland

DRIVING DIRECTIONS   Harpers Ferry is off Route 340, between Frederick, Maryland, and Winchester, Virginia. From D.C., take I-270 north to Frederick, then 340 west. Approximate distance from D.C., 50 miles.

PUBLIC TRANSPORTATION   Amtrak provides regular service from Washington.

ACCOMMODATIONS   *Cottonwood Inn,* Route 2, P.O. Box 61-S, Charles Town, 25414, 725-3371, $$ CP • *Hillbrook Inn,* Route 2, P.O. Box 152, Charles Town, 25414, 725-4223, $$$–$$$$ CP • *The Carriage Inn,* 417 East Washington Street, Charles Town, 25414, 728-8003, $$–$$$ CP • *The Dunn Country Inn,* Route 3, P.O. Box 33J, Martinsburg, 25401, 263-8646, $$–$$$ CP • *Boydville,* 601 South Queen Street, Martinsburg, 25401, 263-1448, $$$ CP • *Bavarian Inn and Lodge,* Route 480 at the Potomac River Bridge, Box 30, Shepherdstown, 25443, 876-2551, $$–$$$ • *Thomas Shepherd Inn,* P.O. Box 1162, Shepherdstown. 25443, 876-3715, $$ • *Piper House,* Route 65, Sharpsburg, MD 21782, 797-1862, on Antietam battlefield, $–$$ CP • *Inn at Antietam,* P.O. Box 119, Sharpsburg, MD 21782, 432-6601, also on the battlefield, $$–$$$ CP.

DINING   *The Anvil,* 1270 Washington Street, Harpers Ferry, 535-2582, $$ • *The Garden of Food,* High Street, Harpers Ferry, 535-2202, $ • *Mountain House Cafe,* High Street, Harpers Ferry, 535-2339, $ • *Bavarian Inn* (see above), $–$$$ • *Yellow Brick Bank,* German and Princess streets, Shepherdstown, 876-2208, $$–$$$ • *Mecklenburg Inn,* German Street, Shepherdstown, 876-2126, lunch in a lovely garden, $ • *Charles Washington Inn,* 210 West Liberty Street, Charles Town, 725-1030, simple menu in 1788 home, $$ • *Hillbrook* (see above), 7-course extravaganza by reservation only, $$$$.

SIGHTSEEING   *Harpers Ferry National Historic Park,* 535-6371. Hours: daily 8 A.M. to 5 P.M. Living history interpretations daily in summer, weekends in spring and fall. Election Day annual celebration in mid-October. Cars, $5; persons on foot, $2 • *Antietam Battlefield,* Route 65, Sharpsburg, MD, 432-5124. Hours:

daily 8:30 A.M. to 5 P.M.; June to August 8 A.M. to 6 P.M. Adults, $1; under age 17, free.

INFORMATION Jefferson County Convention & Visitors Bureau, P.O. Box A, (off US 340), Harpers Ferry, WV 25425, 535-2627.

Victorian Week in Cape May

You could call it "Gingerbread by the Sea."

A national landmark and America's oldest seaside resort, Cape May, New Jersey, is a national treasure of Victoriana, boasting 600 prize Victorian houses within 2.2 square miles, an irresistible collage of pastel paint, curlicues and cupolas, ornate railings, columned porches, and towers and turrets looking out to sea.

After the summer crowds recede, Cape May takes time out to celebrate its extraordinary heritage with an annual ten-day early October extravaganza known as Victorian Week. That's the time to come for tours, tours, and more tours—trolley tours and guided walking tours through the quaint streets to fill you in on the town's event-packed 179-year history, house tours that let you see what lies behind those ornate façades, tours by gaslight and by twilight and by dark, when lamp-lit stained-glass windows fill the town with a radiant glow.

You can watch a fashion show of Victorian dress or dress up in your own turn-of-the-century finery for the elaborate Glorious Victorian Dinner, hear lectures on Victorian architecture and arts or restoring Victorian homes, browse for Victorian antiques, or attend an evening of Victorian vaudeville. There are special antique and crafts shows scheduled as well.

It's a one-of-a-kind event that puts you right in the spirit of a one-of-a-kind town.

When you arrive, check the current schedules, then hop aboard the sightseeing trolley or join the walking tours to find out how Victorian Cape May came about. You'll learn that America's largest collection of homes of the 1880s resulted from a fire that all but destroyed the city in 1878. Before that, Cape May was the prime vacation spot on the East Coast, attracting many luminaries, including seven U.S. presidents, who came to stay in its elaborate wooden hotels. The blaze of 1878 was so devastating that 30 acres of the town were laid bare.

Ironically, it was that disaster that prompted so many wealthy people, most from the Philadelphia area, to come in and build on the suddenly available tracts of land. They were further encouraged by the railroad, which offered a year's free transportation to anyone who would help recoup its suddenly vanished tourist trade.

The homes that went up were smaller than the originals, but they were even showier, products of an era when having money meant flaunting it in the form of elaborate exterior decoration. "The fancier, the better" seems to have been the Victorians' motto.

You'll get the best taste of the architecture on the walking tours. The "grande dame" and oldest remaining hotel is the Chalfonte on Howard and Sewall streets. The newest renovation is the Virginia Hotel, which is well past its hundredth birthday. The acknowledged showplace, however, is the Mainstay Inn, once an elegant gambling club, still with its original 14-foot ceilings, tall mirrors, ornate plaster moldings, elaborate chandeliers, and cupola with an ocean view. The current young owners have kept much of the original furnishings, and on most Saturdays and Sundays at 4 P.M. they offer tours and tea in the parlor to show off their place. Check for their Victorian Week schedules.

Only a last-minute cancellation will save you if you have not reserved months in advance to stay at the Mainstay or at the Abbey, its equally fine neighbor across the way. But there are many other delightful Victorian inns to try, and staying in them adds to a Cape May visit. Most serve afternoon tea to guests and in colder weather have cozy and welcoming fireplaces in the parlor. If all else fails, you can always find a motel and settle for teatime tours.

One must on a sightseeing tour is the Physick Estate, an authentically restored 1881 Victorian mansion with 16 rooms, a sunken marble bathtub, a tiled fireplace, and elaborate chandeliers.

It should be noted that all of Cape May's attractions are not of the Victorian variety. The beaches have suffered a bit from erosion and are a lot narrower than they used to be, but there are still four miles of sand and plenty of room for in-season sunning, and a long promenade along the beach is perfect for walking or jogging on a mild fall day.

A short drive will bring you to Cape May Point, where the Atlantic meets Delaware Bay, one of the few places where you can see both the sunrise and the sunset over water. Sunset Beach on the bay is ideal for watching the sun go down, and also is the place to sift through the sand for the plentiful pieces of polished quartz known as Cape May diamonds.

And besides being a treat for Victoriana buffs, Cape May in autumn is happy hunting grounds for bird-watchers. You'll be following in the footsteps of John James Audubon and Roger Tory Peterson if you head for Cape May Point State Park or the 180-acre

Cape May Migratory Bird Refuge, owned by the Nature Conservancy. Both are sanctuaries for spotting birds of prey, such as hawks and falcons, as well as exotic and endangered species, like the least tern, black skinner, and piping plover, which stop for food and shelter before crossing the mouth of Delaware Bay. At the point you'll also find one of the country's oldest lighthouses, dating back to 1744.

Back in town, on Washington Mall, there are three blocks of shops, as well as sidewalk cafes, ice cream parlors, and a bookstore where you can pick up the Sunday papers. Just off the mall is the Pink House, an antique shop that is the ultimate in Victorian frills. All over town are restaurants that are gaining a growing reputation among gourmets.

On the way home, there is a worthwhile detour off Route 49 to Wheaton Village in Millville. This little-touted attraction is a recreated Victorian village on the site of a former glass factory, one of several that prospered in this part of New Jersey a century ago. The 1888 factory has been restored and offers demonstrations of early glassblowing techniques. A crafts arcade is filled with artisans demonstrating such nineteenth-century arts as weaving, wood carving, printing, and pottery making, and an old barn provides an agricultural history of south Jersey, with lots of waterfowl and farm animals to please the kids. Youngsters also love the three-quarter-mile trip around the lake in an old-fashioned train.

The main attraction here, however, is the Museum of Glass, one of the best of its kind. Exhibits follow glassmaking history from the first hand-blown bottles, used for drink, strong and otherwise, to Tiffany, Art Deco, and Art Nouveau designs. Early lamps, pressed glass, cut glass, lead crystal—name your favorite, and you will find it here, among the displays of almost every kind of glassware ever made by hand or machine. It's all the more attractive because the museum is built around a court and has tall windows that make good use of natural light to show off its displays. If you want a souvenir, or an early start on your Christmas shopping, you can buy glassware in the village store and paperweights in a special shop that has a most comprehensive collection, ranging in price from $5 to $5,000.

Glassmaking is another side of the 1880s in southern New Jersey—a bonus on a visit to Victorian Cape May.

Area Code: 609

DRIVING DIRECTIONS Cape May is at the tip of southern New Jersey, the last exit on the Garden State Parkway. From D.C., the shortest way is to take the Cape May–Lewes Ferry, a 70-minute ride across Delaware Bay. Take Route 50/301 across the Chesapeake Bay Bridge, follow Route 301 to Route 404 east, which merges with Route 18 and Route 9 east to Lewes. For ferry schedules and current rates, call (302) 645-6313. To travel by car, take I-95 north across the Delaware Memorial Bridge into New Jersey, then follow Route 49 south to Route 47 south, which merges with Route 9 into Cape May. Approximate distance from D.C., 195 miles.

PUBLIC TRANSPORTATION   Bus service from Philadelphia via New Jersey Transit (215) 569-3752; commuter air service to Cape May County airport, 15 minutes away. A car is not necessary in Cape May.

ACCOMMODATIONS   *Mainstay Inn,* 635 Columbia Avenue, 08204, 884-8690, $$$ CP ● *The Abbey,* Columbia and Gurney streets, 08204, 884-4506, $–$$$ CP ● *The Brass Bed,* 719 Columbia Street, 08204, 884-8075, $$–$$$ CP ● *Victorian Rose,* 715 Columbia Avenue, 08204, 884-2497, $–$$$ CP ● *The Queen Victoria,* 102 Ocean Street, 08204, 884-8702, $–$$$ CP ● *Captain Mey's Inn,* 202 Ocean Avenue, 08204, 884-7793, $$–$$$ CP ● *The Summer Cottage,* 613 Columbia Avenue, 08204, 884-4948, $$$ CP ● Write to chamber of commerce for long list of motels.

DINING   *The Mad Batter,* 19 Jackson Street, 884-5970, nouvelle cuisine in a gingerbread house, $$–$$$ ● *Chalfonte Hotel,* 301 Howard, 884-8409, Southern specialties, $$ ● *410 Bank Street,* same address, 884-2127, Cajun, mesquite grill, $$$ ● *Alexander's,* 653 Washington Street, 884-2555, excellent, elegant, $$$–$$$$ ● *Washington Inn,* 801 Washington Street, 884-5697, 1856 home, $$–$$$ ● *The Lobster House,* Fisherman's Wharf, 884-8296, good seafood, long lines, come for lunch, $$–$$$$ ● *A & J Blue Claw,* Ocean Drive, 884-5878, another good seafood choice, $$–$$$ ● *Watson's Merion Inn,* 106 Decatur Street, 884-8363, longtime local standby, $$–$$$$ ● *Louisa's,* 104 Jackson Street, 884-5882, many call this tiny place the best in town, no reservations, $$ ● *Bayberry Inn,* Perry Street and Congress Place, 884-8406, innovative menus, $$–$$$ ● *Frescos,* 412 Bank Street, 884-0366, northern Italian, $$–$$$ ● *Peaches Cafe,* Carpenters Lane between Perry and Jackson, 884-0202, interesting menu, Thai influence, $$–$$$ ● *La Toque,* 210 Ocean Street, 884-1511, French, $$$ ● *Es-Ta-Ti,* Beach Drive and Decatur Street, 884-3504, fine Italian, $$$ ● *Maureen,* 429 Beach Drive and Decatur Street, 884-3774, one of the best, $$$–$$$$ ● *The Globe,* 110 North Broadway, West Cape May, 884-2429, international menu, good reviews, b.y.o.b., $$$ ● Some moderately priced choices: *Pilot House,* 142 Decatur Street, 884-3449, tavern fare, open late, $–$$$ ● *Filling Station,* 615 Lafayette Street, 884-2111, informal, $–$$ ● *Cactus Cantina,* Sunset Boulevard and Broadway, West Cape May, 898-0354, Tex-Mex, $–$$ ● If you want to take a picnic to Cape May Point, *Freda's Gourmet Deli,* Sunset and Broadway, West Cape May, 884-0707, is on the way.

SIGHTSEEING *Victorian Week,* 10 days of special events and tours in mid-October. For full schedule, contact Mid-Atlantic Center for the Arts (MAC), 1048 Washington Street, P.O. Box 340, Cape May, 08204, 884-5404. ● *Trolley Tour* and *Walking Tour* schedules and rates and tours for the *Physick House* also change with the seasons; for current information, pick up the pamphlet "This Week in Cape May" at information centers or contact MAC ● *Wheaton Village,* Route 552, Millville, 825-6800. Hours: daily 10 A.M. to 5 P.M. Adults, $4 ages 6–17, $2; family rates, $9.

INFORMATION Greater Cape May Chamber of Commerce, P.O. Box 109, Cape May, NJ 08204, 884-5508.

The Fairest of Fairs at Waterford

Waterford, Virginia, population 300, still bears a remarkable resemblance to the nineteenth-century village that grew up around a mill on the banks of Catoctin Creek—and that's just the way the residents like it.

When talk of development of the farmlands outside town threatened change, some townspeople had an inspired idea. The Waterford Foundation was formed in 1943 to preserve the open spaces. To raise money toward this goal, they held a crafts fair with their picturesque town as a living backdrop.

Today the annual Waterford Crafts Exhibit and Homes Tour has grown to a giant three-day early October celebration covering every inch of the town, one that has been accurately dubbed "the fairest of fairs." What's more, the timing couldn't be better, for Waterford is near the heart of Loudoun County, the pastoral hunt country just an hour from Washington, and the fair coincides with the fall steeplechase season, providing a double reason for the trip.

Put on your walking shoes—the terrain is hilly—and get ready to meet over 100 top-notch craftspeople demonstrating their skills, from lace making to leatherwork. Visitors are allowed to get into the act, too, and try their hands at stitching on a quilt, throwing a pot on a kickwheel, or working the wooden toys children played with 200 years ago.

Be forewarned: You will need a blindfold not to succumb to the urge to buy some of the handsome wares that tempt at every turn. But then, why pass up the chance? Besides the crafts booths filling buildings and spilling out onto every sidewalk and empty space, thousands of finished crafts are up for sale in the old mill. One barn is full of dried flowers, another is hung with photos and fine art, the Corner Store is stocked with fresh baked goods and homemade jellies, the Hardware Store is transformed into a gallery for a junior art exhibit, and even the Methodist Church gets into the spirit with a display of artwork for bargain hunters.

The arts and crafts are the big attractions, but only the start of the fun. To make it all the merrier, music fills the streets—a string band here, a chamber music group there, a folksinger around the corner. The militia camps in Waterford during the fair, reenacting the skirmish that took place during the Civil War, and you never know when you'll spy a soldier slipping through the trees or a fife-and-drum corps marching through the town.

There are houses to tour, from tiny Quaker dwellings dating from the town's 1733 founding to the imposing eighteenth-century miller's house to Victorian classics built at the turn of the century. Class is in session in the one-room schoolhouse, run about the way it might have been on a typical day in 1880.

Come early if you want to find a place in the parking fields in Waterford, and allow plenty of time to browse and buy. When you need a break, have some cider and a ham biscuit near the mill, a sandwich or some Brunswick stew in the schoolhouse, or head for the barbecue pit outside. There's an apple butter pot simmering nearby, offering yet another fine souvenir to take home.

If you reserve far, far ahead, you may be able to snag one of the handful of rooms in the small, charming bed-and-breakfast establishments in Waterford. Otherwise you have the happy choice of headquartering either in Leesburg, five miles away, or about ten miles farther in Middleburg. Whichever you choose, it's worth taking time to see the other.

Quaint, "old town" Leesburg, named for Francis "Lightfoot" Lee, is another town with the look of the past. The layout of the main streets, some of the stone structures, and one log house date back to 1758, when the town was founded.

Start at the Loudoun Museum for a slide-show orientation, a printed walking tour, and a look at 200 years of town artifacts. Then take a walk on Market, Loudoun, and King streets, where there are fine old homes, and past Courthouse Square, where Loudoun free-holders penned the Loudoun Resolves, a protest of the Stamp Act and a plea for American rights and liberties written two years before the Declaration of Independence.

The Laurel Brigade Inn is the best known of Leesburg's hostelries, but the most appealing may be a tiny newcomer, the Norris House, an 1806 bed-and-breakfast home nicely furnished with antiques. Both inns are within the central historic district.

It will take only an hour to do the old part of Leesburg, leaving time for the town's most impressive sights, the mansions in the nearby countryside. Oatlands, a pillared white Classical Revival beauty, was built at the beginning of the nineteenth century by George Carter, a great-grandson of the famous planter Robert "King" Carter. The spacious rooms are decorated with spectacular ornamental plaster cornices and moldings and furnished with choice French, English, and American antiques. The formal terraced gardens are among Virginia's finest. Once the center of a thriving 3,400-acre plantation, Oatlands is now set on 261 acres that serve as the site for point-to-point races, fairs, and an annual antique-car show.

Morven Park is another storybook estate, built in the 1780s by Maryland Governor Thomas Swann and enlarged in the early twentieth century by Virginia Governor Westmoreland Davis. Besides the superbly furnished mansion with treasures from around the world, formal gardens, and nature trails, Morven offers a carriage museum displaying over 100 horse-drawn vehicles. The grounds here are also the scene of equestrian events, including the Fall National Steeplechase Hunt Races and the Carriage Drive Competition.

Leesburg's choicest shopping is at Market Station, a series of older buildings renovated to house a mix of boutiques, antique shops, and restaurants. It is a sign of the modern development mushrooming just beyond Leesburg's historic core. For antiquers, there are a few shops in town on Loudoun and Market streets, but the stops of most interest are the two locations of the Catoctin Antique Center. One is on South King Street, near the Route 7/15 bypass; the other is on Route 7, east of town.

They're fighting the builders over in Middleburg, the posh village considered the heart of hunt country. Some of Loudoun County's wealthiest residents, America's landed gentry, live on the manicured estates behind split-rail fences in the hill country outside Middleburg, land that has been aptly compared with the lush rolling English countryside.

The residents here cherish their narrow unpaved roads, the better to discourage tourists and developers. One of the best ways to get a feel for the area, in fact, is to take the Washboard Roads tour often printed in local guides.

Middleburg itself is a mixed breed of colonial charm and horsey chic. It was a way station for horsemen traveling to and from the Shenandoah Valley as early as 1728, when it was known as Chinn's Crossing and the present Red Fox Tavern was called Chinn's Ordinary. One frequent visitor was young George Washington, stopping off on his way to the valley as a surveyor for Thomas, Lord Fairfax. Many of the stone buildings from the early days still stand.

But instead of stagecoaches, the roads into town these days bring Mercedes-Benzes and horse vans. Anyone from Jacqueline Kennedy Onassis to John Warner to Paul Mellon might be seen out shopping on Middleburg's Washington Street, where antique stores and boutiques alternate with shops selling shiny boots and saddles. Almost every shop sign features a fox or horse or dog, and many of the clothes and gifts for sale follow the same hunting motifs.

The horse people settle here to breed and train their mounts and take part in the fox hunts, races, and shows that are the social fabric of the county. The hunts are strictly private affairs, but everyone is invited to the colorful steeplechase events that take place throughout the Loudoun countryside in spring and fall. All you need to enjoy the day, Loudoun-style, is a blanket for sitting on the grass and a sumptuous tailgate lunch, which they'll gladly supply for you in town at the Black Walnut shop.

You'll see that some steeplechase spectators like to picnic in style, bringing out portable tables with linen cloths, candles, and the family silver for the occasion. Checking out the culinary spreads is part of the day's entertainment.

Steeplechasing is a natural sport for fox hunters, who learn to jump fences and walls in pursuit of their prey. The name ''steeplechase'' originated in Ireland, where the first recorded horseback chase actually was to a church steeple. On a typical day here there are races over flat ground, over brush jumps, and over timber (split-rail fences). A point-to-point race means exactly that—contestants race from one specified point on the course to another. Some of the horses are bred and ridden by professionals, while others are trained and mounted by their amateur owners, more often for glory and trophies than for monetary prizes.

The races are informal affairs, and viewers are free to sit in the shade or mill about or go up to the fence for a closer view. The racers in their stable colors and the officials in elegant red coats and black riding hats make a pretty picture against the green fields, English racing prints come to life in modern Virginia.

Lodgings in and around Middleburg are choice. You can sleep in a canopy bed at the historic Red Fox Inn or have Colonial decor and modern comfort in the new addition, the Stray Fox, or stop over at

Middleburg Guest Suites, attractive suites right above the shops on Washington Street. Luck House is another possibility, an 1800 Federal home in town that boasts traditional Southern breakfasts.

Out in the countryside, many special inns await. One of the most elegant is Gibson Hall, nine miles to the west in Upperville, the home of a lovely church donated by resident Paul Mellon and the center for the spectacular Loudoun County stable tour held each Memorial Day weekend. Many of us would be happy to be bedded in quarters equivalent to those of Loudoun's favorite steeds!

Also in Upperville is the 1763 Inn, where rustic rooms are in a converted stable set on 50 acres of rolling countryside. The Briar Patch outside Middleburg is a country home offering gracious lodgings on a working farm; the Ashby Inn and the Little River Inn are cozy restored 1800s houses in picture-book small towns; and Oakland Green, a Quaker farmhouse in the country, is a perfect retreat, as well as the only inn in the area offering riding.

Settling on one inn is almost as difficult as fitting in the many attractions of Loudoun County in one weekend. Hunt country is an area that sounds the call for a return trip.

Area Code: 703

DRIVING DIRECTIONS Waterford is near Leesburg in Loudoun County, the horse country west of Washington. From D.C., take Route 7 west to Leesburg, then Route 9 west, and turn right on Route 662 north to Waterford. For Middleburg, take Route 50 west, follow Route 15 north to Leesburg and proceed as above. Approximate distance from D.C. to Leesburg, 35 miles; Waterford, 40 miles; Middleburg, 50 miles.

ACCOMMODATIONS *The Pink House,* Waterford, 22190, 882-3453, $$$ CP ● *James Moore House,* P.O. Box 161, Waterford, 22190, 882-3342, $$ CP ● *Waterford Inn,* Second and Church streets, Waterford, 22190, 882-3465, $$ CP ● *The Norris House Inn,* 108 Loudoun Street, Leesburg, 22075, 777-1806, $$–$$$ CP ● *Laurel Brigade Inn,* 20 West Market Street, Leesburg, 22075, 777-1010, $–$$ ● *Red Fox Inn,* 2 East Washington Street, Middleburg, 22117, 687-6301, $$$–$$$$ ● *Middleburg Guest Suites,* P.O. Box 984, Middleburg, 22117, 687-6301, $$$$ ● *Little River Inn,* Route 50, Aldie, 22001, 327-6742, $$–$$$ CP ● *1763 Inn,* Route 50, Upperville, 22176, 592-3848, $$–$$$$ ● *The Ashby Inn,* Route 1, P.O. Box 21A, Paris, 22130, 592-3900, $$$ CP ● *Oakland Green,* Route 2, P.O. Box 147, Leesburg, 22075, 338-7628, $$$ CP.

DINING *Jordan's Restaurant,* 107 Loudoun Street, Southwest, Leesburg, 777-1471, sophisticated decor and menu, $$–$$$ ● *Laurel Brigade Inn* (see above), $–$$$ ● *Tuscarora Mill Restaurant,* Market Station, 203 Harrison Street, Southeast, Leesburg, 771-9300, $$–$$$ ● *Red Fox Inn* (see above), $$$ ● *Windsor House,* 2 West Washington Street, Middleburg, 687-6800, charming local landmark, also a few rooms to let upstairs, $$–$$$ ● Also try the *Unicorn Pub* at *Windsor House* for burgers and light fare, $ ● *The Upper Crust,* 4 Pendleton Street, Middleburg, 687-5666 ● *Coach Stop,* 28½ Washington Street, Middleburg, 687-5515, unpretentious local favorite, try the Horseman's Special Breakfast, $$–$$$ ● *Ashby Inn* (see above), $$$ ● *1763 Inn* (see above), $$–$$$.

SIGHTSEEING *Waterford Homes Tour and Crafts Exhibit,* sponsored by Waterford Foundation, Inc., Waterford, 882-3018. Three days beginning the first Friday in October, 10 A.M. to 5 P.M. Adults, $10; under 12, free; special rates for advance purchase ● *Loudoun Museum,* 16 West Loudoun Street, 777-0519. Hours: Monday to Saturday 10 A.M. to 5 P.M.; Sunday 1 P.M. to 5 P.M. Free ● *Oatlands,* Route 15, south of Leesburg, 777-3174. Hours: mid-March to late December, Monday to Saturday 10 A.M. to 5 P.M.; Sunday 1 P.M. to 5 P.M. Adults, $5; children, $4 ● *Morven Park,* Old Waterford Road off Route 7, Leesburg, 777-2414. Hours: Memorial Day to Labor Day, Tuesday to Saturday 10 A.M. to 5 P.M.; Sunday 1 P.M. to 5 P.M.; weekends only in May and September to mid-October. Adults, $4; children, $2.50 ● *Steeplechase Racing:* Check tourist office for current schedules. Usually held in early October are Virginia Fall Races at Glenwood Park, Middleburg, and Morven Park Fall Race Meet.

INFORMATION Loudoun County Visitors' Center, Loudoun Museum, 108 D South Street, Southeast, Leesburg, VA 22075, 777-0519. Local call from D.C., 471-6093.

Dropping in on the Du Ponts of Delaware

Louis XVI would feel right at home if he were to drop into Nemours, the palatial pink French chateau built by Alfred I. Du Pont, great-grandson of Louis's minister of finance.

When Louis and his court ran into trouble and Pierre Samuel Du Pont de Nemours fled to the New World in 1800, he founded an American dynasty that would by the 1920s be the nation's wealthiest family, one whose estates would have done credit to royalty. The Du Pont properties now open to the public make for some of the most spectacular sightseeing in the East.

Headquarters for a Du Pont weekend really should be the Du Pont Hotel in Wilmington, which reflects the resources of the family behind the name. It was for a time, in fact, the residence of Pierre S. Du Pont, who didn't marry until he was 40 and divided his time between an apartment on the top floor of the hotel and his nearby Pennsylvania estate, now known as Longwood Gardens.

Built by the company in 1911 as part of its corporate complex in downtown Wilmington at twice the usual cost of a first-class hotel of its size, the block-square white stone Italian Renaissance building remains the epitome of old-world elegance, with polished travertine marble halls, coffered ceilings, carved paneling, and elaborate chandeliers. One notable recent addition is the work of the Brandywine Valley's finest artists, 600 pieces of original art displayed throughout the hotel. Even if you don't stay here, don't miss the dining rooms, the Green Room with its graceful arching two-and-a-half-story windows and gold chandeliers, and the Brandywine-Christina Room, with Italian walnut paneling and a million dollars worth of Wyeth paintings on the walls.

To learn how the Du Pont dynasty began, start at the Hagley Museum, which tells the tale of the first black powder mills along the Brandywine as well as the story of early American industry from the first water-powered mills to the steam-powered engines of the late nineteenth century. The 200-acre grounds of Hagley include the Georgian-style home of Pierre's son, Éleuthère Iréneé, who founded the company that grew into the world's most powerful armaments manufacturer. The founder lived with his domain in full view right out the window of his mansion, known as Eleutherian Mills. Five generations of Du Ponts lived here, and the furnishings of the 12-room home are all the more interesting for revealing their changing tastes.

A barn filled with carriages and wagons, a cooper's workshop, a stone office building, and a French garden also remain to give a complete picture of the world of the nineteenth-century mill owner and his family.

To see what had become of the Du Ponts a century later, take an afternoon tour at Nemours, built in 1910 by Alfred I. It is named for the original family estate in France, and worthy of the European royalty that inspired it. The opulent 77-room mansion is remarkable: Its ornate paneling, carved and gold-leaf-adorned ceilings, crystal chandeliers, priceless antique furnishings, paintings, silver, Oriental rugs, Aubusson carpets, and ornate screens are dazzling in their magnificence. Many of the furnishings have royal origins. One of the chandeliers once hung in Schoenbrun Castle in Austria, where Marie Antoinette grew up. Outdoors, the 1488 English gates came from Wimbledon Manor, the estate given by Henry VIII as a gift to his wife Catherine Parr in 1543, and the Russian Gates were made for Catherine the Great's palace outside St. Petersburg.

There are portraits of the family founder, as well as of Louis XVI and his wife, Marie Antoinette, but also many family photos and paintings of children and much-loved adopted stray pets, evidence that this was, in fact, a warm, family home. Throughout there are reminders of some of the unusual interests of Alfred Du Pont, who, aside from his wealth, was quite an accomplished man—an inventor who held 200 patents, a horseman, and a champion sailor with many trophies. He liked modern devices, and the house included the very latest in bathrooms, as well as its own generator and a room for bottling spring water. There were also gadgets such as an exerciser with a saddle seat that simulates the gait of a horse, a steam cabinet, a bowling alley, a pull-down screen for films, and a billiards room with lights made to swivel so they cast no shadows on the tables.

As if the home were not enough, there are acres of gardens inspired by Versailles, resplendent with reflecting pools and fountains; a 200-foot carillon; and the Temple of Love, with a life-size statue of Diana. Amid the pomp, there is another reminder that this was a family's home in the little gray house called the Wren's Nest, a combination schoolhouse and playhouse for the children on the estate.

Nemours will fill your afternoon and your senses. Come Sunday, you can start fresh among the remarkable American antiques assembled by Henry Francis Du Pont at Winterthur, his estate outside town on Route 52. Du Pont was one of the first to recognize the importance of early American craftsmanship, and in 1923 he began to amass the finest from the period between 1640 and 1840, not only furniture but curtains, bed hangings, rugs, lighting fixtures, silver pieces, and ceramics. Not content with isolated objects, he went on to comb the Eastern seaboard for paneling, fireplaces, mantels, doors, and carved ceilings from the finest homes of the period, dismantling and reinstalling them at Winterthur as proper background for his collections. Eventually there were almost 200 room settings, and after living pleasurably with his antiques for close to 30 years, Du Pont in 1951 turned his home into a museum and educational facility. The 45-minute general tour is a sampler of rooms, a tour of American interiors that span two centuries, shown in chronological order. Special two-hour tours include the celebrated Montmorenci and Readbourne rooms.

Not the least of the pleasures of Winterthur are its gardens, a 64-acre woodland carefully planted to maintain a natural look. Tanbark and turf paths wind through shaded woodland and over rolling hillsides, bringing lovely vistas into view at every turn. In fall the foliage and flowers are spectacular—lavender cups of colchicums covering the hillsides in September joined by fall daffodils and white autumn crocuses in October, all set against a backdrop of scarlet and gold leaves and bright berried shrubs. It's a heavenly stroll on a fine fall day, but there is a tram tour for the less energetic.

Flower lovers will feel they have saved the best for last if Sunday afternoon is devoted to the legendary formal gardens of Pierre Samuel Du Pont (known to all as P.S.) at Longwood in Kennett Square, Pennsylvania, about a 20-minute drive from Winterthur. Local legend has it that Alfred I. built his fabulous Nemours estate because he was jealous of rival cousin P.S.'s showplace, and Longwood is still considered by many to be the most elegant of all the Du Pont estates. In fall, the chrysanthemum display is outstanding. Recently, tours of the Du Pont home here have been offered, but P.S. cared more about plantings than possessions, and his house is modest compared to the splendor of the gardens.

If you have already visited Longwood or Winterthur, you can still spend a rewarding Sunday getting to know the city of Wilmington (see pages 42 through 44) or taking in some of the lesser-known Du Pont landmarks around town.

A drive out Route 100 shows you the best of the beautiful Brandywine countryside, the prime estate country that includes many more Du Pont residences not open to the public. You'll get a view of one of the grandest, the imposing chateau of Irénee du Pont known as Granogue, if you turn off to Smith's Bridge Road. Head just north of town for a Du Pont estate that is now one of the newest Delaware state parks, named Bellevue for the mansion of William Du Pont, which has been renovated into an elegant restaurant. William was a horseman, and the park has many excellent riding and bike paths as a result, along with tennis courts, jogging paths, and extensive grounds.

What else have the Du Ponts left to their state of Delaware? Everything from Route 52, built privately by P.S. in order to provide a smooth ride to Longwood, to Route 13, the major road leading south to Dover and the beaches. The latter route was made possible by Coleman Du Pont, a state and U.S. senator who made a $4 million contribution when he decided his state really ought to have a better north-south artery to conduct him to his business in the capital. Alfred I. contributed toward the road to Philadelphia so that he could drive more easily to concerts and operas in his homemade automobile. This preoccupation with roads and motor cars eventually culminated with the Du Pont Company's becoming a major stockholder in General Motors, adding substantially to the family's fortune.

Dropping in on the Du Ponts is a fascinating experience, one that may convince you that we did have royalty in America after all.

Area Code: 302

DRIVING DIRECTIONS Wilmington is off Route I-95. From D.C., take I-95 north, stay left approaching the Delaware Memorial Bridge, and follow the signs for I-895, Wilmington. From I-895, follow signs marked ''Routes 202 and 52.'' Route 52, Delaware Avenue, leads to the center of town. Approximate distance from D.C., 110 miles.

PUBLIC TRANSPORTATION Amtrak has Metroliner service to Wilmington. Greyhound-Trailways provides bus service. The city can be reached by air via Philadelphia International Airport, about 25 miles away. Shuttle service connects the airport to major city hotels.

ACCOMMODATIONS See Wilmington listings, page 44.

BED AND BREAKFAST *Bed and Breakfast of Delaware*, P.O. Box 177, 3650 Silverside Road, Wilmington, DE 19810, 479-9500.

DINING See Wilmington listings, page 44.

SIGHTSEEING *Hagley Museum*, off Route 141, Greenville, 658-2400. Hours: daily 9:30 A.M. to 4:30 P.M.; Sunday 1 P.M. to 5 P.M. Adults, $6; children, $2.50 ● *Nemours*, Rockland Road, off Route 141, 651-6912. Hours: May to November, Tuesday to Saturday, guided tours at 9 A.M., 11 A.M., 1 P.M., and 3 P.M.; Sunday from 11 A.M.; reservations required. Adults, $7; under 16, not admitted ● *Winterthur*, Route 52, outside Wilmington, 888-4600 or (800) 448-3883. Hours: Tuesday to Saturday 9 A.M. to 4 P.M.; Sunday noon to 4 P.M. General admission: adults, $9; students,

$7.50; under 12, free. Special tours, $12.50 and $6; garden tram tours, $2.50 ● *Longwood Gardens,* Route 1, Kennett Square, PA, (215) 388-6741. Hours: April to October, daily 9 A.M. to 6 P.M.; rest of year, 9 A.M. to 5 P.M. Adults, $8; children, $2 ● *Pierce–Du Pont House.* Hours: daily, April to December, 11 A.M. to 3 P.M. $1.50 plus general garden admission ● *Bellevue State Park,* 2 miles north of Wilmington, off I-95 Marsh Road exit, 571-3390. Daylight hours. Park admission free. Fees for riding and other special activities.

INFORMATION   Great Wilmington Convention and Visitors Bureau, 1300 Market Street, Suite 505, Wilmington, DE 19801, 652-4088 ● Delaware Tourism Office, 99 Kings Highway, P.O. Box 1401, Dover, DE 19901, (800) 441-8846 outside Delaware; (800) 282-8667 within the state.

Riding High
on the Cass Railroad

"Wild and Wonderful," read the license plates in West Virginia. They're right.

The Mountain State has the most wide open spaces and most spectacular scenery to be found in the eastern United States. Two-thirds of the state is covered with wild mountain ranges, ravines, and gorges, once poetically described by Henry David Thoreau as places where "The morning wind forever blows, the poem of creation is uninterrupted."

A visit is a rejuvenation and a joy for urban dwellers any time of year, but in autumn when the hills turn into Technicolor, it is nothing less than fantastic—especially when viewed from the windows of the Cass Scenic Railroad.

The Cass was a logging railroad. The present tracks, now incorporated into a unique state park, are the last 11 miles of 3,000 miles of logging lines that once covered the state. Whistling off from the depot in the onetime lumbering town of Cass, the railroad's steam engines pull open cars converted from old lumber flatcars uphill to the 4,842-foot summit of Cheat Mountain, the spot known as Bald Knob, the state's second-highest peak. The 22-mile climb is a four-and-a-half-hour round-trip winding up, down, around, and through woodlands that are a fingertip-close kaleidoscope of autumn color— yellow hickories and poplars, bright orange sumacs and sassafras, crimson maples and dogwoods, and a mix of scarlet and gold on sugar maples—that positively dazzles the eye.

By the top, the climate has changed so dramatically, you might as well have driven 800 miles north to Canada. Be sure to bring a jacket.

Along with the ride comes a running commentary over the public address system, and a stream of colorful asides from the brakemen posted in each car. You'll learn about the days at the turn of the century when these tracks were laid to reach a valuable stand of red spruce atop Cheat Mountain, turning tiny Cass into a boomtown. The lumberjacks brought from Canada and the northern states descended periodically to spend their pay and, when it was all gone, climbed back up the mountain to start all over again.

All that's left of Cass today is a handful of houses and the Cass Country Store, once the company store of the West Virginia Pulp and Paper Company and the largest wood structure east of the Mississippi. Now the store makes the most of the railroad traffic with gifts, food, and a couple of little museums.

When your ride is over and while you are in the neighborhood, you may want to visit the futuristic home of the National Radio Astronomy Observatory in Green Bank. This national research center and its huge telescopes seem out of place here in the countryside, but it's definitely the right place if you want to learn about radio astronomy. There is a 15-minute movie and a narrated bus tour.

Hikers and bikers can hook up with the Greenbrier River Trail below Cass, a 75-mile-long former railbed of the C & O Railway now maintained by the state for recreation. The location along the river is a fine one.

Nor is a train ride the only way to view the remarkable scenery in this part of wild, wonderful West Virginia. Cut over from Route 28 to Route 219 and take Route 150 for the 25-mile, semicircular drive known as the Highland Scenic Highway, which takes you through cranberry backcountry and over the Williams River for more unforgettable mountain views.

At the southern end of the highway is the Cranberry Mountain Visitor Center, where you can learn about the additional sights and activities waiting in this section of the Monongahela National Forest. Don't miss the Cranberry Glades, where a boardwalk gives easy access to the bogs and a look at such exotic flora as bog rosemary, buckbean, a carnivorous plant called the horned bladderwort, and many species of orchids, beard flowers, and beaked rush. Just to the west of the glades off Route 39, a three-quarter-mile trail takes you 250 feet down a steep ravine past the three falls of Hills Creek. The final waterfall, almost five stories high, is the second highest in the state.

Surrounding the Cranberry Glades are 53,000 acres of backcountry wilderness, a favorite haunt for hikers, campers, and fishermen going after the trout in the Cranberry and Williams rivers.

For Civil War buffs, Droop Mountain Battlefield State Park is a few miles south of Hillsboro. It was the site of one of the most fiercely contested battles of the war. Eight thousand men took part in the bloody battle to drive the Confederates out of the fertile lands of the Greenbrier Valley. Today the lookout tower offers a peaceful view of the valley, lovely in autumn or when the rhododendrons bloom in July.

Pulitzer prize–winning author Pearl Buck's home, a National Register Historic Site, is also nearby, on a mountainside in Hillsboro. The white clapboard home where Buck was born in 1892 still has some of its original Victorian furnishings. The posted hours aren't always observed, so it's best to phone and check before you visit.

The most convenient lodgings in this immediate area are cottages and a small inn at Cass, a motel in Marlinton, some local bed and breakfasts, or the condominium accommodations atop the mountain at Snowshoe Ski Resort. Willis Farm, one of the options, is also a center for mountain biking expeditions.

But to add a touch of civilization and charm to your trip to the mountains, you might want to make your headquarters in the valley about 30 miles south in Lewisburg. The white-columned General Lewis Inn is a winning old place, dating back to 1830 when stagecoaches like the one now sitting out front used to travel along the James River and Kanawha Turnpike (now Route 60), bringing visitors to the mountains. This simple inn is full of beams and fireplaces, country antiques and old-fashioned warmth. There are curios everywhere and a "memory hall" hung with tools and memorabilia of the early mountain settlers. On a chilly day, the fire will be going in the sitting room, and they'll be serving tea and scones, the latter heaped with thick rich cream and strawberries. At dinner, the fare turns Southern—fried chicken, pork chops, Virginia ham, and homemade corn sticks and biscuits.

Little Lewisburg is one of the oldest towns in West Virginia, and the whole center of town is a National Historic District. Originally called either Camp Union or Fort Savannah, it was renamed in 1774 to honor General Andrew Lewis, a local Indian fighter hero, and became an important way station on the turnpike. The Civil War battle of Lewisburg in 1862 was won by the North, but the town remained a Southern outpost for most of the war.

Today's Lewisburg is a spiffy cluster of fine old homes with wide porches and churches dating back to colonial times. The Old Stone Church, circa 1796, is surrounded by pioneers' graves, many bearing names still associated with the area. The local walking tour, available at the inn, takes you past many early homes on Washington Street and its surrounding avenues, to the 1837 Greenbrier

County Courthouse and the North House Museum, an 1820 mansion containing collections of early local memorabilia.

There are some interesting shopping stops on Washington Street as well—a couple of promising antique shops; a small gallery; the Vintage Furniture Shop, specializing in fine reproductions of eighteenth-century furniture; and Quilts Unlimited, which has two stores, one for antique quilts and one for those newly made by local artisans. The quilt shops are run by Joan Fenton, a city girl who fell in love with the mountains, and who has built her small-town business into the country's largest source for mail-order quilts. If you can't make the trip, write and she will send you close-up color snapshots of dozens of patterns.

If you are looking for more sights around Lewisburg, Organ Cave, named for its majestic limestone formations that resemble a giant church organ, is only a few miles away. The caves have historic as well as natural interest. Ammunition for the Confederate army was made here; and Robert E. Lee's troops took shelter and held religious services in the mammoth cave.

For a totally different kind of attraction just outside town, you can visit the famous Greenbrier, one of America's landmark resorts. The hotel is grand, and the mountain views are lovely—but even the Greenbrier can't touch the majesty of the climb up Cheat Mountain aboard the old Cass Railroad.

Area Code: 304

DRIVING DIRECTIONS Cass is off Route 28/92 between routes 250 and 219. From D.C., take Route 66 west, then I-81 south. At Staunton, Virginia, take Route 250 west to Bartow and turn left to 28 south, watching for the turnoff to Cass between Greenbank and Dunmore. Approximate distance from D.C., 230 miles. From Route 219, turn north on Route 28/92 at Marlinton.

ACCOMMODATIONS *General Lewis Inn,* 301 East Washington Street, Lewisburg, 24901, 645-2600, $–$$ ● *Marlinton Motor Inn,* US 219, Marlinton, 749-4711 $$ ● *Willis Farm Inn,* Route 219, Slatyfork, 26291, 572-3771, modest accommodations, delicious home cooking, $ CP ● *The Current,* P.O. Box 135, Hillsboro, 24946, 653-4722, simple homey bed and breakfast, $ CP ● *Whistlepunk Inn,* P.O. Box 70, Snowshoe Mountain, 26290, 572-1126, inn rooms and condos, $–$$$ (more during ski season) ● *Cass Cottages,* Cass Railroad State Park, P.O. Box 75, Cass, 24927, (800) CALL-WVA, restored turn-of-the-century rustic log cabins, $ ● *Shay Inn,* P.O. Box 46, Cass, 24927, 456-4652, $ ● *Boyer Motel,* routes 28 and 92, Arbovale, 24915, 456-4667, $.

DINING   *General Lewis Inn* (see above), \$–\$\$ ● *Marlinton Motor Inn* (see above), \$–\$\$ ● *Willis Farm Inn* (see above), \$–\$\$ ● *Red Fox Restaurant,* Whistlepunk Village, Snowshoe Mountain, 572-1111, \$\$–\$\$\$.

SIGHTSEEING   *Cass Scenic Railroad,* Route 28, Cass (between Dunmore and Green Bank), 456-4300. Hours: Memorial Day to Labor Day, Tuesday to Sunday; Labor Day to late October, weekends only; Thursday and Friday rides added first 2 weeks in October; the 4½-hour ride to Bald Knob leaves at noon. Adults, \$11; children, \$5; 2-hour rides to Whittaker Station leave at 11 A.M., 1 P.M., 3 P.M. Adults, \$8; children, \$4 ● *National Radio Astronomy Observatory,* Route 28, Green Bank, 456-2011. Hours: mid-June to Labor Day, Wednesday to Sunday 9 A.M. to 4 P.M.; September and October, weekends only. Free ● *Cranberry Mountain Visitor Center,* off US 219 and Route 39, 846-2695. Hours: Memorial Day to Labor Day, daily 9 A.M. to 6 P.M.; in May, September, and mid-October, weekends. Tours to Cranberry Glades and falls of Hills Creek available in season. Free ● *Droop Mountain Battlefield State Park,* Route 219, Droop, 653-4254. Daylight hours. Free ● *Pearl S. Buck Birthplace Museum,* off Route 219, Hillsboro, 653-4430. Hours: May to October, Monday to Saturday 9 A.M. to 5 P.M.; Sunday 1 P.M. to 5 P.M. Adults, \$3; ages 6–18, \$1 ● *North House Museum,* Route 60, Lewisburg, 645-3398. Hours: Tuesday to Saturday 10 A.M. to 4 P.M. Adults, \$2; ages 6–12, \$1 ● *Organ Cave,* Route 219, Lewisburg, 647-5551. Hours: daily 9:30 A.M. to 7 P.M. Adults, \$5; children, \$2.50 ● *Elk River Touring Center,* Route 219, Slatyfork, 572-3771, mountain bike tours.

INFORMATION   Potomac Highlands Convention & Visitors Bureau, P.O. Box 1459, Elkins, WV 26241, 636-8400 ● Pocahontas County Tourism Commission, P.O. Box 275, Marlinton, WV 25954, 799-4636 ● *Lewisburg Visitors Center,* 105 Church Street, Lewisburg, WV 24901, 645-1000.

Mr. Jefferson's Legacy in Charlottesville

Here in gentle, magnolia-studded Charlottesville, Virginia, the lines get long outside Monticello, the home of Thomas Jefferson, but the crowds stand patiently. They've heard it's worth the wait.

Few homes anywhere so radiate the personality of their builders, and in this case the builder was one of America's most remarkable men.

Author of the Declaration of Independence, governor of Virginia, president of the United States, founder of the University of Virginia—none of these titles do full justice to the tall, redheaded man the townsfolk still refer to as Mr. Jefferson. Charlottesville was his birthplace, Monticello his passion, and here is where you must come to get to know something about Mr. Jefferson, the man—not just the brilliant writer, diplomat, and champion of freedom, but the loyal friend, gracious host, avid gardener, and architect who was far ahead of his time.

While Monticello draws the crowds, almost everywhere you go in and around this scenic city at the foot of the Blue Ridge Mountains still bears the Jefferson imprint. The Jefferson-designed rotunda, lawns, and colonnades at the University of Virginia earned a citation from the American Institute of Architects almost two centuries after their creation as the most outstanding achievement in American architecture. Court Square downtown is where Jefferson strolled with his fellow patriots, James Monroe and James Madison, discussing law and liberty. Later, Monroe came to live at Ash Lawn Plantation to be near his friend, settling on a site personally selected by Jefferson, who sent his own gardeners to plant the orchards.

And all the vineyards now thriving in surrounding Albemarle County are carrying on experiments in viticulture that the foresighted Jefferson began in the 1700s. They even call themselves the Monticello Viticultural Area.

You can see Jefferson's legacy anytime of year, but a good reason for braving the crowds in fall is the bonus backdrop of color provided by the autumnal mountains that Jefferson called the Eden of the United States. Columbus Day weekend has an added lure—the Monticello Wine Festival at the Boar's Head Inn.

An excellent place to begin a visit is at the Charlottesville/Albemarle Visitors Bureau, where a fascinating exhibit, ''Thomas Jefferson at Monticello,'' explores the many facets of his life and shows some 400 objects and artifacts, including personal family memorabilia and artifacts discovered during recent archaeological excavations on the Monticello grounds. Many objects are being displayed for the first time. The exhibit gives you background that makes a visit to Monticello far more meaningful.

The best plan to beat the crowds at the home is to get up early enough to reach Monticello soon after the gates open at 8 A.M. A bus will take you from the ticket booth to the 867-foot hilltop where Jefferson enjoyed a commanding view of the countryside he loved best.

For 40 years, from the day he inherited the land and gave it the name Monticello ("little mountain") at the age of 24, Jefferson continually dreamed about and planned for perfecting his home. He was responsible for every detail of its design, construction, furnishing, and several remodelings.

Jefferson chose a classical design rather than the Georgian architecture popular in his day. Except for the dome, familiar from countless photographs, the architectural plan gives a 35-room house the appearance of a one-story home.

The house was a wonder in its time, causing one visiting French nobleman to write, "Mr. Jefferson is the first American who has consulted the Fine Arts to know how he should shelter himself from the weather." Enter and you are in the unmistakable presence of genius, in a home of unmatched grace and elegance, flooded with natural light, yet with a sense of intimacy within each room.

Jefferson's keen mind, interest in the scientific, and delight with gadgets can be seen everywhere: in the dumbwaiter used to transport wine from the cellar and the revolving serving door that allowed the servants to set out food without entering the dining room; in a set of glass doors connected to open simultaneously when the first is set ajar; and in the seven-day clock in the entrance hall that recorded the day as well as the hour. Like the 14 skylights that bathe the house with light, they were innovations in their time.

His practical bent is evidenced by Monticello's stairs, which are narrow and tucked away out of sight. Jefferson thought the then common practice of installing elaborate stairways a waste of floor space.

His own sanctum—bedroom, sitting room, library, and study—is a high point of the tour. Above the bed is a long, narrow closet with porthole windows for light and ventilation, reached by a stepladder kept in a closet at the head of the bed. He used the revolving chair, Windsor bench, and revolving-top table for reading and writing, sitting in a half-recumbent position to ease his rheumatism. A telescope is installed in the south window; a pair of globes, terrestrial and celestial, stand on shelves flanking the doorway.

Jefferson's library once held 6,000 volumes. They went to the federal government in 1815, forming the nucleus of the present Library of Congress. The volumes now at Monticello are a selection of duplicates.

His attention to his garden design was as inventive as his interest in architecture. Both ornamental and vegetable gardens and two orchards were part of his plan for a self-supporting estate, and the gardens have been restored to his meticulously laid-out design, with 250 varieties of vegetables and 122 kinds of fruit. The stables and slave quarters, smokehouse, kitchen, and other outbuildings are currently being researched and further restored.

From Monticello, it is a short drive to Ash Lawn, the home of

Jefferson's friend James Monroe. The modest yellow frame Colonial is cozy and filled with family memorabilia. The grounds, with their peacocks and boxwood gardens, are exceptional. Special events, concerts, plays, and crafts displays are often held here.

You may have to face another line if you want the traditional Southern buffet of fried chicken, black-eyed peas, biscuits, and apple cobbler, served up daily for lunch at the Ordinary, a converted log house adjoining Michie (pronounced "mickey") Tavern. Tours are offered in the tavern itself, one of the oldest in Virginia, moved to its present site from a well-traveled coach road northwest of town. Many of the original furnishings and utensils remain, and a rare hammered dulcimer still stands in the upstairs ballroom, where it provided music for dancers two centuries ago.

To see more of Mr. Jefferson's town, proceed downtown to Court Square, where the original Albemarle Court House was built in 1762 and where the sight of three future American presidents—Jefferson, Madison, and Monroe—chatting on the green was not unusual. Many of the historic buildings here have been renovated into business and legal offices and shops. Paula Lewis, at Fourth and East Jefferson, is a worthwhile shopping stop for quilts, folk art, and antiques, and Signet Galleries, on Fifth, offers fine handmade crafts and clothing.

Almost 100 artists work in Charlottesville. You can see and talk to more than 40 of them in their studios at the McGuffey Art Center at 201 Second Street, Northwest.

More shops await two blocks south of Court Street on Main Street, which has been turned into a pedestrian mall. Have a look into Alley Antiques for country furniture and the Hardware Store complex of shops, including Stoney Mountain Fleece for rag rugs and "sheepy" gifts. There is also a little cafe here that is a good bet for lunch. You may well want to return to some of the excellent little restaurants on Main Street for dinner.

In the lush horse country outside of town, fall is a busy season. The oldest steeplechase race in America, the American Grand National, is held at Foxfield Race Course west of Charlottesville each year, and the Farmington Hunt Club annual fall horse show takes place in October.

You can also stay in the countryside in a variety of lovely lodgings. Prospect Hill is a romantic 1732 plantation house with rooms in the former slave quarters, while Clifton is a gracious mansion dating from 1799 that once belonged to Thomas Mann Randolph, husband to Thomas Jefferson's daughter, Martha, and an early governor of Virginia. High Meadows is a landmark home with two sections, 1832 and 1882, and furnishings appropriate to each. The specialty here is the wine-sampling weekend, with tastings plus dinner with complimentary house wine.

Guesthouses, the local bed-and-breakfast registry, offers many listings on country estates, as well as in fine antebellum homes in town.

The countryside is also the place to visit the vineyards that are helping to fulfill Jefferson's vision of native Virginia wines. Of the eight vineyards in the region, Montodomaine is one of the largest wineries, Barboursville claims the distinction of being the picturesque ruins of a home designed by Thomas Jefferson, and Oakencroft boasts proudly of being the only winery with a female owner and winemaker.

You will have the chance to sample and buy all of the local products at the annual Monticello Wine Festival, held at the Boar's Head Inn on Columbus Day weekend. But the wine is still young, so don't judge it by French or even California standards. The most appealing thing about these novice winemakers is their enthusiasm for their work.

If you want a balloon's-eye view of Monticello and the Virginia mountains, you can arrange for a hot-air balloon ride at the Sports Club at Boar's Head Inn.

For a final appreciation of Jefferson's genius, visit the magnificent campus of the University of Virginia. Guided tours go out frequently from the Rotunda, the famous landmark he designed with dome and columns inspired by the Parthenon. Today it is a monument to Jefferson, displaying his statue and copies of the drawings and writings of the "academical village" he envisioned and brought to life.

The Rotunda steps lead out to the Lawn, tiers of greenery flanked by facing columned arcades. The most coveted student lodgings are those in these historic arcades, awarded each year to honor students.

Beyond the arcades are gardens enclosed by serpentine walls and more arcaded rows of rooms, known as East and West Range, for graduate students. A poor student named Edgar Allan Poe lived in West Range arcade until his gambling debts forced him to withdraw. His room is open to visitors.

The Rotunda was begun in 1821, and Thomas Jefferson saw the first students enroll in the school in 1825, just one year before his death. Among his many accomplishments, he considered his role as founder of the university one of the greatest. For his own gravestone epitaph he wrote, "Here was buried Thomas Jefferson, Author of the Declaration of American Independence, of the Statute of Virginia for Religious Freedom and Father of the University of Virginia." These mattered more to Jefferson than titles like governor or president.

Jefferson also wrote, "All my wishes end where I hope my days will end . . . at Monticello." He got his wish. Thomas Jefferson is buried just down the path from the home he loved, and where he died at age 83 on the Fourth of July 1826, the fiftieth anniversary of the Declaration of Independence.

Area Code: 804

DRIVING DIRECTIONS Charlottesville is at the intersection of routes I-64 and 29. From D.C., take I-66 west to Route 29 south. Approximate distance from D.C., 125 miles.

ACCOMMODATIONS *Boar's Head Inn and Sports Club,* Route 250, 22905, 296-2181, elegant, longtime local landmark, $$$ ● *Silver Thatch Inn,* 3001 Hollymead Drive, Route 29 north, 22901, 978-4686, charming inn and restaurant, $$–$$$ CP ● *Clifton,* Route 9, P.O. Box 412, 22901, 971-1800, 1799 mansion, elegant, $$$–$$$$ CP ● *Omni Charlottesville Hotel,* West Main Street, 22901, 971-5500, on the downtown mall, $$$ ● *200 South Street,* at that address, 22901, 979-0200, beautifully furnished restored home in town, $$–$$$ CP ● *Prospect Hill,* Route 3, P.O. Box 430, Trevilians, 23093, (703) 967-0844, wonderful restored plantation, fine food, $$$$ MAP ● *High Meadows,* Route 20, Scottsville, 24590, 286-2218, restored historic home, noted for wine-tasting programs, $$–$$$ CP.

BED AND BREAKFAST *Guesthouses,* P.O. Box 5737, Charlottesville, VA 22905, 979-7264 or 979-8327.

DINING *C & O Restaurant,* 515 East Water Street, 971-7044, $$–$$$$ ● *Silver Thatch Inn* (see above), country French, $$–$$$ ● *Le Snail,* 320 East Main Street, 295-4456, Continental, $$–$$$ ● *South Street,* 106 South Street, 979-9300, seafood in a restored warehouse, $$$–$$$$ ● Old Mill, Boar's Head Inn (see above), $$–$$$ ● *Memory & Company,* 213 2nd Street, Southwest, 296-3539, noted local chef, lunch Monday to Friday, dinner Friday, $$, and Saturday, $$$ ● *Lavande,* 633 West Main Street, 296-6099, French, $$–$$$ ● *Book Gallery,* Emmet and Barracks roads, 977-2892, art exhibits, outdoor dining, $$–$$$ ● *High Meadows* (see above), by reservation only, $$$ ● *Prospect Hill* (see above), by reservation only, $$$.

SIGHTSEEING *Monticello,* Route 53, 295-8181. Hours: March to October, daily 8 A.M. to 5 P.M.; rest of year 9 A.M. to 4:30 P.M. Adults, $7; children, $2 ● *Ash Lawn–Highland,* Route 795, 293-9539. Hours: March to October 9 A.M. to 6 P.M.; rest of year 10 A.M. to 5 P.M. Adults, $6; children $2 ● *Historic Michie Tavern,* Route 53, 977-1234. Hours: daily 9 A.M. to 5 P.M. Adults, $5;

children, $1. President's Pass for all three attractions: adults, $16 ●
University of Virginia Rotunda and Central Grounds, 924-3239.
Guided tours, free ● *Thomas Jefferson at Monticello*, exhibit at
Charlottesville/Albemarle Visitors Bureau, Route 20 south,
293-6789, 9 A.M. to 5 P.M. Free.

INFORMATION Charlottesville/Albemarle Visitors Bureau,
Route 20 south, P.O. Box 161, Charlottesville, VA 22902,
293-6789. Hours: daily 9 A.M. to 5 P.M.

Autumn Adventures in the Poconos

Once upon a time, the unusual little town of Jim Thorpe, Pennsylvania, formerly known as Mauch Chunk, was a tourist mecca
dubbed the Switzerland of America for its extraordinary location,
tucked in a steep gorge between high mountains along the Lehigh
River.

The town's fortunes waned, but the scenery did not. Renamed
and rapidly restored to its nineteenth-century look and feel, Jim
Thorpe is enjoying a renaissance that merits a visit—especially in
autumn, when 18,000 square miles of surrounding wilderness in the
western Poconos light up in a million shades of crimson, gold, and
russet.

The town is particularly festive during its annual foliage festival
the second weekend in October. And while you are learning about a
curious little chapter of American history, you can sample a bit of
outdoor adventure, taking in the flaming foliage via steam train,
bicycle, mule back, river raft, or from a mountaintop. For those
who want to get rid of their aggressions, there's still another option
nearby—the chance to play the curious adventure game known as
Skirmish.

Strolling the streets of town, lit up by the glowing hills that enfold
it, is a treat in itself in autumn. Because it was hemmed in by mountains, Mauch Chunk grew vertically instead of horizontally. Many
of the buildings, like the 1869 St. Mark's Episcopal Church, are
built directly against the side of the mountain. Stop at the tourist
welcoming center in the 1888 New Jersey Central Railroad Station
for a walking tour that will tell you the story of Mauch Chunk's rise
and fall.

The town's original prosperity derived from its status as a river port that was the shipping center for the rich deposits of anthracite coal being mined in the surrounding mountains. You can still see the tow path of the old Lehigh Canal, which was dug to connect to the Delaware Canal in Easton so that the coal could be shipped out. English, Welsh, and Irish immigrants were attracted to the area, and building boomed in the town that soon became the county seat of Carbon County.

The early reliance on canals ended in the 1850s as Mauch Chunk became a prominent rail transfer point for coal, largely through the formation of the Lehigh Valley Railroad by Asa Packer, a local self-made millionaire and a philanthropist.

The first railroad in America actually was built between Mauch Chunk and Summit Hill, an 18-mile gravity track known as the Switchback. At the start it was used to transport coal into town, then to bring tourists up for the view. Gravity brought the cars downhill, mules towed them back to the top.

In the early 1900s, a trolley car was added to carry tourists to Flagstaff Park, atop the mountain just outside town, once again for the fabulous views. During the big band era, the famous Dorsey Brothers, natives of nearby Lansford, played here in the "Ballroom in the Clouds."

The decline of the coal industry brought a halt to Mauch Chunk's prominence, and hard times followed. In the 1950s, a small effort to revitalize began, with local citizens asked to contribute a nickel a week to a redevelopment fund. About that time the famous American Indian athlete, Jim Thorpe, died in poverty, and his wife, having heard about the town's spirit, offered his name in exchange for a proper burial and memorial. In 1954 three adjacent areas, Mauch Chunk, Upper Mauch Chunk, and East Mauch Chunk, combined to form one borough renamed Jim Thorpe. Thorpe's Memorial, a 20-ton granite mausoleum, can be seen a half-mile east of town on Route 903.

The new town hoped that the recognition that followed its name change would encourage an economic recovery, and finally that has indeed begun to happen. Mauch Chunk, the little town that once boasted of its 13 millionaires, is beginning to reclaim some of its past glory.

Among the prominent downtown buildings to be seen on a walking tour are the handsome Lehigh Coal and Navigation Building, dating back to 1884, and St. Mark's Episcopal Church, which boasts Tiffany windows; gold, marble, and brass furnishings; and a three-story wrought-iron elevator. The stone Carbon County Courthouse is worth a visit also for its elaborate oak-paneled skylighted courtroom, but it is open only on weekdays. And the fine 1881 Opera House is undergoing restoration.

The imposing local jail, a citadel on West Broadway, was infamous for its association with the "Molly McGuires," the violent forerunners of the labor union movement. Five of its members were hanged here. The last, Tom Fisher, left a handprint on the wall of cell 17, which he declared would remain forever as proof of his innocence. The outline is still visible today despite efforts to remove it.

Race Street, which took its name from the race, or track, that ran water down the street's center to the mill at the foot of the hill, contains a row of 16 houses known as Stone Row, almost unchanged in appearance since they were built in the 1840s. Stone Row had become run-down, but much of it is undergoing renovation, and delightful new shops are occupying many of the old homes.

Millionaire's Row is the lineup of fine homes on both sides of Broadway built by the wealthy of Mauch Chunk between 1860 and 1890. Wealthiest of all was Asa Packer, president of the Lehigh Valley Railroad and founder of Lehigh University, whose treasure-filled 1860 Victorian mansion on a hill overlooking town is open for guided tours. Next door, the restored home of Harry Packer, Asa's youngest son, is open for touring and available as well as an elegant bed-and-breakfast lodging, though weekends are devoted to murder-mystery shenanigans and carry a high price tag in a town that boasts of happily moderate rates.

Best bet for lodging is the tiny Hotel Switzerland, whose bar is the social center of Jim Thorpe. The pretty rooms upstairs are country-fresh. Increasingly, owners of some of the Victorian beauties in town are also taking in bed-and-breakfast guests. The tourist office has a complete current listing.

Shops are multiplying in Jim Thorpe, and you'll find some pleasant browsing awaiting on Race Street and Broadway. The restored Hooven Mercantile Company, a former spice and coffee warehouse on Susquehanna Street, offers shops as well as the small Scale Model Railroad and displays of local memorabilia. Among the variety of crafts for sale is one unique to the region—coal sculpture and jewelry, which you can see at the Coal Bin.

A short stroll away in Asa Packer Park, a 15,000-pound hunk of black diamond carbon coal is on display, a sample of why the town once prospered.

While you are wandering, have lunch at the Black Bread Cafe on Race Street and dessert at the Sweet Shop or Tory's Ice Cream & Soda Parlor, both on Broadway. At the latter, you can browse in the Bookworm, the bookshop upstairs. Another fine stop for refreshments is Priscilla's Kaffee Haus on Race Street, where gourmet coffees and teas and homemade pastries are on the menu.

When you've seen the in-town sights, take a drive to Flagstaff

Park for the fantastic 65-mile view from 1,400 feet atop Flagstaff Mountain.

Plan the rest of your stay according to your inclinations. The railroad station is the departure point for nostalgic steam train rides into the fall countryside. The old switchback trail is a prime lure for hikers, and scenic raft trips are offered through the Lehigh gorge. Once the spring high water recedes, the trips are labeled "floats" and described as "great for beginners." At Pocono Adventures, you can sign on for a mule ride into the autumn wilderness, for two hours or for two days. Or you can sign on for bicycle tours or rent a mountain bike in town.

And then we have Skirmish, billed as a "friendly war game," actually an adult version of Capture the Flag, with two teams competing to capture each other's flags from bases in a wooded area. Combatants use specially designed air pistols to splat their opponents with colored liquid—not everyone's idea of fun, but then some people love it and come back again and again. No question that it's different.

And so is Jim Thorpe, a small town being brought back to its former charm in a mountain setting that needed no improvement. Mark it down as a fascinating autumn destination.

Area Code: 717

DRIVING DIRECTIONS   Jim Thorpe is on Route 209, reached off Route 9, the Pennsylvania Turnpike Extension. The scenic route from D.C. is to take I-95 north to I-695 outside Baltimore and connect with I-83 north. At Harrisburg, turn east on I-81 and continue east as it merges with I-78. (Do *not* follow I-81 north to Hazleton.) Just before Allentown, take Route 9, the Turnpike Extension, to Route 209 west into town. Alternate route: Follow I-95 to Philadelphia, connect with I-76 north, then I-276 west to Route 9 north and proceed as above. From the northeast, take Route 80 to Route 9 south and proceed as above. Approximate distance from D.C., 223 miles.

ACCOMMODATIONS   *Hotel Switzerland,* 5 Hazard Square, 18229, 325-4563, $–$$ CP ● *Tiffany's Grand Victoria Bed & Breakfast,* 218 Center Street, 18229, 325-8260, an 1857 home in a quiet neighborhood, $ CP ● *Victoria Ann's Bed & Breakfast,* 68 Broadway, 18229, 325-8107, delightful courtyard; be prepared for a minimuseum of dolls in the living room, $–$$ CP ● *Harry Packer Mansion,* Packer Road, 18229, 325-4432, midweek $$ CP; Friday and Saturday nights are "Mystery Weekends" year-round, $$$$

MAP • Two full-scale resorts in the nearby Poconos are *Lodge at Split Rock,* Lake Harmony, 18624, 722-9111, big resort-condo complex with motel, hotel, and condo lodgings, $$$$ MAP • *Mountain Laurel Resort,* White Haven, 18661, 443-8411, modern complex with indoor pool and gym, riding, children's programs, $$$ MAP.

DINING *Hotel Switzerland,* (see above) 325-4563, $–$$ • *Flagstaff Mountain Park Resort,* Jim Thorpe, 325-4554, glassed-in porch with great mountaintop view, $–$$ • *Dean Anthony's,* 1122 North Street, 325-4432, Italian, $–$$ • *A Touch of Vanilla,* Mountain Laurel Resort (see above), $$–$$$ • *The Lantern,* routes 209 and 93, Nesquehoning (just outside Jim Thorpe), 669-9433, ignore the decor, the food is great, $–$$.

SIGHTSEEING *Asa Packer Mansion,* Packer Road, 325-3229. Hours: Memorial Day through October, daily, noon to 5 P.M.; weekends only in spring. Adults, $2.50; ages 6–17, $1.50 • *Harry Packer Mansion,* Packer Road, 325-3229. Hours: May to November, Tuesday to Sunday noon to 5 P.M. Adults, $2.50; ages 6–17, $1.50 • *Flagstaff Mountain Park,* 3 miles south on Route 209. Hours: daily 10 A.M. to 9 P.M. in summer; from 11 A.M. in fall. Observation platform, $1 • *Rail Tour, Inc.,* Central Railroad Station, P.O. Box 285, 325-4606, 40-minute steam train rides daily, July 5 to Labor Day, weekends spring and fall. Adults, $3.50; ages 4–10, $2 • *St. Mark's Episcopal Church,* Race Street. Hours: tours, Tuesday through Sunday, Memorial Day to October 31, 1 P.M. to 4:20 P.M. Free • *Pocono Whitewater Adventures,* Route 903, 325-3655, rafting trips, bicycle tours, and Skirmish games (Skirmish is limited to players over age 16). Phone or write for current offerings and rates • *Jim Thorpe River Adventures, Inc.,* P.O. Box 4066, 325-2570, rafting trips, inquire about current offerings • *Pocono Adventures on Mules,* Star Route, 325-2036, 2-hour to all-day muleback rides. Check current schedules and rates • *Blue Mountain Sports,* 34 Susquehanna Street, 325-4421, mountain bike rentals, hourly and daily rates.

INFORMATION Carbon County Tourist Promotion Agency, P.O. Box 90, Railroad Station, Jim Thorpe, PA 18229, 325-3673.

On Top of the World in Shenandoah

Virginia's Skyline Drive is a wonder. It wiggles its way heaven-high astride the Blue Ridge Mountains for 105 miles, smack through the exquisite wilderness of Shenandoah National Park, with tiers of dusky mountain ridges honing into breath-catching view at every bend.

Down below, the lush rolling Piedmont horse country stretches away to the east. To the west lies the Shenandoah Valley of fable and song, and the Shenandoah River, dividing in order to fork its way around the 40-mile stretch of Massanutten Mountain.

There's plenty of time to enjoy the views. The pace on the drive is a leisurely 35 miles per hour, there are only four entrances in over 100 miles, and there are 71 outlooks along the way, allowing you to pull off to contemplate the scenery or take a walk in the woods whenever the spirit moves you.

A beauty spot year-round, Shenandoah Park takes on an extra glow in autumn, and even the crowds can't spoil the glory as the golds and crimsons of the season begin working their way down from the mountaintop, bathing the hills in radiant color.

If you are able to stay in one of the two park lodges, Skyland and Big Meadows, you'll have a ringside seat at your window. There are log cabins, too, if you want to be off into the woods with your own fireplace to take the chill off the brisk fall mountain evenings.

But not to worry if the park lodges are full. All of the Shenandoah Valley is aflame in October, and the views are fabulous even outside the park, especially on the roads cutting across the mountains, like Route 211, where the apple sellers are out in force, adding still more color with festoons of Confederate flags behind their baskets of ripe, red fruit.

You could spend a happy weekend just contemplating the serene countryside at Jordan Hollow Farm, a restored Colonial horse-farm-turned-country-inn in Stanley, about 12 miles from the Skyline Drive. The original farmhouse serves as a cozy dining room, where the Continental fare is top-notch, and the 16 bedrooms in a new lodge have rustic charm and admirable views from their porches. This is still a working horse farm with both lessons and trail rides available.

Not far away in McGaheysville, Shenandoah Valley Farm and Inn offers six moderately priced and very private guest cottages on the grounds of a 150-acre cattle farm with magnificent grounds and views.

Two excellent resorts are also nearby, Bryce Mountain and Massanutten, each offering handsome condominium lodgings, golf and tennis, and striking mountain views. Massanutten also has hotel accommodations.

Having settled in, you'll find plenty of activity to keep you busy both in and out of the park.

Shenandoah was a unique experiment in returning an overused area to its original beauty. It was authorized as a national park in 1926, and the state then purchased and donated to the federal government nearly 280 square miles cradling 194,327 acres of the Blue Ridge Mountains. The goal was to reclaim this once-magnificent area where the forests were shrinking and game was disappearing because of oversettlement.

Thinning soil had driven out half the settlers, and the other half had to be relocated before the park could be dedicated in 1936. The recreational facilities and the Skyline Drive were both "Depression babies," man-made monuments to nature built by Franklin Roosevelt's Civilian Conservation Corps. Over the years more than 95 percent of the land has returned to forest filled with more than 100 species of trees. The deer, bear, bobcat, turkey, and other animals that were becoming rare or absent have also returned. The largest remaining open area, Big Meadows, is being kept in its pristine condition to retain the abundance of wildflowers, strawberries, and blueberries that attract both wildlife and humans.

Besides gazing at the views in the park, there are many naturalist-guided programs and self-guided nature trails. Over 500 miles of footpaths give you a close-up view of nature at its best. There are walks for everyone, from short strolls to 95 miles of the Appalachian Trail. One of the most popular trails is Old Rag Mountain, which has been called the most spectacular in the northern Virginia Blue Ridge. It features a rock "obstacle course," a 7.2-mile circuit under and around large boulders and through a narrow natural rock tunnel. Another favorite is the 6.25-mile section of the Appalachian Trail from Fishers Gap to Skyland, which edges Franklin Cliffs for an astonishing valley view, then crosses a ridge between Hawksbill and Naked Top Mountain. A side trail leads to the summit of Hawksbill, at 3,860 feet the highest point in the park.

Wherever you wander, you'll find unspoiled nature, mountain creeks, waterfalls, a rich variety of plants and wildlife, and 200 species of birds.

Horseback riders can rent mounts at Skyland Lodge and enjoy the scenery along 150 miles of horse trails, and canoeists can go down into the valley to enjoy the mountain views from the waters of the Shenandoah River. Shenandoah River Outfitters of Luray will provide the canoes.

Some of the great sights in the Shenandoah Valley are underground in the seven huge limestone caverns beneath the valley's floor. The best known and most spectacular is Luray Caverns, where the soaring formations and crystal pools are a true natural wonder. Some of the shapes are eerie, others are nature's whimsy, bearing an uncanny resemblance to giant slabs of bacon and fried eggs. Most amazing of all is the Great Stalacpipe Organ, the world's largest musical instrument, a series of huge stalactites that produce melodious concert music when they are struck with rubber-tipped hammers.

You can bring your camera with you into the caves, by the way. One section is lit with 25,000 watts, allowing for photos without a flash.

Part of the Luray complex, which includes motel, tennis courts, and golf course, is a museum of 75 historic cars and carriages, with displays dating all the way from a 1755 Conestoga wagon to a 1946 Daimler.

Luray is the king of caverns, but when you see one cave you haven't quite seen them all. Shenandoah Caverns is smaller, but it holds its own wonders, especially the sparkling Diamond Cascade and the vaulted-ceilinged Grotto of the Gods. While you are in the neighborhood, stop at Tuttle & Spice General Store for the free mini-museum of 1880s antiques offered by collectors Ed and Maxine Heberlein.

If you want more sightseeing, head for the Hall of Valor Civil War Museum at New Market Battlefield, one of the clearest displays of the course of the war, especially the battles in Virginia.

An alternate way back east to D.C. past the apple stands on Route 211 brings you to the village of Sperryville, a delightful stop for antiquing. On the third weekend in October, the annual Apple Harvest Celebration fills the town with booths and crafts, buggy rides, entertainment, and food. It's the perfect place to watch apple butter being made and to stock up on cider and apples from the nearby orchards. A few miles farther in Washington, Virginia, the Inn at Little Washington offers elegant and memorable dining.

But the memories that will linger longest are those of heavenly autumn vistas of the Blue Ridge Mountains. Driving at peak level on the Skyline Drive leaves you feeling on top of the world!

Area Code: 703

DRIVING DIRECTIONS From D.C., take I-66 west to the northern end of the Skyline Drive at Front Royal. Approximate distance from D.C., 76 miles. For other destinations in the valley, continue west on I-66 to Route 81 south. Other entrances to the drive are at routes 211, 33, and 250/I-64.

ACCOMMODATIONS *Skyland Lodge,* P.O. Box 727, Shenandoah National Park, 22835, 999-2221, open late March to mid-December; motel rooms, $$, cottages, $–$$ ● *Big Meadows Lodge,* P.O. Box 727, Shenandoah National Park, 22835, 999-2221, May to October, motel rooms, $$; cottages, $; main lodge, $–$$; suites, $$ ● *Lewis Mountain,* Shenandoah National Park, 22835, 743-5108, mid-May to October, $. All park rates are higher in October, lower in early spring, November, and December ● *Jordan Hollow Farm Inn,* Route 2, P.O. Box 375, Stanley, 22851, 778-2285, $$ ● *Shenandoah Valley Farm and Inn,* Route 1, P.O. Box 142, McGaheysville, 22840, 289-5402, $ ● *Bryce Resort,* P.O. Box 3, Basye, 22810, 856-2121, ask about weekend sports packages, $$$$ ● *Massanutten Village,* P.O. Box 1227, Harrisonburg, 22801, 289-9441, $$$–$$$$ for hotels; condos vary with size ● *The Inn at Little Washington,* Middle and Main streets, Washington, 22747, 675-3800, $$$$ CP. See also lower Shenandoah Valley, page 36.

DINING All of the above. Box lunches are available at park lodges if ordered at breakfast time.

SIGHTSEEING *Shenandoah National Park,* headquarters, US 211 east of Luray, 999-2229. Hours: daily. Admission, $5 per car to enter park ● *Luray Caverns,* Luray, 743-6551. Hours: spring and fall, daily, 9 A.M. to 6 P.M.; mid-June to Labor Day to 7 P.M.; winter weekdays to 4 P.M., winter weekends to 4 P.M. Adults, $9; ages 7–13, $4; under 7, free ● *New Market Battlefield Park,* New Market, 740-3102. Hours: daily 9 A.M. to 5 P.M. Adults, $4; children, $1.50 ● *Shenandoah Caverns,* New Market, 896-CAVE. Hours: spring and fall, daily 9 A.M. to 5 P.M.; summer to 7 P.M.; winter to 5 P.M. Adults, $7; children, $4.50.

INFORMATION Superintendent, Shenandoah National Park, Luray, VA 22835, 999-2229 ● Shenandoah Valley Travel Association, I-81, Exit 67, P.O. Box 1040, New Market, VA 22844, 740-3132.

Carving a Niche in Easton

The signposts are little carved ducks, the pointers painted on the sidewalks are the outspread wings of geese.

There's no mistaking who's king in Easton, Maryland, come early November, when the annual Waterfowl Festival gets under way, and you needn't even be a bird lover to enjoy the show.

Some 18,000 people now flock to the Eastern Shore each autumn for this weekend celebration of waterfowl art and carvings and photography that fills the town to overflowing. A visit leaves little doubt as to the special niche this very American folk art has carved for itself among collectors and admirers.

Whether you go home with a $1,500 prize decoy, a $15 carved tern, or a $50 hand-painted map of Chesapeake Bay, you'll have a festive day. As a bonus, there are those luscious Chesapeake Bay oysters in their November prime, not to mention the prime views of live V-shaped formations of ducks and geese overhead this time of year, honking in for their annual winter stay.

Some of the world's best carvers come to show and sell their work in Easton, and some of the finest antique decoys go up for display and sale at an annual auction. The Gold Room of the Tidewater Inn turns into an art gallery for paintings by the nation's most renowned waterfowl artists, while the Blue Room displays art for the budget-minded, priced below $500. A special building is set up for carvers and painters from the Eastern Shore.

The Talbot County Historical Society shows off work by photographers, while the Academy of the Arts presents changing exhibits relating to the carver's art. At the high school, the big "Buy, Sell, and Swap" display brings scores of dealers and collectors ready to make a deal on antique decoys, rare books, and all manner of memorabilia. The Easton Middle School becomes a gift shop for the weekend, devoted to waterfowl-related arts and crafts, which means anything from stained glass and ceramics to needlework, leather, and clothing, all with bird and hunting-dog motifs. Most are items not available in commercial shops.

The 1,000 volunteers who run the show, which has raised over $1.7 million for conservation causes, have managed to organize a potential mob scene into relative order. Efficient shuttle buses are in constant motion ferrying visitors from one site to another, so you can leave your car in the high school parking lot and forget about the traffic hassles in town. Those ducky signs in orange and blue clearly mark the bus stops.

They can't do much about the long lines waiting outside the two buildings housing the stars of the show, the carvers. Originally wildfowl carvings meant working decoys, lifelike models of ducks and geese and shorebirds that were used by hunters to lure the birds. The ducks and geese actually floated in the water, the shorebirds were mounted on rods and stuck in the sand as if scanning the surf for food.

The best of these decoys are recognized today as whimsical, nostalgic works of folk art, and their prices have risen dramatically. Prizes that used to be found at flea markets for small change may now sell for $1,000 and up. Among the most sought-after pieces are those made pre–World War II, before the advent of mass-produced decoys. Collectors also treasure signed decoys by acknowledged masters like Lem and Steve Ward, brothers from Crisfield, Maryland, who worked in the 1960s. Knowledgeable aficionados say that you can still buy a pretty good old decoy for a few hundred dollars, but extremely rare pieces have gone for over $30,000 at auction.

As interest in the bird carver's art has grown, the craft has evolved to become closer to realistic sculpture, amazing in its intricacy and detail. The work of many top contemporary carvers is beautiful and can be appreciated by anyone who enjoys artistic workmanship, regardless of the subject matter.

If the lines for exhibits get to you and you want a break, stop for some of the cold oysters al fresco served at stands set up by the local Lions club, then have a stroll through town. All of Easton is decked out for the occasion, but with a sense of humor about it all. There are displays everywhere poking gentle fun at the hunters, like a rubber boat with a giant goose dressed in camouflage at the helm. In the boat is his prey, a trussed pair of hunters. Hunters, incidentally, are often the most ardent conservationists, abiding strictly by legal limits and working hard to preserve the wetlands, so as to encourage the abundant flocks that give them so much sporting pleasure.

Shop windows in Easton are filled with carved ducks and geese and shorebirds of every size and species. Inside the shops you can find almost anything imaginable with bird motifs—goosey sweatshirts, pillows, skirts, and pocketbooks; gold jewelry in the shape of ducks on the wing; Dhurrie rugs with ducky designs; ties and even toilet seats adorned with birds in flight.

While this is not the ideal time for a peaceful stroll through Easton, a walk still can give you a good idea of the flavor of the town that is the hub of the lower Eastern Shore. Easton grew inland from the water, centered on a church and a court of justice. The Third Haven Meeting House on South Washington dates back to 1682 and is said to be the nation's oldest frame building devoted to religious worship. It was built at the head of the Tred-Avon River so that congregants could come to services by boat.

The Talbot County Court House on North Washington is a 1791 successor to the building put up in 1710 to serve Talbot County. It became the focus of the settlement that was actually known as Talbot Court House until 1786, when residents petitioned for incorporation. Many fine early homes remain, like Foxley Hall, a 1775 home on Goldsborough and North Aurora streets, the Joseph Neale House and Premises, two next-door late 1700s homes at 18 and 20 West Street, and the 1803 Thomas Perrin Smith House at 119 North Washington.

If you want to see more of Easton, you can pick up a walking tour at the historical society and follow along Washington and its parallel neighbors West and Harrison, as well as the intersecting streets of Dover and Goldsborough.

Festival tickets include a visit to the Chesapeake Bay Maritime Museum in St. Michaels, a fine place to get a sense of the role water has played in Chesapeake history, and to see the largest floating fleet of historic bay boats in existence. The museum's landmark is the Hooper Strait Lighthouse, one of the last three remaining cottage-type lighthouses on the bay. A stroll around St. Michaels, a village that retains much of its nineteenth-century character, is also rewarding.

Two other popular attractions during the weekend are retriever demonstrations at area ponds, showing the uncanny skills of the hunting dog, and the world championship goose-calling contest, held at the high school auditorium.

However fascinating the wildfowl exhibits may be, save part of a day for a look at the real thing, the waterfowl that flock so abundantly here in late fall and winter. The Chesapeake Bay region is one of the main intersections of the migratory paths of more than 37 species of waterfowl, including the biggest of the migrating birds, whistling swans, which may weigh as much as 25 pounds. While spotting and identifying birds on the wing is a skill that takes years to develop, you don't need first-name acquaintance to appreciate the bevies of beauties to be seen overhead, on the ponds, and in the marshes.

The best place for close-up views is the Blackwater National Wildlife Refuge, to the south of Easton, 12 miles below Cambridge. This stretch of 314,263 acres, mostly rich tidal marsh, was set aside in 1932 as a protected haven for migratory wildfowl. It was originally established as a refuge for ducks, but soon also became a favorite wintering area for Canadian geese using the Atlantic flyway. In autumn, at the peak of the annual migration, some 60,000 geese and 35,000 ducks can be found here. Among the residents that have been spotted spending the winter are the whistling swans, tundra swans, snow geese, and some 20 duck species, including colorful mallards, black ducks, blue-winged and green-winged teal, wigeons, and pintails.

Other feathered residents include the great blue heron and the bald eagle; the endangered national bird is found here in its greatest numbers in the East north of Florida. Other endangered species sometimes seen here are the peregrine falcon and the red-cockaded woodpecker, which has been known to nest in the area. Ospreys arrive in spring and stay through fall, using the nesting platforms that have been placed throughout the marsh.

The refuge is also a year-round home for towhees, woodpeckers, brown-headed nuthatches, bobwhites, and woodcocks, and such mammals as white-tailed deer, raccoons, opossums, skunks, red foxes, gray squirrels, and the Delmarva fox squirrel.

You can see the wildlife along a five-mile drive among the ponds, woods, fields, and marshes. There are walking trails as well, and an observation tower overlooking the junction of the Big and Little Blackwater rivers and their marshlands.

Blackwater is an appropriate end to a wildfowl weekend, a chance for a live appreciation of the grace that inspires the Easton bird carvers.

Area Code: 301

DRIVING DIRECTIONS   Easton is on Route 50, south of the Chesapeake Bay Bridge. Take Route 50/301 east across the bridge and turn south on Route 50. Approximate distance from D.C., 73 miles.

ACCOMMODATIONS   See page 110 for accommodations in Easton and neighboring Oxford and St. Michaels. Rooms here are booked months ahead for the Waterfowl Festival weekend, so here are a few more options: *St. Michaels Motor Inn,* Route 33, St. Michaels, 21663, 745-3333, $–$$$ ● *Harbourtowne Resort,* off Route 33, St. Michaels, 21663, 745-9066, resort-motel, $$$ ● *St. Michaels Harbour Inn and Marina,* 101 North Harbor Road, St. Michaels, 21663, 745-9001, $$–$$$$ ● *The Bishop's House,* 214 Goldsborough Street, Easton, 21601, 820-7290, B&B home, $$$– $$$$ CP ● *John S. McDaniel House,* 14 North Aurora Street, Easton, 21601, 822-3781, modest B&B, $–$$ CP ● Area motels include the following: *Comfort Inn,* Route 50, Easton, 21601, 820-8333, $$ ● *Atlantic Budget Inn,* Route 50, Easton, 21601, 822-2200, $ ● *Econo Motor Lodge,* Route 50, Easton, 21601, 822-6330, $ ● *Marinor Motor Lodge,* Route 50, Easton, 21601, 822-4600, $–$$.

BED AND BREAKFAST   *The Traveller in Maryland,* P.O. Box 2277, Annapolis, MD 21404, 269-6232 in Maryland, 261-2233 toll-free in D.C.

DINING *Tidewater Inn,* Dover and Harrison streets, 822-1300, elegant, $$–$$$ ● *Peachblossoms,* 6 North Washington Street, 822-5220, seafood and pasta, $$–$$$ ● *Washington Street Pub and Raw Bar,* 20 North Washington Street, 822-9011, informal, $$ ● Three of Easton's best dining choices are in the restored Avalon building, 42 East Dover Street. They are *Legal Spirits Tavern,* 822-5522, casual, $–$$$; *Cecile's,* 822-2500, chandeliers and stained glass, Continental menu, $$–$$$; *Chambers Penthouse Restaurant,* 822-5521, attractive, informal, $$–$$$. See also page 110 for St. Michaels and Oxford.

SIGHTSEEING *Easton Waterfowl Festival,* usually the second weekend in November. Information and current rates, P.O. Box 929, Easton 21601, 822-4567. Headquarters at the Tidewater Inn ● *Historical Society of Talbot County,* 25 South Washington Street, Easton, 822-0773. Hours: Tuesday to Saturday 10 A.M. to 4 P.M.; Sunday 1 P.M. to 4 P.M. Closed Sunday in January and February. Adults, $2; students, $.50 ● *Chesapeake Bay Maritime Museum,* Navy Point, St. Michaels, 745-2916. Hours: daily 10 A.M. to 5 P.M.; weekends only April to October, 10 A.M. to 5 P.M.; closed rest of year. Admission included with Waterfowl Festival ticket; otherwise $4 ● *Blackwater National Wildlife Refuge,* Route 1, P.O. Box 121, Cambridge, 228-2677. Visitors center open daily 7:30 A.M. to 4 P.M. Wildlife Drive and outdoor facilities open dawn to dusk. Free.

INFORMATION Talbot County Chamber of Commerce, 7 Federal Street, P.O. Box 1366, Easton, MD 21601, 822-4606.

The Inn Crowd in Bucks County

William Penn, who had his pick of Pennsylvania, chose to build his country home along the Delaware River in Bucks County, reportedly telling some friends that it was even lovelier than the English countryside he had left behind.

This bucolic enclave of hills, streams, covered bridges, and mellowed stone farmhouses has been drawing people ever since. At the turn of this century, the pastoral views inspired one of the nation's first art colonies. Later they lured some of America's top creative talents, people like Oscar Hammerstein II, Moss Hart, George S.

Kaufman, James Michener, and Pearl Buck, who chose Bucks County for their country homes.

Nowadays it is inn lovers who flock to Bucks County, where choosing among the historic homes now serving as lodgings is one of life's pleasanter dilemmas. Should it be Barley Sheaf Farm, the mellowed 1740 stone farmhouse where George S. Kaufman used to entertain the Marx Brothers and Lillian Hellman, or Oscar Hammerstein's Highland Farms, where Stephen Sondheim was a frequent guest and the late Henry Fonda was married under the grape arbor? High Victorian style and a five-course dinner at Evermay, or an intimate stone cottage done in country French at the Inn at Phillips Mill?

The list goes on and on—and so do the pleasures of a Bucks County visit: walking along the canal, riding a mule barge, leisurely gliding in a canoe down the Delaware, roaming through galleries and antique shops, visiting historical sites, or just gazing at some of the most enchanting back-roads scenery in the East.

You might start your visit Saturday morning in New Hope, the picturesque artists' colony that is the heart of Bucks County. Here, a labyrinth of paths and alleyways offers almost 100 shops and galleries for browsing. New Hope, however, is far from undiscovered, and you'll understand why an early start is advisable when you see the number of tourists converging here as the day goes on.

Still, there is good reason for the crowds. Here's where you can take that nostalgic ride on the last operating mule-drawn canal barge in the country, or watch early hand-printing being done at the Old Franklin Print Shop. And tucked among the gift and gewgaw shops are some fine antique and art dealers. A few special shops and galleries to note are Golden Door (a historic stone building) for Bucks County traditional landscape paintings, A Mano for country crafts, Dulman Larsen for contemporary art and sculpture, and Three Cranes for Oriental pieces and interesting clothing.

The sightseeing spot here is the Parry Mansion, with 10 rooms displaying the furnishings and decor that might have been used by the family whose successive generations lived here for 182 years. Come evening, the Bucks County Playhouse, the famous old theater in a restored gristmill, will likely have something interesting on tap.

When the New Hope sidewalks begin to overflow with shoppers, it's time to visit the tourist office at the corner of Main and Mechanic to stock up on maps and guides and then head out for the shops that run almost nonstop along Route 202 to Doylestown. Peddler's Village, a nicely landscaped Colonial-style complex, has over 60 shops crammed with wares of every kind, and even more shops adjoin in the Yard, a Victorian mélange of 14 boutiques. Right across the street the Lahaska Antique Courte has 14 shops filled with all kinds of collectibles plus a try-your-luck flea market.

You'll need no guide to find the many other antique shops along this route, but if you are a serious antiquer, be sure to pick up the printed guide listing close to 50 stores throughout the area. There are three big shows each year. Drop a note to the Bucks County Tourist Commission for this year's dates and locations.

Continue on to Doylestown for a unique sightseeing complex known as the Mercer Mile, the legacy of a genuine American genius—and eccentric—Henry Chapman Mercer. One of the nation's leading archaeologists, he had a passion for collecting early American tools that led to a midlife career change. Mercer became so intrigued with the tools used by the old Pennsylvania German potters and tile makers that he determined single-handedly to perpetuate the dying craft. He apprenticed himself to one of the potters, rented a decrepit kiln, and soon exhibited a talent that brought him a new kind of fame. Mercer tiles can be seen from the casino at Monte Carlo to the Gardner Museum in Boston to the tile floor in the Pennsylvania state capitol at Harrisburg.

Mercer called his enterprise the Moravian Pottery and Tile Works. The factory is now a living museum, but it is the least of Mercer's monuments. The most incredible display of tiles is in his own home, Fonthill, a castlelike concrete fantasy of columns, balconies, beams, towers, arches, and winding stairs. Tiles are everywhere—on columns and beams; serving as headboards, tabletops, and ceilings; and even lining the stair steps.

And then there is the Mercer Museum, housing Mercer's huge collection of 60,000 hand tools for some 130 crafts. There are tools once used by butchers, dairymen, cooks, and coopers; carpenters, weavers, leather makers, and printers; doctors, clock makers, surveyors, and seamstresses. Each trade's tools are set up in separate cubbies surrounding a spiral ramp. The ramp encircles a six-story high-vaulted core where handcrafted objects of every conceivable kind are suspended—chairs, cradles, barrels, whaleboats, baskets, bellows, cigar-store Indians, even a Conestoga wagon.

Fonthill and the museum established Mercer as an unlikely prophet of modern architecture. The museum's ramp arrangement is believed to have been the inspiration for New York's Guggenheim Museum.

Across from the Mercer Museum is Doylestown's newest important attraction, the James A. Michener Arts Center of Bucks County, endowed by and named for the author who is the town's most famous native son. It is handsomely housed in the ornate 1884 complex that once included the Bucks County jail. The prison yard is now a courtyard encircled by a sculpture garden. The arts center, which concentrates on twentieth-century art, has changing exhibits as well as a permanent collection that includes work by the noted early 1900s New Hope School of landscape painters.

Sunday is the time for the back roads and countryside, the stone houses and barns that are the special trademark of Bucks County. Part of the fascination is that no two houses are alike. Even their colors and textures vary according to the native stones used for construction. You'll see mostly limestone and shale in central Bucks and craggier granite in the upper regions. Notice the double houses with twin doors, the big trilevel barns, and the ''bride and groom'' trees that flank many of the doorways. The trees were planted long ago for good luck by newlyweds who hoped their love would flourish along with the saplings.

The main roads are River Road (Route 32) and routes 611 and 413, and you can't go wrong making your way back and forth. One possible route is to follow winding River Road north. The thin strip of land paralleling the road between the canal and the river is officially called Theodore Roosevelt Park, but generally it is just referred to as the towpath, because it was once used by the mules that pulled barges down the canal. Now, hikers and bikers ply the path.

The drive will take you through the sleepy town of Lumberville, where the Cuttalossa Inn is a perfect spot for brunch or lunch beside a waterfall. Then it's on to Point Pleasant, where you may be tempted to pause for an hour to see the river from one of its nicest perspectives—by canoe. Point Pleasant Canoe can provide all the necessary gear, and even novices need not worry about this placid stretch of water.

In Ralph Stover State Park near Point Pleasant you will see the Big Red covered bridge, and there are other covered bridges farther north in Erwinna and Uhlerstown. Stover Mill in Erwinna, its old machinery still intact, is sometimes used as a gallery for local art. Tinicum Park on River Road is the site of the restored Federal-style Erwin-Stover House, and there are picnic facilities here if you want to take a break.

A two-and-a-half-mile detour west of River Road in Upper Black Eddy will bring you to a curiosity, three and a half acres of huge boulders known as Ringing Rocks because many of the rocks, when struck, actually do ring.

From here, continue west on Route 32 to the connection with Route 611 and proceed south, once again through more charming towns such as Pipersville, site of the Cabin Run and Loux covered bridges and another restored mill. Not far away, near Dublin, is Green Hills Farm, where Pulitzer and Nobel prize–winning author Pearl Buck lived and worked for 40 years. Her 1835 stone house is filled with Oriental antiques.

If you take a drive to lower Bucks County, you can see Pennsbury Manor in Morrisville, William Penn's reconstructed seventeenth-century country plantation estate overlooking the Delaware.

And then there is still that matter of choosing a Bucks County lodging of your own. What about the simple country charm and folk art of Pineapple Hill, or the elegant country ambience, pool, and tennis court at Pine Tree Farm? Or would you rather have river views from your room at the 1740 House or live on the gracious estate of seed king David Burpee at Ford Hook Farm?

If you find it hard to decide on a favorite, you'll be in good company. You can join the legions who keep returning happily to Bucks County to make up their minds.

Area Code: 215

DRIVING DIRECTIONS New Hope is on Route 32, River Road. From D.C., take I-95 north into Pennsylvania, then north on Route 32. Approximate distance from D.C., 175 miles. From the north or west, follow Route 202 to Route 32.

ACCOMMODATIONS *Barley Sheaf Farm,* P.O. Box 10, Route 202, Holicong, 18928, 794-5104, $$$–$$$$ CP ● *Evermay on the Delaware,* River Road (Route 32), Erwinna, 18920, 294-9100, $$–$$$ CP ● *The Inn at Phillips Mill,* River Road (Route 32), New Hope, 18938, 862-9919, $$ CP ● *1740 House,* River Road (Route 32), Lumberville, 18933, 297-5661, $$ CP ● *Pineapple Hill,* 1324 River Road (Route 32), New Hope, 18938, 862-9608, $$ CP ● *The Inn at Fordhook Farm,* 105 New Britain Road, Doylestown, 18901, 345-1766, $$$ CP ● *Highland Farms,* 70 East Road, Doylestown, 18901, 340-1354, $$–$$$ CP ● *Pine Tree Farm,* Lower State Road, Doylestown, 18901, 348-0632, $$$ CP ● Inns are small and fill quickly. If all of the above are booked, here are some very pleasant alternatives: *Ash Mill Farm,* Route 202, Holicong, 18928, 794-5373, eighteenth-century farmhouse, $$–$$$ CP ● *Tattersall Inn,* Cafferty and River roads (Route 32), Point Pleasant, 18950, 862-2984, gracious manor house, $$$ CP ● *The Bucksville House,* Route 412 and Buck Drive, Kintnersville, 18930, 847-8948 (a bit of a drive, but cozy and a good buy), $–$$ CP ● *The Whitehall Inn,* Pineville Road, New Hope, 18938, 598-7945, pool, tennis, afternoon tea, and chamber music, $$$–$$$$ CP ● *Isaac Stover House,* River Road (Route 32), Erwinna, 18920, 294-8044, owned by Sally Jessy Raphael, crammed to the rafters with Victoriana, $$–$$$ CP.

DINING *Odette's,* River Road (Route 32), south of New Hope, 862-2432, river views, piano bar, $$$ ● *The Inn at Phillips Mill* (see above), romantic setting, $$$ ● *Evermay* (see above), 5-course dinner, prix fixe $42 ● *Pear & Partridge Inn,* Old Easton Road, Doylestown, 345-7800, highly rated "new American cuisine," $$$ ● *Black Bass Hotel,* River Road (Route 32), Lumberville, 297-5770, perfect riverside setting, $$–$$$ ● *La Bonne Auberge,* Village II, New Hope, 862-2462, classic French, $$$$ ● *Carversville Inn,* Carversville and Aquetong roads, Carversville, 297-8100, country French, $$–$$$ ● *Forager House,* River Road (Route 32), south of New Hope, 862-9477, art filled, informal, $$–$$$ ● *Cuttalossa Inn,* River Road (Route 32), Lumberville, 297-5082, best for lunch or brunch, $$$ ● *Conti's Cross Keys Inn,* routes 611 and 313, Doylestown, 348-9600, longtime local standby, $$$ ● *Golden Pheasant Inn,* River Road (Route 32), Erwinna, 294-9595, restored 1857 inn, highly regarded chef, $$$ ● For less-pricey fare, check out the current crop of little cafes along Main Street in New Hope. Also highly recommended is Hamilton's Grill, just across the river in Lambertville, NJ. See pages 10–11.

SIGHTSEEING *Parry Mansion,* South Main Street, New Hope, 862-5652. Hours: May to October, Friday to Sunday 1 P.M. to 5 P.M. Admission, $2.50 ● *Mule-Drawn Barge Ride,* South Main Street, New Hope, 862-2842. Hours: April to mid-November. Adults, $6.50; children, $3.75. Check for current schedule ● *Mercer Museum,* Pine and Ashland streets, Doylestown, 345-0210. Hours: Monday to Saturday 10 A.M. to 5 P.M.; Sunday 1 P.M. to 5 P.M. Adults, $4; students, $1.50 ● *Fonthill,* East Court Street, Doylestown, 348-9461. Hours: daily 10 A.M. to 5 P.M.; last tour 4 P.M. Adults, $4; students, $1.50 ● *Pearl S. Buck Home,* Dublin Road, Perkasie, 249-0100. Hours: daily tours at 10:30 A.M. and 2 P.M. Adults, $4; ages 6–18, $2 ● *James A. Michener Arts Center of Bucks County,* 138 South Pine Street, Doylestown, 340-9800. Hours: Monday to Friday 10 A.M. to 4 P.M.; Saturday and Sunday 11:30 A.M. to 4:30 P.M. Adults, $3; students, $1.50 ● *Pennsbury Manor,* 400 Pennsbury Memorial Road, Morrisville (near Tullytown), 946-0400. Hours: guided tours Tuesday to Saturday, 9 A.M. to 5 P.M., Sunday noon to 5 P.M.; last tour begins at 3:30 P.M. Adults, $2.50; ages 6–17, $1.

INFORMATION Bucks County Tourist Commission, P.O. Box 912, Doylestown, PA 18901, 345-4551 ● New Hope Chamber of Commerce, 1 West Mechanic Street, 18938, 862-5880.

An Early Thanksgiving on the James River

Forget all those stories about the Pilgrims. Down in Virginia, they'll tell you that the first official Thanksgiving was celebrated not in Massachusetts at all, thank you, but at Berkeley Plantation on the James River in 1619, two years before the Pilgrims celebrated the first Thanksgiving in Massachusetts. Virginians even persuaded a Massachusetts native, President John F. Kennedy, to issue a Thanksgiving Proclamation in 1963 recognizing their state's claim.

But being the gracious folks they are, the Virginians didn't try to change the familiar national observance. They simply added a celebration of their own at Berkeley on the first Sunday in November, providing a perfect opportunity to visit the great plantations along the James, as well as the settlements at Jamestown, where the first permanent English colony in Virginia—and in America—began in 1607.

Some 144 passengers sailed up the James River aboard three tiny ships to found that first settlement. A mixed crew of well-heeled gentlemen, skilled artisans, and indentured servants, they faced hunger, sickness, Indians, and the rigors of the wilderness in their new home. More settlers arrived, but during "the starving time" of 1609–1610, 440 of the 500 inhabitants perished. Yet they learned to conquer frontier living and prospered. Jamestown was the capital of the sprawling Virginia colony and an active community for almost 100 years, until the capital was moved to Williamsburg in 1700, and the idea of representative government was developed here.

About all that remains of the original town is the seventeenth-century Old Church Tower. At Jamestown National Historic Site, the island where the Virginia settlers landed, foundations, artifacts, and graveyards have been excavated, a 1608 glass factory has been re-created, complete with demonstrations of the old craft, and paintings and markers have been created as clues to the world of young "James Cittie." Knowledgeable and oftentimes witty National Park Rangers lead walks and give talks that help put the pieces into perspective. Many of Jamestown's residents have been forgotten, but statues remain to honor Pocahontas, the Indian princess whose marriage to Englishman John Rolfe helped improve relations between their two peoples, and to commemorate Captain John Smith, the explorer who was president of the Jamestown Council from 1608 to 1609. The remains of the settlement called New Towne, established after 1620, help show the further development of the community.

Just next door on the mainland, at Jamestown Festival Park, you can board reconstructions of the three ships—the *Susan Constant*, the *Godspeed,* and the *Discovery*—that made the long ocean voyage to America and marvel that these tiny vessels ever survived. There is a reconstruction of the first fort carved out of the forest, high wooden walls protecting the tiny wattle-and-daub structures that were used for everything from houses to churches and armories. Inside the fort during the summer season costumed interpreters show you the crafts and trades of the era, such as basket making and turning clay from the riverbanks into earthenware pottery.

There is also the reconstructed Indian Village and Pavilions in the Festival Park, offering exhibits and dioramas tracing the events before, during, and after Jamestown's founding.

You could spend an instructive weekend just following the Colonial Parkway north from Jamestown into Williamsburg, the second Virginia capital, now a restored colonial town that has preserved better than any other single spot the life-style of eighteenth-century America. The seeds of the American Revolution were sown here, and the fate of the new nation was sealed with the final victory ending the Revolutionary War at Yorktown, the destination at the far end of the Colonial Parkway.

One way to fit all of this in might be to save the wealth of Williamsburg sightseeing for another visit, but to get the flavor of the town now by staying here. The James River plantations lie about midway between Williamsburg and the present capital of Richmond, 50 miles and an hour's drive away, and either town serves as a good home base for the weekend.

There are some interesting countryside bed-and-breakfast possibilities also in the heart of the plantation area near Charles City. North Bend Plantation, circa 1819, is a Virginia Historic Landmark on 250 acres that was used as headquarters by General Sheridan in 1864. The owners, George and Ridgely Copland, have family roots deep in Virginia history, and their home is filled with fascinating memorabilia. Piney Grove is an intriguing mix of 1800 log cabin and fine residence, recently restored into a welcoming small inn. Two fine restaurants, Coach House Tavern at Berkeley Plantation and Indian Fields Tavern, have also added appealing dining choices to the area.

Route 5, the plantation route between the two towns, is one of the oldest roads in the country. It follows an old Indian trail paralleling the river. As plantations and villages grew up beside the river, an overland route was built connecting them, known as the "new market road" because it literally connected the old markets of Williamsburg with the newer ones in Richmond. The road played a prominent part in both the Revolutionary and the Civil wars.

Heading west from Williamsburg, you are entering the lush agricultural region where the new English colonists began to make fortunes growing tobacco and other crops. Some of Virginia's most magnificent plantations were built here, and some are now open to the public, offering dramatic proof of how much things had progressed in the new colony in just one century.

The undisputed queen of the plantations is Shirley, founded in 1613, and the home of the Carter family since 1723. The superb red Flemish bond brick buildings in the Queen Anne forecourt are recognized as architectural gems unique in America. They were constructed by James Hill for his daughter Elizabeth, who married John Carter, son of planter "King" Carter, uniting two great Virginia families.

The Hills and Carters entertained the Byrds, the Harrisons, Washington, Jefferson, and many other prominent early Virginians here. Anne Hill Carter, mother of Robert E. Lee, was married in one of these rooms to Governor Harry "Lighthorse" Lee. The famous general spent several years in his mother's home, where he received part of his schooling. Hill Carter, Jr., now the ninth generation to live in the home, resides upstairs with his family, allowing the public in to see the stunning great rooms downstairs. The original family portraits, silver, and furniture remain, along with a tall carved walnut staircase remarkable for its lack of visible support.

Shirley's 800-acre estate continues to be a working farm, producing corn, barley, wheat, and soybeans. Besides the main house, many outbuildings have been preserved, among them a large two-story kitchen, laundry, smokehouse, dove cote, stable, and two sturdy brick barns.

Sherwood Forest Plantation stands out for its presidential residents, John Tyler and William Henry Harrison, and for a ghost, the Gray Lady, who has reputedly occupied the Gray Room parlor for 100 years. Legend has it that she would descend a hidden staircase and rock until dawn in a nonexistent rocking chair.

The gracious white-columned and porticoed Colonial home, said to be the longest frame house in America, was built in 1730 and redone by John Tyler when he retired from the White House in 1845. It has been occupied by members of the Tyler family ever since. It also boasts fine furnishings and a grand staircase, as well as a 68-foot ballroom. The house is open only by appointment, but the fine gardens are always available for strolling. The 1,600-acre plantation remains a working farm, as it has been for 140 years.

Two other homes of note are Westover, built about 1730 by William Byrd II, the founder of Richmond, and Evelynton, named for Byrd's daughter and once part of the Westover estate. The gardens, known for their elaborate gates, are the only part of Westover now open to the public. Evelynton has recently been refurbished and opened for tours.

The culmination of a plantation tour is Thanksgiving at Berkeley. The early Georgian mansion built by Benjamin Harrison in 1726 is said to be the oldest three-story brick house in Virginia, and is matched only by the Adams House in Massachusetts for producing two presidents, Benjamin's son, William Henry Harrison, and his great-grandson (also Benjamin). The younger Benjamin Harrison came home to Berkeley to write his inaugural address in the room where he was born. Every president from Washington to Buchanan enjoyed Berkeley's famous hospitality.

The Berkeley brochure claims six "firsts" in American history. The first bourbon was supposedly made here in 1622, and that same year, the first organized American war, an Indian massacre, took place on the grounds. The first commercial shipyard opened here in 1695, the first pediment roof went up in 1726, and while General Butterfield was quartered here with General McClellan in 1862, Butterfield composed the music for "Taps."

But the "first" that is celebrated with much ceremony each year is the one entered in the seventeenth-century records of the Berkeley Company. These papers commission Captain John Woodlief and 38 Englishmen to settle 100 acres in Virginia and to designate the date of their landing as an annual day of thanksgiving, the first official American thanksgiving.

On the first Sunday of November, food booths open and entertainment begins on the Berkeley grounds about 11:30 A.M., along with demonstrations of early colonial and Indian crafts. There are puppets, strolling musicians, Morris dancers, and a preprogram concert to keep everyone happy until the official ceremonies get under way at 1:30 P.M. These include speeches by a long list of dignitaries and a reenactment of the landing and prayer of the first settlers at Berkeley.

There are no turkey dinners, no cranberry sauce or pumpkin pie, which is possibly why the Massachusetts observance attracts a lot more followers.

What Berkeley's ceremonies do offer is another reminder of the importance of Virginia's settlers in building the nation we call America. And that alone is reason enough for thanksgiving.

Area Code: 804

DRIVING DIRECTIONS Virginia's plantation road is Route 5, between Richmond and Williamsburg. From D.C., take I-95 south to Richmond, then turn east on Route 5 to the plantations and Jamestown. Approximate distance from D.C. to Berkeley Plantation, 135 miles.

ACCOMMODATIONS *North Bend Plantation,* Route 1, Box 13A, Charles City, 23030, 829-5176, $$ CP ● *Piney Grove Bed and*

Breakfast, Route 1, P.O. Box 14B, Charles City, 23030, 829-2480, $$$ CP. See also Williamsburg, page 203, and Richmond, page 24.

DINING *Indian Fields Tavern*, Route 5, Charles City, 829-5004, restored home, excellent food, $$–$$$ ● *Coach House Tavern*, Route 5 at Berkeley Plantation, Charles City, 829-6003, $$. See also Williamsburg, pages 203–204, and Richmond, pages 24–25.

SIGHTSEEING *Virginia Thanksgiving Festival, Inc.*, Berkeley Plantation, Route 5, Charles City. Held the first Sunday in November, 829-6018, check current admission fees ● *Colonial National Historical Park*, Jamestown site, 8:30 A.M. to 6:30 P.M., $5 per car, $2 per person; Yorktown site, 9 A.M. to 6:30 P.M., free. These are summer hours; both have shorter hours rest of year. Check with superintendent, P.O. Box 210, Yorktown, 23690, 898-3400 ● *Jamestown Festival Park*, Route 21 and the Colonial Parkway. Hours: 9 A.M. to 5 P.M. Adults, $5.00; children, $2.50 ● *Shirley Plantation*, Route 5, Charles City, 829-5121. Hours: daily 9 A.M. to 5 P.M.; last tour at 4:30 P.M. Adults, $6.00; students, $4.00; children, ages 6–12, $3 ● *Sherwood Forest Plantation*, Route 5, Charles City County, 829-5377. Hours: daily 9 A.M. to 5 P.M. House tours by appointment, $4.75; grounds tour, $2 ● *Berkeley Plantation*, Route 5, Charles City County, 829-6018. Hours: daily 8 A.M. to 5 P.M. Adults, $7; ages 13–18, $4; ages 6–12, $3 ● *Evelynton Plantation*, Route 5, Charles City, 829-5075. Hours: daily 9 A.M. to 5 P.M. Adults, $5; ages 3–11, $2.50 ● *Westover*, off Route 5, Charles City County. Tours of grounds and garden only. Hours: daily 9 A.M. to 6 P.M. $2.

INFORMATION Virginia Division of Tourism, 1021 East Cary Street, Richmond, VA 23219, 786-4484.

WINTER

Overleaf: **Winter at Valley Forge, Pennsylvania.** *Photo courtesy of Montgomery County Convention & Visitors Bureau.*

Christmas Cheer in West Chester

West Chester, Pennsylvania, is a town that wears its history well. Over a period of more than 300 years, the seat of Chester County has acquired a wealth of fine architecture, from stone farmhouses to brick-paved streets of Federal town houses to massive-columned Greek Revival structures designed by the architect of the nation's Capitol. The elaborate columned buildings once caused this little town to be dubbed the Athens of Pennsylvania.

Come Christmas, all of the town is decked out with Victorian decorations and filled with cheer guaranteed to gladden the heart of even the Scroogiest. The annual West Chester Olde Fashioned Christmas celebration in early December offers live music, candlelight tours, goodies and greens from costumed street vendors, special shop window displays, ''Santa's Workshop'' for the kids, holiday menus at local restaurants, and seasonal entertainment from puppets to *The Nutcracker* ballet to Gilbert and Sullivan songs.

Most special of all is the annual Holiday House Tour, scheduled on the first Saturday each December to benefit the local YWCA. There are more than 20 stops on the tour, offering the chance to visit some of the most beautiful of the area's many historic homes. The houses are all the more interesting because so many contain family heirlooms handed down from generation to generation.

To get your bearings, first take a walk in West Chester to see the parade of architectural variety. You'll discover the green serpentine stone that is characteristic of the area, gingerbread Victorian porches, porticoed doorways, iron-lace fences, as well as those famous Greek columns adorning the courthouse, a local bank, and a church. Both the firehouse and the public library are Gothic buildings boasting Tiffany windows. Fine examples of the residential life of the 1800s can be seen in the restored houses on Portico Row, Pottery Row, Stone Row, and Wayne Square.

Having admired the homes from the outside, you'll be able to appreciate them even more on the house tour. Among the stops included in recent years are an early 1800s carriage house, now a gracious home filled with original family antiques and silver; a 1720 farmhouse lovingly restored with its original flooring, walk-in fireplace, mantels, doors, and hardware; and many of the Federal homes on the brick-paved streets in town. Some of these look-alike row houses hold surprises added by their modern owners. Skylights and eclectic furnishings and color schemes blend surprisingly well with the original exposed brick and giant hearths of the antique homes.

You may even visit West Chester's mayor's home, an 1880s slate-roofed Victorian with stencil decorations inside and a kitchen whose oak countertops were salvaged and recycled from an old local store. One Christmas, the colorful tree here was adorned with family treasures accumulated over many years.

All of the houses are decorated with old-fashioned greenery, bows, and lavish trees, making them all the more welcoming for sightseers.

The YWCA building itself turns into a crafts bazaar for the day, featuring handmade gifts, decorations, and candy. The Chester County Art Association also opens its Christmas Shop for business, while the YWCA and the West Chester Recreation Commission are transformed to Victorian soup-and-sandwich parlors offering homemade foods and baked delights.

The Chester County Historical Society Museum, a pleasure to visit in any season, often adds a special exhibit for the holidays. This exquisite small museum offers period room settings, a fascinating collection of antique clocks, furniture, inlaid chests, embroidery, Tucker porcelain, and majolica. The pieces are particularly fine, the kinds of antiques that are often featured on the covers of magazines for collectors.

After doing the sights by day, you can choose among the many special holiday plays and musical performances presented in the evening.

When the pleasures of West Chester are completed, you have more Christmas treats in store at two other traditional Brandywine Valley observances within a few minutes' drive. The Brandywine River Museum, noted for its Wyeth collections, will be offering its annual display of toy trains, children's illustrations, a winter scene populated by the antique doll collection of Ann Wyeth McCoy, and giant trees decorated with whimsical ornaments made from natural materials—the same lovely ornaments that have been selected to adorn the White House Christmas tree in past years.

At Longwood Gardens, the grounds turn into a wonderland of twinkling lights at Christmas, and the conservatory is abloom with four acres of red and white poinsettias and exquisitely decorated trees. To make things even nicer, some 100 musical events are held here throughout the holidays.

And a few minutes across the Delaware border, Winterthur, the famous house-museum of American furniture and furnishings from 1640 to 1840, has its rooms decorated for Christmas, each ready for entertaining with foods that would have been appropriate for its period.

It's a pre-Christmas outing all but guaranteed to send you home filled with the old-fashioned spirit of the season.

Area Code: 215

DRIVING DIRECTIONS West Chester is off Route 202, west of Philadelphia and north of Wilmington. From D.C., take I-95 north to Wilmington, then Route 202 north. Alternate route: Exit from I-95 at Route 272, just after the Susquehanna River Bridge, and follow Route 272 to Route 1 at Nottingham. Continue north on Route 1 to Chadds Ford, then north on Route 202 to West Chester. Approximate distance from D.C., 126 miles.

ACCOMMODATIONS *Fairville Inn,* Route 52, Fairville, 19357, 388-5900, restored 1820s home, lovely decor, new carriage house with private decks, $$$–$$$$ CP and afternoon tea ● *Brandywine River Hotel,* routes 1 and 100, Chadds Ford, 19317, 388-1200, 40-room hotel with the feel of a small inn, $$$ CP ● *Duling-Kurtz House,* South Whitford Road, Exton, 19341, 524-1830, charmingly furnished inn, $$–$$$$ CP ● Some delightful bed-and-breakfast inns in the nearby countryside include *Meadow Spring Farm,* 201 East Street Road (Route 926), Kennett Square, 19348, 444-3903, folksy, warm, $–$$ CP ● *Sweetwater Farm,* Sweetwater Road, P.O. Box 86, Glen Mills, 19342, 459-4711, elegant, $$$–$$$$ CP ● *Campbell House Bed and Breakfast,* 160 East Doe Run Road, Kennett Square, 19348, 347-6756, antique lover's delight—the furnishings are for sale, $ CP ● *The Whitethorne, Bed and Breakfast,* P.O. Box 92, Unionville, 19375, 793-1748, beautiful setting, $$ CP ● Many nice motels in the area; write for lodgings list.

BED AND BREAKFAST *Guesthouses,* RD 9, West Chester, PA 19380, 692-4575 ● *Bed & Breakfast of Chester County,* P.O. Box 825, Kennett Square, PA 19348, 444-1367.

DINING *La Cocotte,* 124 West Gay Street, West Chester, 436-6722, local French favorite, $$–$$$ ● *Pace One,* Thornton-Concord Road, Thornton, 459-9784, restored barn, good bet for Sunday brunch, $$–$$$ ● *Duling-Kurtz House* (see above), attractive setting and good food, $$$–$$$$ ● All of the following are attractive old country inns with atmosphere near West Chester: *Mendenhall Inn,* Route 52, Mendenhall, 388-1181, $$–$$$ ● *Historic Dilworthtown Inn,* Old Wilmington Pike and Brinton Bridge Road, Dilworthtown, 399-1390, $$–$$$ ● *Marshalton Inn,* 1300

West Strasburg Road (Route 162), Marshalton, 692-4367, $$–$$$ • *Chadds Ford Inn,* Route 1, Chadds Ford, 388-7361, $$–$$$ • See also Delaware, page 159, and Chester County, page 118.

SIGHTSEEING *YWCA West Chester Holiday House Tour,* 123 North Church Street, 692-3737, usually first Saturday in December, 10 A.M. to 4 P.M. Tickets by mail or at YWCA Saturday morning at 9 A.M. Call for current date and rates. For complete schedule of Olde Fashioned Christmas events and ticket order information, contact West Chester Chamber of Commerce, 42 East Gay Street, 696-4046 • *Brandywine River Museum,* US 1, Chadds Ford, 388-7601. Hours: daily 9:30 A.M. to 4:30 P.M. Adults, $3; ages 7–12, $1.50 • *Longwood Gardens,* US 1, Kennett Square, 388-6741. Hours: daily 10 A.M. to 5 P.M. Adults, $8; ages 6–14, $2 • *Winterthur Museum,* Route 52, Winterthur, DE, (302) 888-4600 or (800) 448-3883, Yuletide tours by reservation only, Tuesday to Saturday 10 A.M. to 3:30 P.M.; Sunday noon to 5:30 P.M. Adults, $9; under 17, $4.50.

INFORMATION Brandywine Valley Tourist Information Center at Longwood Gardens, Route 1, Kennett Square, PA 19348, (800) 228-9933.

Away from It All in Williamsburg

The colonial dame had lost her sheep.

Just as we emerged from the doorway of our eighteenth-century lodging, she came racing by, long skirts lifted to allow her feet to fly in pursuit of the flock scampering pell-mell down the road ahead of her.

Sights like that aren't unusual in historic Williamsburg, a sure cure for the winter doldrums. Virginia's colonial capital, a town that had a tremendous impact on the early development of our country, is most people's favorite historical attraction, and it's easy to see why. You not only come back with new knowledge and feel for the nation's heritage; you have a lot of fun.

Williamsburg is well known for its holiday festivities, when candlelight, caroling, and holiday trim turn the whole town into a Christmas card come to life. By all means come for Christmas if you can—but to experience a real escape to another time, come back when the throngs have left.

Winter Colonial Weekends change slightly in theme each year, but all offer uncrowded sightseeing by day and famous Groaning Board banquets with merry colonial entertainment to warm a winter's night. Free bus service connecting all the major sights also makes sure you stay snug no matter what the weather. If there's a dusting of snow to add a bit of magic, it's the frosting on the cake.

Historic Williamsburg consists of 173 acres of the original town, which was the center of America's wealthiest colony from 1699 to 1780. In practical terms, that means an area roughly ten blocks long and three blocks wide looking much as it did 200 years ago and packed with sights that can easily fill two days or more. Not the least of the pleasure of strolling Williamsburg's main thoroughfare, Duke of Gloucester Street, is the absence of twentieth-century traffic to spoil the illusion of another time. More than 90 acres of eighteenth-century greens and gardens surround the buildings, lovely in bloom but adding to the appeal even in winter.

This was a planned city, and within the street plan devised in 1699 are 88 original preserved and restored shops, houses, taverns, and public buildings. An additional 50 major buildings, including the Governor's Palace and the Capitol, have been rebuilt according to extensive archaeological research.

Williamsburg's streets and homes take on unusual vitality because of the costumed "residents" who provide the community with life beyond that of a colonial museum piece. Gaolers, militiamen, blacksmiths, coopers, bookbinders, milliners, and silversmiths can all be seen going about their daily routines. While you admire the finery of the much-photographed redbrick Governor's Palace, for example, you may encounter a resident waiting to air a grievance before the governor. In the 20 crafts shops in town, the artisans will gladly explain their techniques. Late in the afternoon, you might hear the music of the fife-and-drum corps going through its daily paces, and you never know just when you may encounter one of the "Life on the Scene" dramatizations given by the resident Company of Colonial Performers, many of them students at William and Mary College, whose handsome Georgian campus adjoins the historic district and is worth a tour on its own.

Your weekend should begin at the visitors center, where an excellent film puts all of the history into perspective, and maps help you get your bearings. Then hop on the free bus back to Duke of Gloucester Street and stroll, savoring the feel of the town and dropping into the various shops and buildings as the spirit moves you.

There are a few "don't miss" stops. A famous Williamsburg highlight is the Governor's Palace, its fine furnishings and gardens betokening the power and prestige of the Crown in colonial Virginia. Later it became the executive mansion for the first two governors of the independent colony, Patrick Henry and Thomas Jefferson.

Equally impressive is the Capitol, where Henry and Jefferson served in the Virginia legislature and where the Resolution for American Independence passed without a dissenting vote in 1776, even though this wealthiest of the colonies had the most to lose if its bid for freedom failed.

Raleigh Tavern, where patriots including George Washington gathered, is another significant site. A couple of standout homes are the Peyton Randolph House on Nicolson and the George Wythe House on Palace Green.

But you needn't feel bound by any special itinerary. The only "right" way to see Williamsburg is at your own pace and according to your own tastes. It's the ambience of the town that matters far more than any single attraction.

This mammoth restoration began in 1926 through the chance meeting of a minister and a millionaire. Dr. William A. R. Goodwin, rector of the Bruton Parish Church, where the people of Williamsburg have worshipped since 1674, sat next to John D. Rockefeller, Jr., at a Phi Beta Kappa dinner and gained his interest in saving the neglected former capital.

Bassett Hall, Rockefeller's own 1700s home just outside the historic area, is now one of the town's touring sights. It is a warm family home, seemingly modest until you note the 14 sets of fine china—a sign of Rockefeller's dislike for dining with the same plates on the table every night—or the fabulous folk art that was the passion of Abby Aldrich Rockefeller. The gallery bearing her name holds more of the collection that was Mrs. Rockefeller's legacy to Williamsburg.

The restoration efforts and the galleries at Williamsburg continue to expand. In 1985 there was the most important addition in some years, the DeWitt Wallace Decorative Arts Gallery, funded largely by a $14 million grant by DeWitt and Lila Wallace, cofounders of the *Reader's Digest*. The ten galleries here enable historic Williamsburg to display some 8,000 of the best items from its astonishing collection of seventeenth-, eighteenth-, and early-nineteenth-century English and American antiques. Many of these pieces have never before been on public view. The DeWitt Wallace Gallery is built partially underground and behind the reconstructed Public Hospital of 1773, which was the nation's first hospital for mental patients.

Within the historic homes are 225 period rooms furnished with 50,000 more choice pieces of the past, from four-poster beds to pottery and pewter and family portraits.

All of this is even more memorable if you are lucky enough to stay in one of the colonial houses right in the heart of history, which you can reserve through the Williamsburg Inn. The dining places in historic Williamsburg are also a step back in time, housed in real colonial taverns and serving up atmosphere along with traditional dishes.

There's so much more to see and do in this area, you could easily spend a week. Jamestown, Yorktown, the grand plantations along the James River are all minutes away. If you come back in spring or summer, there's also the big amusement park at Busch Gardens nearby.

But Williamsburg alone is more than enough reason for a trip. It's a welcome escape to yesteryear.

Area Code: 804

DRIVING DIRECTIONS   Williamsburg is on Route 60, off I-64 between Richmond and Norfolk. From D.C., take Route I-95 south, then I-64 east. Approximate distance from D.C., 162 miles.

PUBLIC TRANSPORTATION   Williamsburg is served by Amtrak and is only 45 minutes from either the Norfolk or the Richmond airport, even closer to Newport News. Limousine shuttle service is available at airports, along with special car rental rates for those with package reservations within Colonial Williamsburg.

ACCOMMODATIONS   Colonial Williamsburg reservations, Box B, Williamsburg, VA 23187, 229-1000 or (800) HISTORY ● *Williamsburg Inn* and *Historic Houses,* $$$$ ● *Lodge,* $$$$ ● *Motor House,* $$$ ● *Governor's Inn,* $$ ● Weekend packages, including two nights' lodging, two meals daily, and admission to Colonial Williamsburg, are considerably less than these rates individually; winter Colonial Weekends are a special bargain; write for current packages. Golf and tennis plans also available in season. For less-expensive lodgings, write for motel listings. Among conveniently located motels are *Holiday Inn East,* Capitol Landing Road at Parkway Drive, 23185, 229-0200 or (800) 368-0200, $$$ ● *Ramada Inn East,* 351 York Street, 23185, 229-4100, $$–$$$ ● *Best Western Patrick Henry Inn,* York and Page streets, 23187, 229-9540, $$–$$$.

DINING   In the historic district: *Christiana Campbell's Tavern,* Waller Street, serves George Washington's favorite, seafood, Southern fried chicken, spoon bread, sweet potato biscuits, $$$ ● *King's Arms Tavern,* Duke of Gloucester Street, quiet and refined,

Virginia ham and roast beef, $$–$$$ ● *Josiah Chowning's Tavern,* Duke of Gloucester Street, Brunswick stew, Welsh rabbit, colonial gambols and bawdy songs in the tavern after dinner, $$–$$$ ● *Shield's Tavern,* Duke of Gloucester Street, a 1989 addition, 18th-century tavern decor, working fireplaces, entertainment, spit-roasted meats and 18th-century menus, $$–$$$ ● Reservations for all, 229-2141 ● *Regency Room,* Williamsburg Inn (see above), elegant, excellent, $$$ ● *Motor House* (see above), for budget meals. All open for lunch, as is the inexpensive *A Good Place to Eat,* fast food in Merchants' Square, *Cascades* near the visitors center, and the *Clubhouse Grill,* overlooking the inn golf course ● Just outside the historic district, *The Trellis,* Duke of Gloucester Street, Merchants' Square, 229-8610, serves notable nouvelle cuisine, $$–$$$.

SIGHTSEEING *Colonial Williamsburg Foundation,* P.O. Box C, Williamsburg, 23187, 229-1000. Admission: Basic pass including transportation, choice of 12 exhibits (excluding Governor's Palace, DeWitt Wallace Gallery, Carter's Grove, Patriot's Tour). Adults, $19; ages 6–12, $12.50 ● *Royal Governor's Pass* includes all exhibits plus 1-hour guided Patriot's Tour for 4 consecutive days. Adults $22.50; ages 6–12, $14.75 ● *Patriot's Pass* includes all, valid for 1 year. Adults, $26; ages 6–12, $17. Museum pass for DeWitt Wallace Gallery and Bassett Hall, adults $11; ages 6–12, $7.25. Individual admissions, all ages: Governor's Palace, $13; Carter's Grove, $8; DeWitt Wallace Gallery, $7.50.

INFORMATION For accommodations and attractions outside the historic district, Williamsburg Area Tourism and Conference Bureau, P.O. Box GB, Williamsburg, VA 23187.

Christmas Lights in Pennsylvania

It's appropriate that Christmas should be a special occasion in Bethlehem, Pennsylvania.

The city's destiny was fixed on a Christmas Eve in 1741, when a group of pious Moravians gathered in a little log house in an unnamed settlement to light candles and sing. They called the town Bethlehem that night, and ever since, Christmas has been celebrated here in the same simple Moravian tradition, with candlelight and song.

The Moravian church is unique in many of its customs. The oldest Protestant denomination, it was established in 1457, 60 years before the Reformation in Europe, by a Bohemian religious reformer, Jan Hus; its members numbered about 200,000 during Martin Luther's time. By the end of the Thirty Years' War the membership had dwindled, but in 1722 the church was revived on the estate of Count Ludwig von Zinzendorf in Saxony, and followers built the town of Herrnhut nearby. From here they came as missionaries seeking converts in the New World.

The Christmas rites they brought with them from their German homeland are still observed in Bethlehem and in another early settlement, the tiny Pennsylvania Dutch town of Lititz. Each Moravian church and home traditionally hangs a multipointed giant star, similar to the finest ones used in German churches. They also display another German tradition, *putz,* an elaborate creation of detailed scenes from the Nativity using many natural materials in the settings. In the churches on Christmas Day, as the story is read, the appropriate scenes are lit. Afterward carols are sung.

A Christmas trip to share these lovely traditions adds a delightful dimension to the holiday, and also provides the opportunity for a family celebration that can include some of the more familiar observances held each year in Hershey, Pennsylvania. Since the Moravian displays are on view from early December until the end of the month, they are an excellent way to extend the joy of the season.

Bethlehem's glowing celebration has brought it the name ''America's Christmas City.'' All of the town is aglimmer with thousands of tiny white lights in the windows of homes and public buildings alike. Atop South Mountain, above the Lehigh College campus, the huge lighted Star of Bethlehem is visible for miles, a beacon drawing thousands for the famed Night Light tours, which give visitors a chance to see the town transformed by twinkling candlelight. Reservations are an absolute must for these popular tours.

The Night Light bus tours are led by guides in traditional Moravian attire who tell the story of the town's unique history as the bus traces the same paths used by early settlers over two centuries ago. The tour sets out from the Christmas visitors center at Broad and Guetter streets and moves through the historic area. On Church Street, it passes the Bell House, the Brethren's House, Central Church, and other Moravian structures remaining from colonial times—all with a single lighted candle in each window. Past the eighteenth-century Industrial Quarter, two more historic buildings, the John Sebastian Goundie House and the 1758 Sun Inn, come into view on Main Street.

Then the route crosses the Hill-to-Hill Bridge, with scores of Christmas trees lighting the way, toward the star shining atop South

Mountain. The Lehigh Valley below, a fairyland of glimmering lights, is pure magic.

Later, take a stroll in town to see the Moravian stars hanging in doorways and inside the vaulted Central Church, where a giant star six feet in diameter is a much-treasured local tradition. Elaborate stars were first made in Herrnhut in 1850. They usually have 26 spikes—18 four-sided points and 8 triangular points—though some showpieces such as the ones here and in Lititz may contain as many as 110 points. The delicate and difficult crafting of these intricate displays is an art that is often passed down from generation to generation. Originally constructed with a rigid metal core, they are now made of paper, softly lighted to give off a white or yellow glow.

The largest Bethlehem *putz* (from a sixteenth-century Saxon word meaning "to decorate") also is set up in the Central Church. Originally created in the mountains of medieval Germany, the *putz* differs from other Nativity representations in its emphasis on settings of natural materials such as moss, plants, rocks, evergreen sprigs, and tree stumps. Planning must start months before Christmas, when moss is collected from the woods and kept cool and moist to furnish a green foundation for the scenery. Canopies of stars are often used to represent the nighttime skies, and there may be simulated lakes made of mirrors.

The *putz* seeks to tell the whole Christmas story from the prophet's message, or Annunciation, to the flight into Egypt, with each scene a separate entity. Each is constructed anew every year by members of Moravian congregations. No two are exactly alike from church to church, since they are an expression of each builder's conception of the Nativity story. The only given is the scene of the Christ Child in the manger with Mary and Joseph in attendance. Other scenes often used show the angel appearing to Mary, the magi following the star, shepherds on a hillside with their sheep, and an angel bearing glad tidings. Two other *putz* scenes may be viewed at the East Hills Moravian Church on Butztown Road, and the Edgeboro Moravian Church on Hamilton Avenue. In addition to the elaborate community *putzes* in local churches, Moravian families usually make their own *putzes*—in miniature—also with natural materials for the landscapes. Families share their creations by visiting each other's homes on Christmas Day.

Though the nighttime scene is the most memorable one, there is much to see in Bethlehem by day in the historic district, the site of the original Moravian settlement, and in the restored buildings of one of early America's most prosperous industrial areas. Gemein House, the oldest of the original buildings, is now the Moravian Museum, filled with mementos of the early settlers. While you are in town, have a meal at the historic Sun Inn on Main Street. You'll be joining a guest roster that includes George Washington, John Adams, and General Lafayette.

Many other special events are held during this period, such as lantern-light evening walking tours of the historic areas and Christmas concerts by local choral groups, including the famous Bethlehem Bach Choir. Send for this year's complete schedule.

If you prefer a small-town setting for an introduction to a Moravian Christmas, the candlelit homes of Lititz have much village charm to offer. A walk down Main Street takes you past more than a dozen houses dating to the mid-1700s. Toward the end of the block are the brick and stucco buildings of the Moravian Church Square, which includes the church itself, as well as the original Brethren's and Sisters' houses and the 1767 Linden Hall, one of the oldest girls' schools in the country.

During the week after Christmas, the Lititz church offers half-hour light shows featuring the scenes of its *putz*.

Among the homes is the stately Victorian mansion built at 19 East Main Street by General John Sutter, who retired here after striking it rich in the California Gold Rush. The general was the first in Lititz to have indoor plumbing, not to mention a large wine cellar stocked with California wines. His home has been authentically restored and is used as an office by the Lititz Farmers First Bank. Sutter is buried in the Moravian Cemetery at the rear of the church. The very pleasant local inn, which dates back to 1754, bears his name.

There are two other nonreligious attractions in Lititz that are favorites at any time of year. In 1861 a local resident, Julius Sturgis, opened the first commercial pretzel bakery in America in one of the town's historic homes. The house, built in 1784, has been restored and contains a museum where visitors can see pretzels being baked in the original 200-year-old ovens. There are tours of the modern pretzel plant also. Guests from eight to eighty have fun here trying their own hands at some fancy pretzel twisting. They are rewarded with diplomas proclaiming their mastery of the art.

Wilbur's Chocolate Factory, with displays of historical candy-making equipment, tempts with demonstrations of how hand-dipped chocolates are made today. Sample boxes are for sale at outlet prices.

Christmas is not the only time when candles mark a holiday in Lititz. If you should ever happen back to this town on the Fourth of July, you'll find Lititz Springs Park lit with one of the country's most unusual Independence Day displays, a mammoth show of candlelight.

If you are looking for more Christmas lights, you'll find them in ample supply just a short drive away in Hershey, Pennsylvania. Hersheypark's Christmas Candylane glows from mid-November with lavish decorations and more than 300,000 lights. There are rides for the children, gift shops overflowing with everything from antiques to local crafts, and Christmas choirs strolling throughout this mock Tudor village.

Next door, Hershey Museum of American Life features a variety of holiday concerts, special exhibits, and activities for the children. Chocolate World visitors center features an animated elf exhibit in addition to its display of Hershey memorabilia, a free chocolate-making tour, and shops crammed with chocolate novelties and old-time ornaments. Hershey Theatre has a changing selection of holiday attractions, from performances of *The Nutcracker* to Broadway musicals.

Throughout town, horse-drawn carriage rides, Santa Claus adventures on old-fashioned trolley buses, holiday buffets, the annual Festival of Food and Light and Teddy Bear Jubilee, culinary demonstrations, and more pack the schedule—and if there's snow, cross-country skiing, sledding, and tobogganing are available at the Hotel Hershey.

For the ultimate dazzle of lights, make a detour on the way to or from Hershey, from Route 78 to Route 183 south to Bernville and down the clearly marked dark country road that takes you to the stupendous display known as Koziar's Christmas Village. It all began in 1948 when William M. Koziar began putting on a show of lights for his neighbors. Soon there were crowds, and the home became known as the Christmas House. The displays grew, and so did the crowds, until the present village was born. The spectacle now boasts more than half a million Christmas lights—along with two huge barns filled with handmade items, souvenirs, and a super-duper toy train display.

Yes, this one is decidedly commercial—but the kids "oohing" and "aahing" haven't been known to complain.

Area Codes: 215 for Bethlehem, 717 for Lititz and Hershey

DRIVING DIRECTIONS   For Bethlehem driving directions, see page 39. From Bethlehem to Lititz or Hershey, follow Route 22 west; it will merge with Route 78. Turn off on Route 501 south to Lititz; turn off on Route 743 south to Hershey. To go directly to Lititz, follow directions to Lancaster, page 104, then take Route 501 north for 7 miles. Approximate distance from D.C., 113 miles. For direct Hershey routes, see page 140. Approximate distance from D.C., 110 miles.

ACCOMMODATIONS   See Bethlehem, page 39. *General Sutter Inn*, 14 East Main Street, Lititz, 17543, 626-2115, $$ ● *The Alden House*, 62 East Main Street, Lititz, 17543, 627-3363, charming B&B in 1850s style, $$–$$$ CP ● *Hershey Hotel and Lodge,* Hershey Resorts, 17033, 533-2171 or toll-free (800) 533-3131, $$$–$$$$ CP (rates go up for New Year's weekend).

BED & BREAKFAST   *Hershey Bed & Breakfast,* P.O. Box 208, Hershey, PA 17033, 533-2928.

DINING   *General Sutter Inn,* Lititz (see above) $$ ● See Bethlehem, pages 39 and 40, Hershey, page 140, Lancaster area, pages 104 and 105.

SIGHTSEEING   *Bethlehem Christmas tours:* Hourlong tours offered daily through December 30, except December 24–25, at 5 P.M., 6:15 P.M., 7:30 P.M., and 8:45 P.M. *Reservations are essential.* Phone the Bethlehem visitors center at 868-1513 to reserve and check current rates ● *Lititz Moravian Church Christmas* Putz *Scene,* Church Square, Lititz, 626-8515. Hours: December 26–31 7 P.M. to 9 P.M., half-hour presentations. Free; donations welcome. Check church for current dates and hours ● *Sturgis Pretzel House,* 219 East Main Street, Lititz. Hours: daily 9 A.M. to 4 P.M. Adults, $.50; children, $.35 ● *Christmas in Hershey,* Candylane Hotline, 800-HERSHEY. Hours: mid-November to late December, weekdays 4 P.M.–9 P.M.; Saturday and Sunday 10 A.M.–10 P.M.. Call for exact dates, fees, and times of activities; most activities closed Christmas Day ● *Koziar's Christmas Village,* off Route 182, Bernville, (215) 488-1110, nightly from Thanksgiving to December 31, 6 P.M.–9 P.M.; Saturday and Sunday from 5:30 P.M. Admission, $3; ages 6–12, $2.50.

INFORMATION   The Visitors Center, Bethlehem Chamber of Commerce, 459 Old York Road, Bethlehem, PA 18018, 867-3788 ● Hershey Visitors Center, 400 West Hersheypark Drive, Hershey, PA 17033, 534-3005.

Strutting in the New Year in Philadelphia

It won't be "Auld Lang Syne" but "Oh, Dem Golden Slippers." On January 1, to the tune of hundreds of strumming banjos, that lively song traditionally leads off the annual Mummers Parade, strutting 20,000 strong down Philadelphia's Broad Street in the world's most spectacular salute to the New Year.

Twenty fancy brigades in dazzling costume, twenty-five string bands, and scores of brass bands join in the marathon festivities. The ten-hour parade kicks off at 7:45 A.M., but since the string bands heralding the splashiest part of the action don't make their appearance until 3 P.M., you don't have to get up early to join the fun.

It's an attraction that lures thousands to spend New Year's in Philadelphia, and no one goes home disappointed. The feathers and finery, the dazzle of colors and the imaginative motifs, from comic-strip characters to cheerleaders to Chinese dragons, add up to an unforgettable show.

Those marchers in their furs and feathers and fancy capes will actually be carrying on a festive amalgam of many of the New Year's customs that were brought to this country from other lands. The Swedes and Finns, for example, shot off guns to ward off evil in the New Year. The English and Welsh visited their neighbors to recite poems, and the Germans added the tradition of *Belsnickle,* the forerunner of Santa Claus, which in turn inspired additional comic masqueraders who rode through streets shouting and firing guns.

The word *mummer* is found in several of these cultures. In England, it referred to groups of youths who dressed up during Christmas week to perform silent plays about St. George and the Dragon, Father Christmas, and other characters. In German, the word *mummerkleid* means disguise.

In Philadelphia, the idea of a holiday "open house" was adopted by masked callers who were given candies, cakes, fruits, and drinks by their neighbors. The natives also initiated the Carnival of Horns, which drew thousands of costumed characters who celebrated the New Year with a cacophony of noisemakers.

In 1876, groups calling themselves Mummers added an annual march to Independence Hall, doing a strut version of a cakewalk that has become a trademark of the parade. The city's official organization of the event may have been more an effort to control the rowdy revelers than a spirit of holiday cheer, but the result nevertheless is one of the most exuberant celebrations in the country.

Each of the clubs that make up the Mummers has its own name—Silver Crown, Early Riser, and Trilby String Band, to cite a few—and each has its own requirements for admittance. Some people become involved because of a club in their neighborhood, others begin learning the contagious strut as children and can't wait to become part of a group.

Wearing the trappings of a Mummer takes dedication, however. Each Mummer creates and designs his own costume, some of the fancier ones costing several thousand dollars. A frame costume carried on wheels with a man inside can weigh as much as 300 pounds and measure 13 or 14 feet high. Other costumes with elaborate head pieces and backpieces strapped on by harnesses weigh as much as 125 pounds. The big parade climaxes a year of work for each participant. Many a last stitch is still being sewn early on New Year's Day.

This unique folk parade alone is worth a trip to Philadelphia, but it is far from the only reason to think about visiting the City of Brotherly Love. The new Philadelphia is a city reborn. Its historic neighborhoods have been revitalized into charming residential communities ripe for strolling. Independence Hall, the Liberty Bell, and the many other historic monuments tracing our country's birth are part of a handsome urban park rightfully billed as "America's most historic square mile." In Center City, half a dozen sleek new hotels have joined the new office towers that are rapidly tranforming the skyline, and there has been a veritable restaurant explosion, turning the city into a culinary capital.

With intriguing new shopping complexes to explore, 150 museums, the fine Philadelphia Orchestra, the bustling Italian market, the mansions of historic Germantown, the famous cheese-steak shops, the pretzel vendors, the world's largest city park, and the nation's oldest zoo, there is enough here to keep you busy for a month of weekends.

City hotels make it even more appealing with weekend and New Year's packages at bargain rates. Bring the kids for a family salute to the New Year, or if you want to make it the ultimate romantic New Year's Eve for two, check into the luxurious Hotel Atop the Bellevue, splurge on dinner amid the intimate charm and elegance of Le Bec Fin, the mid-Atlantic's only five-star restaurant, and go dancing at any one of the posh new hotels. You can sleep late on New Year's Day and enjoy a fine brunch in the Four Seasons Fountain restaurant before you head to the parade.

If you prefer smaller lodgings, two appealing choices await in the historic district. The Independence Park Inn is a stylishly renovated nineteenth-century building, and the Thomas Bond House is a charming Federal-period guest house run by the National Park Service.

A good place to begin your sightseeing is with a stroll through this area, which has been designated as Independence National Historical Park. You can stand right in the room where Benjamin Franklin and John Hancock framed the Declaration of Independence, and see Carpenter's Hall, where the first American Congress met, and Old City Hall, which housed the first U.S. Supreme Court. Don't overlook the intriguing underground museum dedicated to Ben Franklin, where you can see his many ingenious inventions, such as bifocals and library steps, or dial a telephone to hear a Franklin witticism on almost any topic or hear George Washington or John Adams talk about Mr. Franklin's contributions to his country. The telephone number to dial for each past patriot is posted on a giant directory complete with appropriate area codes.

Near the park are the charming restored Colonial town houses and cobbled streets of Society Hill. If you don't want to walk, you can see it all via horse-drawn carriage. Either way, when you want a break from history, head for the shops on Head House Square, a redbrick restored 1775 marketplace, or visit South Street, a mix of young, funky shops and gathering places for city nightlife.

Another quite elegant nearby shopping complex is the Bourse, once a Victorian merchants' exchange, now a series of shops and eateries. While you are in the neighborhood, look into the Curtis Center building, which houses the Norman Rockwell Museum, for an unexpected art treasure. One entire wall of the lobby shows off a Tiffany glass tile mosaic mural, the only one of its kind.

The Gallery Mall, at Ninth and Market, is one of the largest urban malls in the nation, with 110 shops and restaurants. The chic designer shops are clustered on Walnut Street and in the Bellevue, and antiquers won't want to miss the line up of stores on Pine Street, east of Broad Street.

The sightseeing possibilities in this city are all but endless. Walk narrow Elfreth's Alley, one of the oldest residential streets in the country, or visit the tiny Colonial home where Betsy Ross sewed the first American flag. If the weather is mild, walk down to Penn's Landing, on the waterfront, and board some of the tall ships at anchor. If you want to stay warmer, hop on one of the Victorian trolleys leaving from the Convention and Visitors Bureau for a tour through Fairmount Park with its mansions and Japanese teahouse and views of the boathouses on the Schuylkill River, or tour the period homes in Germantown.

If you want to do some museum hopping, head for the broad, flag-lined Benjamin Franklin Parkway, Philadelphia's answer to the Champs Elysées. Climb the stairs that the film *Rocky* made famous for a tour of the Philadelphia Museum of Art and its treasures, which include a knockout section of Oriental art. Nearby is the Rodin Museum, with the largest collection of the sculptor's works to be found outside of France. At the innovative Franklin Institute Science Museum, on the other side of the parkway, you can pilot a plane, steer a ship, or even walk through a giant human heart! The latest addition to this fabulous museum is the world's only Future Center.

In other parts of the city you can visit the world-famous Mummy Room at the University Museum, watch coins being made at the U.S. Mint, or discover the real world of the dinosaur at the Academy of Natural Sciences. The dinosaur exhibit is one of the best in the world and includes all the latest information that scientists have unearthed about these fascinating creatures, disproving many of the old theories about how dinosaurs lived. Kids love the participatory displays that allow you to learn from video discs, dig for fossils, assemble a dinosaur leg, or manipulate a giant jaw. And the TV screens showing how moviemakers have portrayed the dinosaur over the years in monster movies always attract a crowd.

Kids will also have a ball at the Philadelphia Zoo, where they can climb into a gigantic make-believe beehive or up into a tree house with the birds and butterflies.

The New Year's Day parade may also make you want to learn more about the Mummers, who have their own museum in town with a tile façade as colorful as their costumes.

Later in the afternoon when your energy flags, you can be revived by a proper English tea at the Four Seasons or Top of the Bellevue hotel.

Philadelphia offers pleasures of many kinds, but for color, there's nothing to compare with that inimitable march of the Mummers. It will send you home to a banjo beat auguring the happiest of New Year's.

Area Code: 215

DRIVING DIRECTIONS   Philadelphia is reached via route I-95 or 276/76. From D.C., take I-95 north. Approximate distance from D.C., 135 miles.

PUBLIC TRANSPORTATION   Frequent Amtrak trains, plus buses and planes. No car is needed in Center City.

ACCOMMODATIONS   Ask at all hotels for special New Year's or weekend packages and children's rates. Luxury hotels: *Four Seasons,* 1 Logan Square, 19103, 963-1500 or (800) 268-6282, indoor pool, $$$$ • *Hotel Atop the Bellevue,* Broad and Walnut streets, 19102, 893-1776, or (800) 222-0939, $$$$ • *The Rittenhouse,* 210 West Rittenhouse Square, 19103, 546-9000, $$$$ • *Society Hill Sheraton,* 2nd and Walnut streets, 19106, 238-6000 or (800) 325-2525, $$$$ • *Latham Hotel,* 17th and Walnut streets, 19103, 563-7474, $$$$ • *Palace Suites Hotel,* Benjamin Franklin Parkway at 18th Street, 19103, 963-2222 or (800) 225-5842, $$$$ • *Hershey Philadelphia Hotel,* Broad and Locust streets, 19107, 893-1600 or (800) 533-3131, indoor pool, luxury floor with hot tubs, saunas in suites, $$$$ • Moderate-price choices: *Independence Park Inn,* 235 Chestnut Street, 19106, 922-4442, small, attractive, $$$–$$$$ • *Thomas Bond House,* 129 South 2nd Street, 19106, 923-8523, charming historic-home-turned-inn, $$–$$$ • *Quality Inn–Center*

City, 501 North 22nd Street, 19130, 568-8300, $$–$$$ ● *Society Hill Hotel*, 301 Chestnut Street, 19106, 925-1394, $$$ ● *Comfort Inn–Penn's Landing*, Delaware Avenue and Race Street, 19106, 627-7900, $$.

BED AND BREAKFAST *Bed and Breakfast of Philadelphia*, P.O. Box 252, Gradyville, 19039, 358-4747 or (800) 733-4747 ● *Bed and Breakfast, Center City*, 1804 Pine Street, 19103, 735-1137 or 923-5459.

DINING Literally hundreds of possibilities. A few suggestions: *Le Bec Fin*, 1523 Walnut Street, 567-1000, splurge at the city's best, $$$$ ● *The Palace Cafe*, Palace Suites Hotel (see above), $$$$ ● *Deux Cheminees*, 1221 Locust Street, 790-0200, more fine French, $$$$ ● *La Truffe*, 10 South Front Street, 925-5062, French, both traditional and nouvelle, $$$$ ● *Windows on the Water*, Piers 3 and 5, Delaware Avenue, 351-4151, views, entertainment, contemporary American menu, $$$ ● *Ciboulette*, 1312 Spruce Street, top choice, haute cuisine at fair prices, $$$ ● *White Dog Cafe*, 3420 Sansom Street, 386-9224, university area, informal, interesting menu, $$–$$$ ● *Alouette*, 334 Bainbridge Street, 629-1126, mix of French and Thai influences, $$$–$$$$ ● *Apropos*, 211 South Broad Street, at Walnut, 546-4424, bistro atmosphere, imaginative menu, $$–$$$ ● *Marabella's*, 1420 Locust Street, 545-1845, trendy, seafood, burgers, pasta, $–$$ ● *DiLullo Centro*, 1407 Locust Street, 546-2000, elegant decor, fine Italian food, $$–$$$ ● *Il Gallo Nero*, 254 South 15th Street, 546-8065, a less-pricey Italian favorite, $$–$$$ ● *Dante's & Luigi's*, 762 10th Street, 922-9501, modest old-timer near the Italian market, $–$$ ● *Strolli's*, 1528 Dickinson Street, 336-3390, no decor, Italian bargain, reservations necessary, $ ● *The Commissary*, 1710 Sansom, 569-2240, "in" spot, includes Southwest and Cajun at *USA Café*, $–$$; self-service at *Downstairs*, $; hot sandwiches at the *Piano Bar*, $ ● *DiNardo's Famous Crabs*, 312 Race Street, 925-5115, the name says it, $–$$$ ● *City Tavern*, 2nd and Walnut, 923-6059, revolutionary history, good choice for lunch, $, or dinner $$–$$$ ● *Dickens Inn*, 421 South 2nd Street, 928-9307, pub atmosphere, roast beef, Yorkshire pudding, $$–$$$. For a feast of sights, sounds, and food selections at lunchtime, visit the stalls at Reading Terminal Market, the nineteenth-century marketplace still thriving at 12th and Arch streets.

SIGHTSEEING *Mummer's Parade*, January 1, 7:45 A.M. to 5 P.M. on Broad Street. Grandstand seats, $5, $3, and $2 from visitors center or City Recreation Department, 1450 Municipal Services Buildings, 15th and JFK Boulevard, Philadelphia 19107, 636-1666 ● *Independence National Historical Park*, 3rd and Chest nut streets, 597-8974. Hours: daily 9 A.M. to 5 P.M. Free • *Betsy Ross House*, 239 Arch Street, 627-5343. Hours: daily 9 A.M. to 5 P.M. Free • *Olde City Trolley Tours*, leaves from visitors center, 16th Street and JFK Boulevard, 879-4044. Check for current schedules and rates • *Philadelphia Museum of Art*, 26th Street and Benjamin Franklin Parkway, 763-8100. Hours: Tuesday to Sunday 10 A.M. to 5 P.M. Adults, $4; under age 18, $2; free on Sunday until 1 P.M. • *Franklin Institute Science Museum*, 20th Street and Benjamin Franklin Parkway, 564-3375. Hours: Monday to Saturday 10 A.M. to 5 P.M.; Sunday noon to 5 P.M. Adults, $5; ages 4–11, $4 • *Rodin Museum*, 22nd Street and Benjamin Franklin Parkway, 763-8100. Hours: Tuesday to Sunday 10 A.M. to 5 P.M. Donation • *Academy of Natural Sciences*, 19th Street and Benjamin Franklin Parkway, 299-1000. Hours: Monday to Friday 10 A.M. to 4 P.M.; weekends to 5 P.M. Adults, $4.50; children, $3.50 • *University Museum*, 33rd and Spruce streets, 898-4000, Tuesday to Saturday, 10 A.M. to 4:30 P.M.; Sunday 1 P.M. to 5 P.M. Donation • *Mummers Museum*, 2nd Street and Washington Avenue, 336-3050. Hours: Tuesday to Saturday 9:30 A.M. to 5 P.M.; Sunday noon to 5 P.M. Adults, $1.50; children, $.75 • *Norman Rockwell Museum*, 601 Walnut Street, 922-4345. Hours: daily 10 A.M. to 4 P.M. Adults, $1.50; children under 12, free; no charge to see mosaic in building lobby • *Philadelphia Zoo*, Fairmount Park, 34th Street and Girard Avenue, 387-6400. Hours: Monday to Friday 9:30 A.M. to 5 P.M.; weekends to 6 P.M. Adults, $4.50; children, $2.50 • *U.S. Mint*, 5th and Arch streets, 597-7350. Hours: May to September, Monday to Saturday, daily 9 A.M. to 4:30 P.M.; October to December, closed Sunday; January to March, closed Saturday and Sunday. Free • *Philadelphia Carriage Company*, 500 North 13th Street, 922-6840. Guided tours of historic areas from Independence Hall, February to December, daily, weather permitting. Phone for current hours and rates. See also page 58 for Germantown attractions.

INFORMATION Philadelphia Convention and Visitors Bureau, 1515 Market Street, Philadelphia, PA 19102, 636-1666. In the city, the visitors center is located at 16th Street and JFK Boulevard. Hours: open daily 9 A.M. to 5 P.M. except holidays. For information packet, call toll-free (800) 321-WKND.

Winter Wonder in West Virginia

Winter in the Mountain State is the magic season when brooks and waterfalls freeze to shimmering crystal, every tall tree and mountain is crowned by whipped-cream white, and sugar-coated panoramas await around every bend of the road.

In the area called the Potomac Highlands, the snows are bountiful, an average of 200 inches annually, and so are the mountaintops, 110 of them with an elevation over 4,000 feet. That means winter pleasures galore, whether you want to schuss down the slopes, make tracks cross-country, take a turn on ice skates or a sled, snowshoe through the woods, or simply stay indoors in front of a cozy fire, enjoying the snowscape outside the window. With several state parks, four downhill mountains, and five cross-country ski areas to choose from, there is something here for everyone.

Canaan Valley State Park offers the closest drive and the most variety. This unique 15-mile-long, 5-mile-wide basin stands 3,200 feet above sea level, capped with mountains reaching up to 4,200 feet.

The skiers found it early. The Washington, D.C., Ski Club used to come for the phenomenal snowdrifts they called Little Tuckerman's, in honor of the famous ravine on New Hampshire's Mt. Washington. In 1954 a rope tow was built, and the first commercial ski area south of the Mason-Dixon line opened for business. Later the area was chosen as the West Virginia state park system's winter sports center.

Today, as a four-season resort park, it offers a major ski area, eight miles of cross-country trails, a toboggan run, and an outdoor skating rink well lighted for après-ski fun. A 250-room lodge provides comfortable motel-type rooms with a view. The main lodge has a big, welcoming fireplace in the lobby, a snack bar for light lunches, and the big Aspen Dining Room, offering moderate prices and a picture window overlooking the night action on the lighted skating rink. Downstairs, a new indoor pool, exercise room, sauna, and Jacuzzi await. Cabins are also available, including cozy fireplaces.

In recent years Canaan's ski area has added a quad chair lift, a 2,000-foot expert trail ominously named Gravity, night skiing, and extensive snow-making to augment Mother Nature in her slow seasons. And the facilities are still being improved. With a vertical drop of 850 feet, the mountain now offers 21 trails and good professional ski instruction. It's an ideal place to learn the sport, and a particularly welcome destination for families, since shuttle bus service from the lodge transports eager-beaver youngsters who want to hit the slopes before their parents are ready to venture out into the cold. There is also a nursery providing care for infants and toddlers, and the special Ski 'n Play program for children ages three to six.

The park recreation staff also provides indoor activities for small fry, from crafts lessons to games, and there are family movies at night. Novice ice skaters of all ages will find instruction available, and rentals are offered for sleds as well as skates.

Blackwater Falls State Park is only about ten miles from Canaan Valley in Davis, a village with the look of a Western frontier town and some alternate lodgings for those who might choose not to stay in the parks.

Blackwater Falls does offer its own lodge and dining room, as well as a dramatic outlook. The 65-foot waterfall that tumbles down the rocks into the gorge in summer becomes a frozen still life in winter. You can view the falls from the panoramic overlooks provided around the park or, better yet, put on your long johns and boots and take a walk through the silent snow to enjoy the wonder of winter.

Blackwater Falls State Park also has a cross-country skiing center and trails; good skiers can take a 7.8-mile trail connecting to Canaan Valley. Both state parks offer rentals and lessons, as well as the rare chance to break into fresh powdered snow disturbed only by the early morning tracks of deer and snowshoe rabbits. Beginners should be aware that there is no grooming of the trails, however, and choose their courses accordingly.

For both the unpracticed and the most-experienced on cross-country skis, the White Grass Ski Touring Center provides additional options. Almost ten miles of its meadowland trails and wooded slopes are machine-groomed, and there are many challenging downhill trails for advanced skiers and those who use the Telemark skis that incorporate some of the features of both downhill and cross-country equipment.

Timberline, a newer downhill area near Canaan, attracts many for its two-mile beginner run, attractive modern lodge and restaurant, and condominium lodgings near the foot of the triple chairlift. Several other condominium complexes near Davis offer spacious rentals, as well.

True big-league skiing awaits for those who are willing to drive farther south into the mountains to Snowshoe. The area that calls itself Island in the Sky sits atop a 4,848-foot-high ridge with views that seem to go on forever. Snowshoe Mountain has an elevation of 3,250 feet, challenging trails (including the legendary 6,180-foot Cupp Run), and a ski-village ambience, complete with restaurants, nightlife, and such niceties as hot tubs and indoor pools. Lodgings are in condominium units within distance of the lifts and all the activities. If you want a different perspective of the mountains, rent a horse at the stables at the bottom of the hill for a scenic ride through the winter woods. For those who want the challenge and the fun of a sophisticated ski area, this is definitely the place.

Skiers in the D.C. area also might remember that Snowshoe is part of the Allegheny Front, which catches the storm clouds as they move east from the Great Lakes, so that the snows here come early and stay late, long after spring has arrived in the capital.

Down the hill just a bit from Snowshoe is Silver Creek, a ski resort with a nine-story hotel at the base of its own ten-trail slopes. This smaller resort is especially well suited to beginners.

If you choose this route and also want to get in some cross-country skiing, you will find rentals and trails just down the hill and south a few miles at the Elk River Touring Center in Slatyfork.

A final recommendation is in order for those whose favorite winter sport is cuddling by the fire. You won't find a more romantic spot than Cabin Lodge, north of Davis in Aurora, West Virginia. This three-bedroom log cabin tucked away beside a brook amid snow-covered spruce and hemlock is the kind of quaint and cozy hideaway you might wistfully conjure up while gazing out at the snow from a city window.

They work hard in West Virginia to keep the roads clear so you can enjoy the winter snowscapes and outdoor fun, but nonetheless plan on plenty of extra time for the mountain highways. The views here are so spectacular that it's hard to resist the urge to pause and gaze, or to capture it all with a camera.

Area Code: 304

DRIVING DIRECTIONS   From most locations to the east, West Virginia's mountains are best approached from I-81 south in Virginia. From D.C., take I-66 west to Strasburg, Virginia, then Route 81 south. For Canaan, exit at Route 33 and continue west to Route 32 north. Approximate distance from D.C., 185 miles. For Showshoe, continue south on I-81 to Staunton, then west on US 250, south on Route 42 to Goshen, then Route 39. At Marlinton, turn north on Route 219 to Showshoe. Approximate distance from D.C., 245 miles. A bit longer route to Snowshoe, but one with better roads, is to continue on I-81 to Route I-60/64 west, then turn north on Route 219 at Lewisburg. From Canaan to Snowshoe, follow Route 33 to Elkins, then Route 219 south.

PUBLIC TRANSPORTATION   Air service to Elkins, 35 miles from Canaan, 48 miles from Snowshoe; or to Lewisburg, 65 miles from Snowshoe. Amtrak serves White Sulphur Springs, just outside Lewisburg.

ACCOMMODATIONS *Canaan Valley Lodge,* Canaan Valley Resort State Park, Davis, 26260, 866-4121 or 800-CALL WVA, $–$$ • *Blackwater Falls Lodge,* Blackwater Falls State Park, Davis, 26260, 259-5216 or 800-CALL WVA, $ • *Twisted Thistle,* bed-and-breakfast, 4th Street, Davis, 26260, 259-5389, $ • *Bright Morning Bed and Breakfast,* Main Street, Davis, 26260, 259-5119, $$ CP • *Black Bear Woods Inn and Condominium Resort,* Route 1, P.O. Box 55, Canaan Valley, Davis, 26260, 866-4319, (800) 553-BEAR out of state, indoor pool, cross-country slopes, $$$–$$$$ • *Deerfield Village,* Route 1, P.O. Box 152, Canaan Valley, Davis, 26260, 866-4698, (800) 342-3217 out of state, condo rentals, $$$$ • *Timberline Resort,* P.O. Box 625, Canaan Valley, Davis, 26260, 866-4801, (800) 843-1751 out of state, slopeside condo rentals, $$$. (Note that most 1-bedroom condos sleep four; all are much less in summer.) • *Cabin Lodge,* Box 355, Aurora, 735-3563, $$$ • *Snowshoe Village,* Snowshoe, 572-5252, variety of condominium accommodations, discuss your own needs, $$–$$$$ • *Whistlepunk Village,* Snowshoe Mountain, 572-1126 or (800) 624-2757, inn and condominiums, health club, indoor pool, outdoor Jacuzzi, $$$–$$$$ • *The Inn at Snowshoe,* Linwood Road, Slatyfork, 572-2900, motel at the base of the mountain road, indoor pool, Jacuzzis, $–$$$ • *Willis Farm Lodge,* Slatyfork, 572-3771, modest homey lodgings, good home cooking, adjoining Elk River Touring Center, $–$$ • *The Lodge at Silver Creek,* P.O. Box 159, Silver Creek, 572-4000, (800) 624-2119, high-rise condominium lodgings, $$–$$$.

DINING *Canaan Valley Lodge* (see above), $–$$ • *Blackwater Falls Lodge* (see above), $–$$ • *Oriskany Inn,* Route 32, Canaan Valley, traditional favorite, $$–$$$ • *Bear's Den,* Black Bear Resort (see above), $$ • *Golden Anchor,* Route 32 south, Canaan Valley, 866-CRAB, seafood with mountain views, $–$$ • *Bull & Frog,* Route 32, Canaan Valley, pleasant, 866-4555, $$ • *Sirianni's Pizza Cafe,* Main Street, Davis, 259-5454, local favorite, $ • *Bright Morning* (see above), bountiful breakfast buffets, $ • *The Red Fox Inn,* Whistlepunk Village, Snowshoe, 572-1111, best on the mountain, also good for Sunday brunch, $$–$$$ • *Skidder Pub,* Timberline Lodge, Snowshoe Village, burgers, salads, $ • *Goodtime Bobby's Eating and Drinking Emporium,* Mountain Lodge, $$.

SPORTS Check current prices and conditions at all ski areas. *Canaan Valley Ski Area,* Canaan Valley State Park, Route 1, P.O. Box 39, Davis, 26260, 866-4121, (800) CALL-WVA out of state •

Blackwater Ski Touring Center, Blackwater Falls State Park, P.O. Drawer 490, Davis, 26260, 259-5216, (800) CALL-WVA out of state ● *White Grass Ski Touring Center,* Route 1, P.O. Box 37, Davis, 26260, 866-4114.

INFORMATION   Potomac Highlands Travel Council, P.O. Box 1459, Elkins, WV 26241, 636-8400 ● Tucker County Chamber of Commerce, Route 32, P.O. Box 565, Davis, WV 26260, 259-5315.

Celebrating George at Valley Forge

Martha Washington must have baked a mean birthday cake back in the 1700s. No doubt both she and the general would be pleased to know that over 250 years later, George's birthday remains cause for celebration—and that cake made from Martha's own recipe is one of the main attractions at the annual observance held at Valley Forge, Pennsylvania.

Since Valley Forge country also offers plenty of scenery, shopping, and history beyond the military, it makes a perfect Washington's Birthday weekend outing.

It could not have been a happy birthday for George Washington, quartered with his army at Valley Forge during the freezing winter of 1777–78. During their six-month encampment after triumphant British troops had bested the Americans and occupied Philadelphia, the tired, ill-equipped, and poorly trained Continental army retreated, only to battle new enemies at Valley Forge—hunger, disease, and the fury of a winter that proved fatal to 2,000 of the 12,000-man force. Nevertheless, the survivors revived their spirit and forged a fighting unit that emerged to defeat the British army at the Battle of Monmouth in nearby New Jersey on June 19, 1778. The park is a monument to their triumph against terrible odds, a victory that buoyed the army for the battles still ahead.

The big National Historical Park at Valley Forge traditionally marks Washington's birthday weekend by re-creating the days of that fateful winter. Valley Forge takes on a military air on Saturday, when Boy Scouts converge on the park for their annual pilgrimage, living on the grounds in quarters like those of the original encampment. Everyone is invited to visit their camp that day at the Muhlenberg Brigade huts.

Costumed in authentic colonial uniforms, soldiers from the re-created Second Pennsylvania Regiment move in on Sunday to occupy the rude log huts where the Continental army lived. Their colorful living-history interpretation of encampment life includes firing demonstrations, military music and drills, and camp crafts, including outdoor cooking.

The talks, usually given on Monday, are historical eye-openers, a personal look at Washington and his officers, their personalities, and their contributions to the war effort. Monday is also the day when women of the Valley Forge Historical Society follow Martha's "Great Cake" recipe and serve up portions to visitors at their museum. Visitors also get copies of the recipe for the giant yellow cake studded with fruit and nuts. It calls for 40 eggs, "five pounds of flower [sic]," and a lacing of half a pint of wine plus some fresh brandy.

Besides the special events, the Valley Forge Visitor Center presents its regular 15-minute movie on the role of the area during the War for Independence and the many historic sites in the beautiful park that are open to the public.

Pick up a self-guiding tour map, and drive the marked route through the 2,800-acre complex. If the February fields are blanketed with snow, you might even consider a jaunt on cross-country skis.

Depending on how serious you are about your history, you can spend anywhere from two to four hours touring the sights, which include extensive remains and reconstructions of major forts and lines of earthworks; the Artillery Park, where cannons were massed and gun crews were trained; Washington's headquarters in a seventeenth-century home; quarters of other officers; and the Grand Parade, where General von Steuben rebuilt the army and where the happy news of French support was announced on May 6, 1778. These, plus the reconstructed huts, monuments, and markers help to re-create vividly the story of the men at Valley Forge who helped shape our nation's future.

Don't forget a stop at the lovely Washington Memorial Chapel on the grounds, known for its stained-glass windows, and the Museum of the Valley Forge Historical Society, which offers exhibits relating to the Revolution worth a look even when there is no birthday cake on the menu.

When your park explorations are done, many other pleasures await in Valley Forge country. One of the most fascinating is the home of John James Audubon, now part of the Mill Grove Audubon Wildlife Sanctuary just beyond the park entrance. Take the Route 422 expressway north across the Betzwood Bridge, exit at Audubon/Trooper, turn left at the first light, and proceed straight ahead to the scenic estate that was the first American home of the famed naturalist, the first to portray authentically birds and other wildlife from living subjects and their habitats. You'll find samples of his beautiful art here, including the enormous folios of *Birds of America* rarely seen by the public, and his restored studio and taxidermy room. The colorful murals on the downstairs walls are also extraordinary, done in 1954 as a tribute to Audubon's local adventures. The six miles of scenic marked trails along the Perkiomen Creek take you through the settings that inspired young Audubon to begin his illustrious career.

From Mill Grove, turn left at the end of the drive and follow the road (it eventually becomes Route 363) north about ten miles to Route 73. About a mile farther on your right you'll find signs directing you to the entrance of the Peter Wentz Farmstead. The eighteenth-century German-style house has been restored in detail to the way it appeared when it was Washington's headquarters before and after the battle of Germantown. The house is attractive enough to have merited a cover of *House & Garden*. One of its surprising features is the bold stenciling that decorates the walls, an early-American equivalent of wallpaper. In season, the Wentz complex is a working farm, and year-round there are demonstrations of period crafts on Saturday afternoon.

Another interesting spot at the intersection of routes 363 and 73 is the Ironmaster's House and Museum, where ironmaster Harry Houpt conducts free tours of his mini-museum filled with the colonial ironwork that was a specialty of this area. He will also take you through his own shop.

Valley Forge country abounds with shopping possibilities, beginning with the neighboring King of Prussia mall, one of the nation's largest. More unusual wares can be found on Route 73 heading toward Skippack Village. The Cedars Country Store on Route 73 has been in continuous operation since 1849, and along with the usual stock of a country store, there are some tempting country collectibles for sale, both here and in adjoining shops.

Many more temptations await about three miles west, at Skippack Village. Country antiques and accessories are the specialty, but you'll find almost every kind of antique and craft in the dozens of shops lining the main street of this quaint eighteenth-century village. It's a bit touristy, but the crowds are small when you visit out of season. Skippack also offers pleasant restaurants for a lunch break to fortify yourself for further forays into the stores.

When evening comes, there are many good restaurants in historic quarters in the area, plus an entertainment that is quite a surprise here in Quaker Pennsylvania. The show at Lily Langtry's, the nightclub at the Valley Forge Sheraton, offers Las Vegas–style revues, toned down only a little for local sensibilities. The hotel also offers "theme rooms" that might be just the thing if you have a fantasy or two to play out.

For a springlike end to a winter weekend, take the half-hour drive to Kennett Square and Longwood Gardens, where the four-acre indoor conservatory is already resplendent with spring bloom. It's a guaranteed spirit lifter in February, an encouraging sign that it won't be long before Valley Forge itself will trade its stark winter coat for a pink-and-white canopy of 50,000 dogwood trees in bloom.

Area Code: 215

DRIVING DIRECTIONS   Valley Forge is west of Philadelphia at routes 202 and I-276, the Pennsylvania Turnpike. From D.C., take I-95 north to Route 202 near Wilmington, and proceed north to Valley Forge. Approximate distance from D.C., 125 miles.

PUBLIC TRANSPORTATION   Valley Forge is served by Philadelphia transportation just 30 minutes away.

ACCOMMODATIONS   *Guest Quarters at Valley Forge,* Chesterbrook Corporate Center, Wayne, 19087, 647-6700 or (800) 424-2900, suites at room prices, $$$$; weekends, $$$ CP ● *Stouffer–Valley Forge Hotel,* North Gulph Road, King of Prussia, 19406, 337-1800, toll-free (800) HOTELS-1, nicest of the local hotels, $$$$; weekends $$ ● *Valley Forge Hilton,* 251 West DeKalb Pike (US 202), King of Prussia, 19406, 337-1200, (800) 445-8667, $$$, ask about weekend packages ● *Sheraton Valley Forge,* Route 363, King of Prussia, 19046, 337-2000 or (800) 325-3535, $$$; weekends $$ ● *Budget Lodge at Valley Forge,* 815 West DeKalb Pike, King of Prussia, 19046, 265-7200, $ ● *Joseph Ambler Inn,* 1005 Horsham Road, Montgomeryville, 19454, 362-7500, fine 1734 inn on 12 acres, furnished with antiques, $$–$$$ CP.

BED AND BREAKFAST   *Bed & Breakfast of Valley Forge,* P.O. Box 562, Valley Forge, PA 19481, 783-7838.

DINING   *Kennedy-Supplee Mansion,* 1100 West Valley Forge Road, King of Prussia, 337-3777, elegantly restored 1852 mansion on the park grounds, excellent food, $$$ ● *Jefferson House,* 2519 DeKalb Pike (Route 202), Norristown, 275-3407, attractive mansion setting, $$–$$$ ● *Picket Post Restaurant,* 100 Old Gulph Road, Gulph Mills, 525-8716, candlelit dining in home that was headquarters for Aaron Burr during winter of 1777–78, $$–$$$ ● *The Baron's Inne,* 499 North Gulph Road, King of Prussia, 265-2550, Swiss specialties, Colonial decor, convenient, $$–$$$ ● *The Audubon Inn,* 2801 Egypt Road, Audubon, 666-5553, another oldie, dating to 1710, $–$$$ • *Trolley Stop,* Route 73, Skippack, 584-4849, $–$$$ • There are also several restaurants, chain and otherwise, in the large King of Prussia shopping mall near Valley Forge.

SIGHTSEEING *Valley Forge National Historical Park,* Valley Forge, 783-7700, information desk, 783-0220. Hours: daily 8:30 A.M. to 5 P.M.; summer hours until 6 P.M. Admission free; fee for guided bus tours • *Valley Forge Historical Society Museum,* Route 23, Valley Forge National Historical Park, 783-0535. Hours: Monday to Saturday 9:30 A.M. to 4:30 P.M.; Sunday 1 P.M. to 4:30 P.M. Adults, $1; under 10, free • *Mill Grove,* Audubon and Pawlings roads, Audubon, 666-5593. Hours: Tuesday to Sunday 10 A.M. to 5 P.M. Free • *Peter Wentz Farmstead,* off Route 363, 584-5104. Hours: Tuesday to Saturday 10 A.M. to 4 P.M.; Sunday 1 P.M. to 4 P.M. Free • *Longwood Gardens,* Route 1, Kennett Square, 388-6741, conservatory open 10 A.M. to 5 P.M. Adults, $8; children, $2.

INFORMATION Valley Forge Convention and Visitors Bureau, P.O. Box 311, Norristown, PA 19404, (215) 278-3558.

Getting a Lift at Wintergreen

He loves the wide-open spaces, but she'd rather sightsee or shop. Or she's a hotdog skier, but he'd rather relax by a pool. Or maybe it's the kids who want to romp in the snow, while Mom and Dad prefer to read or cuddle in front of the fire.

When temperaments don't match, planning a winter weekend can be a problem, but not at Wintergreen, Virginia's spectacular mountaintop resort. There's everything or nothing to do here, all in a matchless setting astride the Blue Ridge Mountains.

Wait until you see the views from this classy complex set on more than 10,000 sky-high acres. With over half of its own land set aside as permanent undisturbed forest and borderlands that include the Blue Ridge Parkway, a 2,400-acre U.S. Park Service reserve, and the George Washington National Forest, Wintergreen's unspoiled vistas go on forever from a ridgeline that reaches an altitude of 3,850 feet.

It would be worth the trip if you did nothing but gaze out your picture window at the hazy blue ridges spreading out in the distance, especially since the windows are in stylish privately owned condominiums that range from spacious studios to lavish mountain chalets with as many as six bedrooms. Depending on your mood, you can choose a quiet retreat hidden in the trees or be right in the middle of the action on the ski slopes, so the skiers can schuss out the door in the morning leaving everyone else in peace. Almost all of the accommodations give you a fireplace and deck of your own, and while the tab isn't cheap, it's made a lot more affordable with the option of making your own meals, a special saving where families are concerned. You don't even have to worry about the cooking if you emulate some of the veteran guests who come bearing frozen casseroles made in advance at home.

They care a lot about the environment at Wintergreen, and all the homes are tasteful, built of natural wood in modernistic architecture that has been carefully regulated to blend into the setting. Not every one knows that rates here go by the number of bedrooms, not by the views, so by all means request a prime location.

If you prefer country-inn ambience, you can find that here as well at Trillium House, a warm, modern 12-room inn right in the midst of the complex.

Snowbirds won't have to complain about sissy slopes at Wintergreen if they ski the Highlands, where three expert trails offer vertical drops of 1,000 feet and respectable runs over 4,000 feet long. They won't even allow you on the Wild Turkey run until you demonstrate your proficiency at parallel turns. There's plenty of other terrain for all abilities on the other seven trails, and snowmaking over 83 acres keeps the hills powdery even in winters when Mother Nature doesn't bless the Virginia slopes. Half the trails are well lighted for night skiing, and five chair lifts, including one triple-seater, help hold down the waits in line. In past seasons the mountain has offered another bonus, a free first lesson for beginners.

If you don't want to risk your limbs or brave the cold, however, just grab your bathing suit instead and head for the Wintergarden Spa. Facilities here include a big indoor swimming pool, as well as hot tubs, a Jacuzzi and sauna, and a convenient informal cafe, the Garden Terrace, for lunch with a mountain view. There's also an exercise room if you feel the need for a workout afterward.

Inveterate shoppers need go no farther than the Mountain Inn to whip out their credit cards. The center of activity and site of the excellent Copper Mine Restaurant, where lounge entertainment continues into the evening, the inn adjoins a small shopping gallery that includes home furnishings and mountain crafts, as well as a good selection of sportswear. There's a food market on the grounds also, but you'll do a lot better in price if you buy your groceries before you take the two-mile drive to the top of the mountain.

For dining variety, the Verandah offers Virginia specialties and seafood, light fare is served at the Grist Mill, or you can head down the hill for a special culinary treat, the down-home country cooking at Rodes Farm Inn. This nineteenth-century brick farmhouse is chockablock with rural charm—red-checked cloths on the tables, handmade quilts on the walls, and a fireplace in every room. The story goes that Rodes Farm came into being when Nelson County native Marguerite Wade welcomed the new developers of Wintergreen back in the 1970s with a nice lunch of fried chicken, home-made bicuits, and all the fixings. Knowing a good thing when they tasted it, they soon made plans to open an inn with Marguerite running the kitchen. Her chicken, roast beef with gravy, barbecued ribs, and country ham have become all but legendary, and no trip to Wintergreen is complete without a Rodes Farm breakfast with Marguerite's thick homemade apple butter waiting to be spread on the hot biscuits.

Wintergreen's final big advantage is location. Many ski areas are so remote that there isn't much to do nearby. But an hour's drive from this plush aerie zips you to Charlottesville, just 43 miles away, and tours of Thomas Jefferson's Monticello, James Monroe's Ash Lawn, and the splendid campus of the University of Virginia. It's only a mile to the Blue Ridge Parkway or another easy drive over to Route 81 and the Woodrow Wilson home in Staunton, the Hall of Valor Civil War Museum at New Market, and the historic campuses of Washington and Lee and Virginia Military Institute in the charming little town of Lexington.

There is one definite problem with Wintergreen, however, and that is deciding which season here is the best. Winter sports and snowscapes are followed by dogwoods in bloom and such a profusion of wildflowers that seminars and field trips are scheduled in spring. As soon as the weather permits, the golf course opens, offering 50-mile views and cool mountain breezes. There are 18 tennis courts, an outdoor pool, stables with horses for rent, fish ripe for catching in mountain streams, and miles of hiking trails, including a section of the Appalachian Trail. Come autumn, the views rival those of the Blue Ridge Parkway—and without the traffic.

Wintergreen lifts the spirits no matter when you come. If you're smart, you will sample all the seasons before you decide on a favorite.

Area Code: 804

DRIVING DIRECTIONS   Wintergreen is off I-64 west of Charlottesville. From D.C., take Route 66 west, then Route 29 south to Route 64 west. At exit 20, pick up Route 250 in Crozet, continue west to Route 6 east, then turn left and continue for 8.7 miles. Where Route 6 splits with Route 151, follow Route 151 south 5.4 miles to Route 664, turn right, and watch for Wintergreen, 4.5 miles ahead. Approximate distance from D.C., 168 miles.

PUBLIC TRANSPORTATION Air and Amtrak service to Charlottesville, 43 miles away. Limousine service available from Charlottesville.

ACCOMMODATIONS AND INFORMATION *Wintergreen,* Wintergreen, VA 22958, 325-2200, wide range of condominiums and many package plans available for skiing, golf, and tennis, $$$– $$$$. For reservations only, toll-free (800) 325-2220 ● *Trilium House at Wintergreen,* P.O. Box 280, Nellysford, VA 22958, 325-9126, $$$ CP.

DINING *Copper Mine,* $$–$$$ ● *The Verandah,* $$–$$$ ● *Garden Terrace,* $$–$$$ ● *Grist Mill,* $–$$ ● *Rodes Farm Inn,* $–$$.

Beyond the Inner Harbor in Baltimore

Oh, how things have changed in this Cinderella city.

Not too long ago, the only reason most tourists stopped in Baltimore was because they were stuck in traffic on the way to Washington or Philadelphia. But ever since the urban miracle that totally transformed the Inner Harbor area, the tourists come flocking—so many, in fact, that in a recent year once-dowdy Baltimore outdrew Disney World in number of visitors. These days, an out-of-season visit is a good idea to avoid the crowds!

The tourists come primarily for Harborplace and the Gallery, the shiny glass pavilions on the water housing hundreds of shops and restaurants that are a constant source of fun, festivity, and good food. They also come to gawk and grin at the 8,000 species of fish, mammals, and birds in the National Aquarium; to board the historic ships in the harbor; and to find out about everything from earth to outer space at the Maryland Science Center, with its planetarium and IMAX theater, the other star Inner Harbor attractions.

But for newcomers who venture farther afield the real discovery is the pleasures that lie beyond the Inner Harbor. That's where the real Baltimore awaits, a big warm historic mix of neighborhood moods from ethnic to elegant to colonial charm, offering a rich variety of color, cuisine, heritage, and arts that catch many visitors totally by surprise.

First-timers will still want to start with the miraculous Inner Harbor, until recently an area of rotting wharfs so decayed that native H. L. Mencken described it as "smelling like a billion polecats." One and a half billion dollars and a lot of vision have turned it into the spark of a city revival that is visible for blocks beyond, as more new office towers, hotels, and shopping complexes continue to rise, totally changing the face of the city. You can get an eagle's-eye view of all the changes from the top of I. M. Pei's World Trade Center on Pratt Street.

Get an early start to avoid the lines at the National Aquarium. It's worth a wait, however, because it's quite a show, beginning with your ride up a moving ramp into a rain forest, and continuing as you descend a spiraling walkway to the Atlantic Coral Reef and Open Ocean exhibits. You are eye to eye with the colorful denizens of the deep all the way. Another highlight is the Sea Cliffs exhibit, where puffins and razorbills are at home, fascinating birds with an uncanny ability to "fly" underwater in search of food. The newest addition is a building housing marine mammals, including those perennial favorites, whales and dolphins.

It takes a morning to do justice to the aquarium, and if hunger pangs strike when you are done, you could conveniently proceed right across to Harborplace. Deciding what to eat here is a major undertaking. There are dozens of snack stands, restaurants, and markets in the Light Street Pavilion, still more cafes at the twin Pratt Street Pavilion. Should it be a mix of goodies from stands like the Flying Fruit Fantasy and Shuckers Oyster Bar, or calzone at Mama Ilardo's? Or will it be a sit-down French meal at Jean Claude's Cafe or the Greek Taverna Athena—or the famous desserts at Vaccaro's?

In a way it is appropriate that Harborplace should be located in Baltimore, a city long known for its variety of ethnic foods. Seven public markets featuring fresh fruits and vegetables, meats, and seafood from Chespeake Bay are open here, the *newest* of them over 100 years old. The first and still the largest is Lexington Market, a downtown landmark since 1782 and the oldest public market in the country. This is an authentic market, not one created just for tourists, though many a knowledgeable visitor does join the locals in line for the delectable chowder and crab cakes at Faidley's. Since the markets are not open on Sunday, you may want to detour here for Saturday lunch.

At some point, you'll probably want to return for the other popular sights around the Inner Harbor—the Maryland Science Center with its planetarium, IMAX theater, computers, and hands-on exhibits, and the harbor ships, the most famous being the *Constellation*, the oldest commissioned warship in the U.S. navy.

At Harborplace, the shops await, from standards like Benetton or Pappagallo to specialty boutiques, filled with games, kites, music boxes, or a selection of wares with a bear motif. The vendors here also offer every kind of souvenir imaginable, emblazoned "Baltimore Is for Crabs." There are upscale stores like Ann Taylor and Brooks Brothers across the way at the Gallery, and still more to see at Market Place and the Brokerage, new developments adjacent to Harborplace offering entertainment, and even more restaurants and shops.

Antique buffs should note that the city's Antique Row is away from the city center, between the 700 and 800 blocks on North Howard Street and the 200 block of West Read Street.

For a superb view of the harbor and the busy working port of Baltimore, climb the stairs behind the Science Center to the colonial streets of Federal Hill. You'll be standing on the spot where 4,000 local citizens celebrated the ratification of the U.S. Constitution. The recently restored homes in this and many other of Baltimore's older neighborhoods are evidence that the spirit of revival begun at the harbor has been contagious. Take a long walk or a short drive downhill around Sharp Street for a look at one of the city's prides, the Otterbein Homesteading Project. Residents bought up the blighted eighteenth-century row houses here for a dollar each, and carefully restored them, turning the area into a beautiful and vibrant historic district.

Fell's Point, the oldest port area in the city, has also had a major renaissance in recent years. It still looks remarkably like the salty seafaring community that was laid out in 1763, with its cobbled streets and charmingly restored eighteenth- and nineteenth-century residences and shops. Someone called it a cross between Georgetown and Dublin. One of the most appealing of the city's lodgings is the Admiral Fell Inn, three Fell's Point town houses put together to make an elegant hostelry on the site of an old seaman's hotel.

Pick up a walking tour at the Admiral Fell that points out some of the more interesting neighborhood sights, including Broadway Market, a miniature version of Lexington Market dating back to 1784; the Robert Long House, the oldest home in the area, now restored and furnished by the Society for Preservation of Federal Hill and Fell's Point. Adjoining Brown's Wharf, the city's oldest warehouse, is new construction along the water with architecture that is hard to distinguish from the old, housing even more new shops and cafes. As you stroll, check out the galleries and shops and little theaters, the cafes and clubs that are sprouting like wildflowers,

turning Fell's Point into a lively center for young nightlife. Among
the restaurants, Bertha's is known for mussels, Admiral's Cup for
cozy pub atmosphere. A number of cafes offer music; take a stroll
and listen for your favorite.

For a total change of scene, hop the trolley or the bus that goes
from the Inner Harbor up Charles Street, newly spruced up as a
cultural corridor of galleries and shops leading to Mt. Vernon Place.
This square of parks and fountains, laid out in 1827 and centered on
a 160-foot Washington Monument that predates the one in the nation's capital, is the heart of the elegant, arts-centered part of Baltimore. The 22 buildings around the square and those in some 40
blocks surrounding it are the cream of Baltimore's late-nineteenth-
and early-twentieth-century architecture, and include the homes of
some of the city's most noted earlier residents—Johns Hopkins,
Enoch Pratt, and George Peabody, to name a few.

The noted Peabody Conservatory of Music is found on Mt. Vernon Place, and next to it is the Peabody Library, a five-tiered, skylighted Victorian beauty maintained by Johns Hopkins University
and containing original manuscripts by Beethoven, Purcell, and
Handel. Nearby, on West Monument Street, is the Maryland Historical Society, where you can see the original manuscript of the
''Star-Spangled Banner,'' as well as a display of toys, costumes,
silver, and furniture.

The prize of Mt. Vernon Place is the magnificently restored Walters Art Gallery, a mini-palace that has been rightfully called one of
America's great museums. On its four floors are the treasures
amassed by Henry and William Walters, a father and son whose
collections are dazzling in their range and profusion, paintings from
every major period of art, plus sculptures, armor, stained glass,
Roman sarcophagi, Russian icons, Renaissance bronzes, Sèvres
porcelain, jewelry, and silver. A new wing to be completed in 1991
will add display space for some 7,000 pieces of Oriental art.

An equally amazing Baltimore art collection was gathered by two
sisters, Claribel and Etta Cone, and you'll find it at the Baltimore
Art Museum. Just continue north on Charles Street past the attractive turn-of-the-century row houses of Charles Village near the
Johns Hopkins campus, and you'll come to the museum, where the
Cone Collection of Impressionist art is housed in its own wing. It
contains many fine pieces, but the real jewel of the collection is the
selection of works by Matisse—42 oils, 18 sculptures, 36 drawings,
155 prints, and 7 illustrated books. You also might want to stop at
the museum's American Wing to see the outstanding exhibit of
early furniture. And the Museum Café, overlooking a sculpture garden, is a fine choice for brunch, lunch, or dinner.

Among the other prime attractions in Baltimore are the homes of
some of its favorite sons, Edgar Allan Poe, H. L. Mencken, and

Babe Ruth. The last offers not only baseball lore but a nostalgic view of the era when colorful Ruth was the Sultan of Swat. Two more only-in-Baltimore sights are the B & O Railroad Museum, where you can explore the nation's first passenger station and climb aboard some magnificent antique trains, and Fort McHenry, where the sight of the high-flying giant star-spangled banner that inspired Francis Scott Key to write the national anthem stills brings a proud swell of patriotism.

Two unusual collections that may interest aficionados are on display at the La Crosse Hall of Fame Museum on the Johns Hopkins campus and the Jockey Hall of Fame at Pimlico Racetrack, the site of the spring Preakness, one of the nation's top races.

Come evening, there is music in the city's striking Joseph Meyerhoff Symphony Hall, as well as opera at the Lyric Opera House, a reproduction of Germany's Leipzig Music Hall. The Morris Mechanic Theatre in the downtown Charles Center is a major stop for national touring companies as well as a favorite for pre-Broadway tryouts, and the Center Stage is the respected local regional theater company. Concerts are also presented at the Peabody Conservatory of Music and by the Chamber Music Society of Baltimore at the Museum of Art.

When it comes to fine dining in Baltimore, the top choices are the romantic Conservatory atop the Peabody Court Hotel and the elegant and intimate Hampton's at the Harbor Court Hotel. Note that both hotels have attractive, moderately priced cafes as well. Tio Pepe, Maison Marconi's, and the Prime Rib, longtime local favorites, continue to draw crowds, and there are many interesting choices along Charles Street, known now as Restaurant Row.

But some of the best of Baltimore eating is found in the city's many modest ethnic neighborhoods. A few recommendations: Sabatini's and Capriccio in Little Italy; Haussner's, a mini-museum of rococo art in the German area of town; and Ikaros in Greektown. For crab cakes, Obrycki's (open only April to November), Angelina's, and Something Fishy came in behind Faidley's in a recent local poll. Too new to rate at press time was the Eastern Shore at Harrison's Pier, a branch of the highly regarded Tilghman Island restaurant.

Scores of luxury hotels have risen to accommodate the growing tourist trade in Baltimore. Once again, Harbor Court and Peabody Court get the nod for elegance. Welcome among the newcomers are some small gracious accommodations, such as the Admiral Fell, Shirley-Madison, and Society Hill inns, that bring a bit of country-inn ambience to the neighborhoods of the city.

The Inner Harbor has made all of Baltimore come alive, and it is the lure that keeps so many visitors coming. But it is the pleasures beyond the harbor that keep them coming back.

Area Code: 301

DRIVING DIRECTIONS   Baltimore is reached via routes I-95, I-83, and I-70. From D.C., follow I-95 north or take the Baltimore-Washington Parkway. Approximate distance from D.C., 37 miles.

PUBLIC TRANSPORTATION   Frequent Amtrak and bus service and many air connections via BWI airport.

ACCOMMODATIONS   Many hotels offer better rates on weekend package plans, especially off-season—be sure to ask. *Peabody Court Hotel,* 612 Cathedral Street at Mt. Vernon Square, 21201, 727-7101, elegant, on city's nicest square, $$$$ ● Across from the Inner Harbor: *Harbor Court Hotel,* 550 Light Street, 21202, 234-0550, small and exquisite, $$$$ ● *Hyatt Regency,* 300 Light Street, 21202, 528-1234, $$$$ ● *Stouffer Harborplace Hotel,* 202 East Pratt Street, 21202, 547-1200, $$$$ ● *Brookshire Hotel,* 120 East Lombard Street, 21202, 525-1300, all suites, $$$$ ● *Baltimore Marriott Inner Harbor,* Pratt and Eutaw streets, 21201, 962-0202 ● *Day's Inn,* 100 Hopkins Place, 21201, 576-1000, $$$ ● *Holiday Inn Inner Harbor,* 301 West Lombard Street, 21201, 685-3500, $$$ ● Some budget choices: *Tremont,* 8 East Pleasant Street, 21202, 576-1200, and *Tremont Plaza,* 222 St. Paul Place, 21202, 727-2222, both (800) 638-6266, all suites, $$–$$$ ● *Comfort Inn,* 24 West Franklin Street, 21201, 727-2000, $–$$ ● *Susse Chalet,* 4 Philadelphia Court, 21237, 574-8100, motel, $–$$ ● More intimate B&B hotels in city neighborhoods include: *Admiral Fell Inn,* 888 South Broadway, Fell's Point, 21231, 522-7377, charming, in lively neighborhood, $$$ CP ● *Society Hill Hotel,* 58 West Biddle Street, 21201, 837-3630, Victorian charm near Meyerhoff Symphony Hall, $$$ CP ● *Society Hill–Hopkins,* 3404 St. Paul Street, 21218, 235-8600, $$$ CP ● *Society Hill–Government House,* 1129 North Calvert Street, 21202, 752-7722, restored 1800s mansions, $$$ CP ● *Shirley-Madison Inn,* 205 West Madison Street, 21201, 728-6550, 1880 Victorian near Mt. Vernon Square, $$–$$$ CP.

BED AND BREAKFAST   *Amanda's Bed and Breakfast Reservation Service,* 1428 Park Avenue, Baltimore, 21217, 225-0001 ● *The Traveller in Maryland, Inc.,* P.O. Box 2277, Annapolis, 21404, 269-6232, in D.C. (301) 261-2233 ● *Maryland Reservation Center, Inc.,* 66 Maryland Avenue, Annapolis, 269-7550; outside MD, (800) 654-9303.

DINING   *The Conservatory,* Peabody Court Hotel (see above), $$$$ ● *Peabody's,* Peabody Court Hotel (see above), light fare, $$

● *Hampton's,* Harbor Court Hotel (see above), $$$$ ● *Cafe Brighton,* Hampton Court Hotel (see above), $$ ● *JaFe,* Brookshire Hotel (see above), Japanese and French, good reports, $$–$$$ ● *Museum Café,* Baltimore Museum of Art, Art Museum Drive, 235-3930, international menu, best when you can see the sculpture garden, $$ ● *Eastern Shore,* Harrison's Pier 5, 783-5553, crabs and fried chicken are the specialties, $–$$$ ● *Tio Pepe,* 10 East Franklin, 539-4675, Spanish, $$–$$$ ● *The Prime Rib,* 1101 North Calvert Street, 539-1804, American menu, $$$ ● *Maison Marconi,* 106 West Saratoga, 752-9286, seafood in 1800s town house, $–$$$ ● *Olde Obrycki's Crab House,* 1729 East Pratt Street, near Fell's Point, 732-6399 (open only April to November), $–$$$ ● *Ikaros,* 4805 Eastern Avenue, 633-3750, Greek, $–$$ ● *Grille 58,* Society Hill Hotel (see above), $$–$$$ ● *Bertha's,* 734 South Broadway, Fell's Point, 327-5795, mussels, $–$$$ ● *Admiral's Cup,* 1645 Thames Street, Fell's Point, 675-6988, $$–$$$ ● *Something Fishy,* 606 South Broadway, Fell's Point, 732-2233, pricey seafood, just go for the crab cakes, $$–$$$ ● *Capriccio,* 845 Fawn Street, Little Italy, 685-2710, $$–$$$ ● *Sabatini's,* 901 Fawn Street, Little Italy, 727-9414, $–$$$ ● *Haussner's,* 3244 Eastern Avenue, 327-8365, German, $–$$$ ● *Angelina's,* 7135 Harford Road, Beltway exit 31, 444-5545, Italian, also known for crab cakes, $–$$$ ● *Brass Elephant,* 924 North Charles Street, 547-8480, northern Italian, $$–$$$ ● *Louie's Bookstore Cafe,* 518 North Charles Street, 962-1224, classical music, eclectic menu, $–$$ ● *Kawasaki,* 413 North Charles Street, 659-7600, Japanese, sushi bar, $–$$ ● *Owl Bar,* Belvedere Hotel, 1 East Chase Street, 547-8220, pub for light fare, $.

SIGHTSEEING *Inner Harbor,* Pratt and Light streets, includes the following: *Harborplace,* two pavilions of food and shops. Admission, free. *National Aquarium,* Pier 3, Pratt Street. Hours: daily 10 A.M. to 5 P.M.; Friday to 8 P.M.; from May 15 to September 15, Saturday and Sunday also to 8 P.M. Adults, $7.75; students, $6; children, $4.75. *Maryland Science Center & Planetarium,* 601 Light Street, 685-5225. Hours: Monday to Thursday 10 A.M. to 5 P.M.; Friday and Saturday 10 A.M. to 10 P.M.; Sunday noon to 6 P.M.; June 25 to September 1, daily 10 A.M. to 8 P.M. Adults, $6.50; children, $5.50; planetarium, $1 extra. U.S. Frigate *Constellation.* Hours: mid-September to mid-June, daily 10 A.M. to 4 P.M.; June 15 to Labor Day to 8 P.M.; Adults, $2; children, $1 ● *Mt. Vernon Place,* Charles and Monument streets, attractions around this square include *Peabody Library,* 17 East Mt. Vernon Place. Hours: Monday to Saturday 9 A.M. to 5 P.M. Free ● *Walters Art Gallery,* 600 North Charles Street, 547-9000, Tuesday to Sunday 11 A.M. to 5 P.M. Adults, $3; under 18, free ● Other special city sights: *Baltimore*

Museum of Art, Charles and 31st streets, 396-7101. Hours: Tuesday to Friday 10 A.M. to 4 P.M.; Saturday and Sunday 11 A.M. to 6 P.M.; Thursday to 9 P.M. Adults, $2; under 21, free. Free on Thursday ● *Babe Ruth House/Maryland Baseball Hall of Fame,* 216 Emory Street, 727-1539. Hours: April 1 to October 1, daily 10 A.M. to 5 P.M.; rest of year to 4 P.M. Adults, $2.50; children, $1.25 ● *H. L. Mencken House,* 1524 Hollins Street, 396-7997. Hours: Wednesday to Sunday 10 A.M. to 5 P.M. Admission, $1.75 ● *B & O Railroad Museum,* Pratt and Poppleton streets, 237-2387. Hours: Wednesday to Sunday 10 A.M. to 4 P.M. Adults, $3.50; children, $2.50 ● *Fort McHenry,* foot of East Fort Avenue, 962-4299. Hours: daily 8 A.M. to 5 P.M.; summer to 8 P.M. Adults, $1; under 17, free ● *Lexington Market,* Lexington and Eutaw streets, 685-6169. Hours: Monday to Saturday 8:30 A.M. to 6 P.M. Free ● *Edgar Allan Poe House,* 203 North Amity Street, 396-7932 ● *Top of the World* observation deck, World Trade Center, 837-4515. Hours: Monday to Saturday 10 A.M. to 5 P.M.; Sunday noon to 5 P.M. Adults, $2; ages 5–15, $1.

INFORMATION   Baltimore Area Convention and Visitors Association, 1 East Pratt Street, Baltimore, MD 21202, 837-4636 or (800) 282-6632.

Tracking the Snow in Western Maryland

When they tell you there is snow awaiting in Garrett County, Maryland, believe it, even if there is nary a snowflake where you live.

We found out for ourselves driving west on Route 40 from Cumberland, Maryland, one fine February day, when the sun was shining, the sky was blue, and the ground was bare. Then we started to climb—and climb and climb—and a few minutes later as we crossed the county border, we were looking at a powdery white landscape and were knee-deep in the middle of a snowstorm.

Garrett County, which accurately calls itself Maryland's Best Kept Secret, is the triangular far end of the state, sandwiched between West Virginia and Pennsylvania, and its terrain has more in common with its mountainous neighbors than with the rest of its own state. The second-largest and most sparsely populated of Maryland's counties, it lies within the Appalachian Plateau, and contains five main mountain ridges with an average elevation of 2,300 feet above sea level. The highest point, Backbone Mountain, stands some 3,340 feet high.

Besides the mountains, trees and lakes are the dominant features of the 662-square-mile Garrett landscape. Three state forests comprising some 75,000 acres of wilderness and six state parks add up to more trees than people and plenty of wide-open space for enjoying nature.

Deep Creek Lake, a man-made wonder covering nearly 3,900 acres, is the state's largest freshwater lake. Created in 1925, the lake is now owned by the Pennsylvania Electric Company and leased to the Maryland Inland Fish and Game Commission for a fee of one dollar a year for public recreational activities.

In spring and summer the boaters and fishermen and swimmers hold sway in Garrett County, in autumn the leaf watchers take over, but come winter, this is a snow lover's paradise. The Allegheny Front, which captures moisture moving east from the Great Lakes, accounts for the perennial winter coat of white, even when lowlanders haven't seen a sign of snow.

Wisp Ski Area takes advantage of all that white stuff with 23 downhill trails along the slopes of Marsh Mountain, part of the Allegheny Range. With a respectable elevation of 3,080 feet, a vertical drop of 610 feet, and trails up to two miles long, it is a small mountain, but challenging enough for all but the most expert. It is ideal for learners, and should the average 90 inches of snow fail to accumulate, skiing is still guaranteed by extensive snowmaking that covers 90 percent of the mountain. Most of the trails also are lighted for night skiing to prolong the fun.

Cross-country skiers and hikers will also find good going amid gorgeous winter scenery in Garrett County parks. There are cleared and marked trails in New Germany State Park, Deep Creek State Park, and Herrington Manor State Park, the last a scenic five-mile route around Herrington Lake. Trails also can be found at Swallow Falls State Park, where the scenic falls were the site of a 1918 camp used by automotive pioneers Henry Ford, Thomas Edison, and Harvey Firestone. Muddy Creek Falls in Swallow Falls Park is a dramatic 64-foot tumble to the rocks below that turns into a fairytale scene frozen in motion in winter.

Another way to enjoy the superb winter scenery is on horseback. Western Trails, on Route 219 on the way to Swallows Falls, will be glad to oblige with horses by the hour, or half-day and whole-day trail rides.

This is also prime territory for snowmobilers, who have 35 miles of trails to themselves. And hardy fishermen don't give up when the ice covers Deep Creek Lake. They just chop a hole in the ice, drop their lines, and go right on catching yellow perch, pike, and pickerel. The ice fishermen patiently tending their lines add a colorful note to the frozen landscape.

While Garrett is mainly a mecca for winter-sports enthusiasts, there is a little bit of sightseeing nearby when you want to come in from the cold. The center of things is Oakland, a pleasant little town boasting the "Church of Presidents," the St. Matthew's Episcopal Church on Liberty Street, where Presidents Grant, Harrison, and Cleveland worshiped while vacationing nearby at Deer Park, once a fashionable resort. President and Mrs. Cleveland spent one week of their honeymoon here in 1886.

The Queen Anne–style B & O Railroad station, built in 1884 in Oakland, is one of the oldest in the country. John W. Garrett (for whom the county was named) was then president of the Baltimore and Ohio Railroad and did much to further its development. During his presidency, the railroad built large summer resorts in Deer Park and Oakland. The coming of the railroad also was responsible for the growth of Mountain Lake Park—just east of Oakland off Route 135—which became a noted resort attracting thousands each summer for cultural events. Many wealthy families built fine Victorian homes and came for the whole summer to attend the many dramatic and musical presentations held in a 5,000-seat amphitheater and to hear speakers like President William Howard Taft, William Jennings Bryan, and the evangelist Billy Sunday. A number of the elegant old homes are being restored, and a portion of the town has been declared a historic district.

The Pennington Cottage, located east of Mountain Lake Park on the south side of Route 135 (the old Oakland and Deer Park Road), is the last reminder of the grand old days of Deer Park. The elaborate fourteen-room, three-story summer home stands on the grounds of the old resort and now operates as a restaurant and bed-and-breakfast inn.

Things are more modest in Garrett County these days, and one of the definite advantages it offers are lodging rates that are quite reasonable compared with those in some ski areas.

More attractions await to the north of the county in the little town of Grantsville, an Amish-Mennonite community whose Main Street was along the old National Pike, built in 1813. Two local landmarks are the 1797 Stanton's Mill, the county's oldest operating gristmill, and the graceful Casselman Bridge, which was the longest single-span stone-arch bridge in the country when it was built in 1813.

The biggest draw in Grantsville is Penn Alps, a Mennonite-operated restaurant in a remodeled 1818 log stagecoach stop. Bountiful Pennsylvania Dutch cooking is served up here, and after dessert you can browse through a shop full of Allegheny handicrafts. Crafts demonstrations are held in the summer months, and the early-July quilt show always brings lots of visitors to town.

More old-fashioned food and ambience can be found down the street at the Casselman Hotel, an 1824 lodging also built to serve stagecoach travelers and still serving overnight guests. Antiques are for sale here, as well as an assortment of tempting sweets in the Bake Shop. Other tasty souvenirs are the hickory-smoked meats, sausages, or bologna; local maple sugar; and homemade jams from Yoder's Country Market and Meat Packers in Grantsville.

While Garrett County serves up outdoor fun throughout the winter season, it saves its most festive efforts for last. The season's traditional end is the Winterfest at Wisp, which includes sleigh rides, ski races, and such good-natured competitions as tugs-of-war, volleyball, horseshoes, wrist wrestling, bubble-gum blowing, and snowmobile climbs. The big event comes on the last Saturday night, when a fireworks display and torchlight parade light up the mountain. It's quite a gala way to say good-bye to winter.

Area Code: 301

DRIVING DIRECTIONS Garrett County is west of Cumberland, Maryland, reached via Route 40 from the east, Route 219 north and south. From D.C., take I-270 north to Frederick, then follow Route 70 west to Route 40 west. At Keysers Ridge, take Route 219 south to Oakland. Approximate distance from D.C., 180 miles.

ACCOMMODATIONS *Wisp Resort,* Marsh Hill Road, McHenry, 21541, 387-5581, slopeside hotel and condos, indoor pool; ask about ski packages, $$ ● *Alpine Village,* Route 219 on Deep Creek Lake, Oakland, 21550, 387-5534, pleasant motel lodge and chalet apartments, $ CP ● *Will o' the Wisp Resort,* Route 219 on Deep Creek Lake, Oakland, 21550, 387-5503, indoor pool, $$$ ● *Holiday Inn,* Grantsville, 21536, 895-5993, indoor pool, $–$$ ● *Casselman Hotel,* Main Street, Grantsville, 21536, 895-5055, no frills, country atmosphere, $ ● *Deer Park Inn,* Route 4, P.O. Box 58, Deer Park, 21550, 334-2308, Victorian landmark, $$–$$$ CP ● *Red Run Inn,* Mayhew Inn Road, Oakland, 21550, 387-6606, simple rooms atop the barn, $$–$$$ CP; some condos for rent, $$$$ ● Many basic motels and bed-and-breakfast lodgings available in the area; write for full list.

BED AND BREAKFAST *The Traveller in Maryland, Inc.,* P.O. Box 2277, Annapolis, MD 21404, 269-6232; in D.C. (301) 261-

2233 ● *Amanda's Bed & Breakfast Reservation Service,* 1428 Park Avenue, Baltimore, MD 21217, 225-0001.

DINING *Silver Tree Inn,* Glendale Road near Alpine Village, 387-4040, chalet with fireplace, veal specialties, $–$$ ● *Chimney Corner,* routes 50 and 219, Redhouse, 334-2040, historic log building, country fare, $–$$ ● *Four Seasons,* Will o' the Wisp Resort (see above), $$–$$$ ● *Penn Alps,* Route 48, Grantsville, 895-5985, reasonable Pennsylvania Dutch specialties, $ ● *Casselman Inn,* Main Street, Grantsville, 895-5266, cozy, baking a specialty, $ ● *Deer Park Inn* (see above), $$–$$$ ● *McClive's,* Deep Creek Drive, McHenry, 387-6172, overlooking McHenry Cove and Wisp ski area, $$ ● *Red Run Inn* (see above), crab specialties, views, $–$$$.

INFORMATION Deep Creek Lake–Garrett County Promotion Council, Court House, Oakland, MD 21550, 334-1948.

Carnival Time in the Poconos

Ever meet a Sno-Poke? This fuzzy, friendly snowperson loves all kinds of winter sports, from riding a sled or snowmobile to gliding on ice skates or skis.

You can find the Sno-Poke, the official costumed winter mascot of the Pocono Mountains, and join him in any or all of the above activities at the nine-day Pocono Winter Carnival, held each year from late February to early March.

The carnival includes all of the 18 ski areas in the Poconos and features a number of ski races and other special events for spectators. Some of the racing is serious; some is strictly for laughs, like the annual waiter/waitress event, which requires balancing a tray of water-filled champagne glasses while maneuvering an obstacle course around Stroudsburg Mall.

But Winter Carnival is far from just a spectator's show, and you needn't be an expert to take part in the merriment. Such events as "sloppy slaloms," family races, torchlight ski parades, uphill races, a costume parade on skis, and all-night skiing are open to everyone, along with indoor events like a roller-skating party and a Snowflake Ball. Cross-country ski races and snowmobile tours and races are also on the busy agenda, and there are special events for small fry, from children's plays to preschoolers' skating parties.

Carnival or not, you'll find the Poconos are a lively center of winter fun. The peaks are gentle, but skiing is always reliable as long as the nights go below freezing, since all of the major areas have extensive snowmaking equipment to ensure good conditions. Lights on the slopes make it possible to keep schussing after the sun goes down at Camelback, the largest of the areas, at Big Boulder, and at several other ski slopes.

But if you choose one of the many-faceted resorts that are a specialty in this area, you may never even make it to the big ski slopes. Besides those famous honeymoon havens with the heart-shaped bathtubs, the Poconos abound with major resort complexes where ice skating, skiing, snowmobiling, sleigh rides, stables, and cross-country trails may all be available on the premises, right outside your door.

Even if the weather is uncooperative, weekend fun here is guaranteed, because along with their outdoor facilities some of the major resorts offer big indoor sports pavilions. All have swimming pools, and some also have tennis courts, ice- and roller-skating rinks, and fitness centers, many of which are open to nonguests for a fee.

One of the most beautiful Poconos resorts is Sky Top Lodge, standing on a mountaintop overlooking 5,500 unspoiled acres. Fresh from a stylish renovation, it is gracious and grand, a place where gentlemen wear coats and ties for dinner, and service is impeccable. Despite its old-world ways, the atmosphere is not stuffy, and the prices are not exorbitant, considering the wealth of facilities included, plus three meals daily and afternoon tea.

Pocono Manor, another grand old resort, on 3,000 acres, is also being nicely refurbished. Its Nordic Touring Center, with 40 miles of groomed trails, is one of the area's best. Mountain Laurel, a modern resort complex conveniently located off the intersection of routes 9 and 81, may interest families for its supervised children's center.

If country inns are more your style, you'll have to look hard for a lovelier one than the Inn at Meadowbrook. The house is light and airy, with big windows to take in views of the lovely grounds; rooms are tasteful and charmingly furnished with brass beds or four-posters, ruffles, and wicker. The stable next door offers trail rides and riding lessons in an indoor arena.

Three more winning choices are in the town of Canadensis. The Overlook Inn is welcoming, done in soft shades of blue, with lots of plants and pillows, comfortable seating in front of the fire, and a game room–library that invites guests to mingle. Old Village Inn has stylishly decorated rooms upstairs over a pretty restaurant with an international menu, and Pine Knob is cozy country, warmed with personal touches like the owner's collections of quilts and cookie jars.

A bit unique is French Manor, an inn that fits its name, a Normandy mansion on a lofty hilltop with views that go forever. The manor takes pride in its multicourse French dinners. And the Sterling Inn is a bit of both worlds, inn ambience in a mini-resort complex.

For the best of the local scenery, take in the views from either Pocono Manor or Sky Top, or take the scenic drive through Big Pocono State Park in Tannersville to the top of Camelback Mountain. Then drive east to the Delaware Water Gap, the deep tree-covered gorge that is the entrance to the Poconos. This three-quarter-mile-high natural wonder, carved by the Delaware River, is part of a 70,000-acre national recreation area that offers canoeing, hiking, and picnicking in summer and cross-country trails in winter. Even when everything is blanketed with snow, you can pull on your boots and make tracks through the woods for the short walk to Dingman and Silver Thread falls. The crashing waters are a sight worth the trek.

This is not a region for quaint little towns, but if shopping is your favorite winter pastime, there are plenty of options to keep you busy in the Poconos. Route 390 between Cresco and Mountainhome is a good place to start. Among the interesting shops are Jabara, with discount prices on fine Portuguese linens, ceramics, and sweaters, and Viva, with a stock of unusual clothing and home accessories. Come upstairs over the Theo. B. Price hardware store to the Country Store for the area's best selection of folk art and country gifts, and to Christmas Memories for holiday spirit, music boxes, and interesting ornaments year-round.

Another unusual stop is the Pocono Mineral and Gem Company in Colony Village, south of Canadensis, where there is a mini-museum of natural gems, plus a fine selection of gem jewelry at reasonable prices. Antiquers should head for the Other Woman in Mountainhome, as well as Kelly's in Swiftwater, and the Sunday market at Collectors Cove off Route 33 south of Stroudsburg, where over 100 dealers participate.

Several Pocono shops give you a show with your shopping. Callie's Candy Kitchen in Mountainhome has chocolate-covered everything, from strawberries to potato chips, plus a laugh-a-minute candy-making demonstration from the colorful Mister Callie. Thirty-seven kinds of yummy soft pretzels are the offerings at Callie's Pretzel Factory, where you're invited to taste samples, watch the "pretzel bender" in action, and try bending one of your own. A few miles north in LoAnna, you can watch the making of pottery and china giftware at Holley Ross Pottery, and candle makers are at work at American Candle in Bartonsville.

Come nighttime, the same resorts that provided so much to do by day turn the spotlight on dancing and lively entertainment.

Though the fireworks and parades and races are extra incentives for making the trip, the Poconos are a carnival all winter long.

Area Code: 717

DRIVING DIRECTIONS Most Pocono locations are reached from I-80. From D.C., take I-95 north to I-695, then I-83 north to Harrisburg. Connect here with I-81 north to I-80 east. The closest of the resorts and ski areas (Big Boulder and Jack Frost) are around Lake Harmony and White Haven; approximate distance from D.C., 225 miles. Camelback Mountain and other resorts are 20–25 miles to the east off I-80.

PUBLIC TRANSPORTATION Wilkes-Barre/Scranton Airport, 38 miles away. Bus service from Philadelphia.

ACCOMMODATIONS *Sky Top Lodge,* Sky Top, 18357, (800) 345-7SKY, in PA (800) 422-7SKY, $$$$ AP ● *Pocono Manor,* Pocono Manor, 18349, (800) 233-8150, $$$$ MAP ● *The Sterling Inn,* South Sterling, 18460, 676-3311, (800) 523-8200, $$$$ MAP ● *The Inn at Meadowbrook,* Cherry Lane Road, RD 7, P.O. Box 7651, East Stroudsburg, 18301, 629-0296, $–$$ CP ● *The Overlook Inn,* Dutch Hill Road, Canadensis, 18325, 595-7519, $$$$ MAP ● *The Pine Knob Inn,* Route 447, Canadensis, 18325, 595-2532, $$$$ MAP ● *Old Village Inn,* North Skytop Road, Canadensis, 18325, 595-2120, $ CP ● *The French Manor,* P.O. Box 39, Huckleberry Road, South Sterling, 18460, 676-3244, $$$$ MAP ● *Mountain Laurel Resort,* P.O. Box 126, White Haven, 18661, (800) 458-5921 $$$$ MAP.

DINING *Pump House Inn,* Skytop Road, Route 390, Canadensis, 595-7501, $$–$$$ ● *Hampton Court Inn,* Route 940 east, Mt. Pocono, 839-2119, $$–$$$ ● *Overlook Inn* (see above), $$–$$$ ● *Pine Knob Inn* (see above), $$–$$$ ● *The Inn at Tannersville,* Route 611, Tannersville, 629-3131, $–$$$ ● *A Touch of Vanilla,* Mountain Laurel Resort (see above), $$$ prix fixe ● *Fox Hill Inn,* Fox Run Lane, East Stroudsburg, 223-0303, $$–$$$.

SIGHTSEEING AND INFORMATION *Pocono Winter Carnival:* Begins late February. For current year's schedule, detailed information on area ski resorts, and full lodging listings, contact the Pocono Mountains Vacation Bureau, Box K, 1004 Main Street, Stroudsburg, PA 18360, 421-5791 or (800) POCONOS.

A Taste of Spring in Maryland

Some wait for the robin's song, but more eager watchers for spring's first signs keep their eyes on the maples.

Even while nights are still freezing and snow is on the ground, warming sun during the day is enough to trigger the rising of the sap in the maple trees, heralding the start of maple-sugaring season, a welcome assurance that old man winter is on the way out.

Demonstrations of how the sap is turned to tasty maple syrup are an annual event for two mid-March weekends at Cunningham Falls State Park, not far from Frederick, Maryland. It's a chance to watch a longtime American custom, have a welcome break out of doors, and get acquainted with a spirited historic town. Antiquers will find special incentive for the trip in New Market, the tiny town six miles from Frederick that is Maryland's antiques capital.

At the park, rangers are in residence, ready with an indoor film explaining the skills of sugaring that were first taught to early American settlers by the Indians, followed by firsthand outdoor demonstrations of how it's done.

The sap running into the buckets nailed to the trees seems as clear and thin as sugar water, but just let it simmer long enough in the big kettles tended by the rangers, and before you know it, tempting smells are rising and the liquid is thickening into familiar sticky-delicious golden maple syrup. Everyone is fascinated to see how much sap it takes to boil down into a small amount of syrup, which explains why this delicacy comes with such a high price tag.

Watching the process is an educational taste of spring, and you can buy take-home samples of maple candy and maple syrup made in Maryland's woodsy Garrett County. Lunch is for sale, too—hamburgers, hot dogs, or the perennial best-seller, pancakes, lavished with you-know-what.

If the weather is cooperatively springlike, Cunningham Falls Park offers 43 wooded acres for walks, picnics, and a look at the 78-foot cascading waterfall for which the park was named.

This state-run park is on the south of Catoctin Mountain, adjoining Catoctin Mountain National Park, a 10,000-acre preserve where the presidential retreat at Camp David is located. Since the National Park Service took over in 1936, the once-depleted forests of black locust, wild cherry, sassafras, and yellow poplar have grown back into their full glory, and Camp David is hidden deep among the dense trees—so you won't be able to see it.

What you *can* see in this park are many panoramic views from the mountain. Don't miss the 11-mile scenic drive, marked out on the folder given away at park headquarters.

Catoctin offers its own early-spring adventures as well, such as ranger-led "charcoal hikes," spiced with tales of the time when charcoal was made on the mountain, and orientation classes teaching the skills of using a map and a compass in the woods. If you come back in summer, rangers will be leading hikes, giving talks, and demonstrating the moonshiner's art at the Blue Blazes Whiskey Still. And the residents of the Catoctin Mountain Zoo begin receiving visitors in April.

If woodland rambles don't suit the March weather or your fancy, head instead for in-town pleasures in Frederick and New Market.

Frederick's history goes back to 1745, but it was poet John Greenleaf Whittier who immortalized the town's "clustered spires" of church steeples in 1863, when he wrote about a spunky local patriot, 90-year-old Barbara Fritchie. Fritchie is the lady who, furious at Confederate troops shooting at .Old Glory, shamed mighty "Stonewall" Jackson by imploring, "Shoot if you must this old gray head, but spare your country's flag." A reconstruction of her redbrick house and the shop, where she sold gloves made by her husband and gingersnaps, is open for touring.

Like its legendary heroine, Frederick has refused to allow age to dim its spirit. Once a major crossroads on the old National Pike, the town had faded in prominence and the center of town was looking decidedly run-down, what with the ravages of time and the competition of shopping centers. Frederick responded with a vigorous revitalization program that spruced up storefronts, planted platoons of trees and flower boxes along brick-paved sidewalks, and put underground the maze of unsightly overhead wires that were spoiling the colonial look of things. The changes are so pleasant that many an urbanite has been inspired to move here and commute to a job in Baltimore or Washington, each about 45 miles away. The appearance of trendy shops and restaurants beside the establishments of longtime storekeepers on Market Street is evidence of the changing population.

A town walking tour of the 33-block historic district is available at the visitors center on Church Street. A good place to start is Court Square, where 12 judges from Frederick County met in November 1765 to issue one of the first official protests against the British Stamp Act, a full eight years before the Boston Tea Party. The nineteenth-century courthouse, recently converted to serve as city hall, replaced the original building that burned in 1861.

The old city hall has its own bit of history to tell. It was here that the city fathers met in urgent session to hear the demands of Confederate General Jubal Early, who demanded ransom in return for sparing the city. Frederick dug down to the tune of $200,000, but Early never got to spend it, since Union troops were waiting for him just outside the city. The Battle of Monocacy delayed him enough to stave off a planned rebel invasion of Washington, D.C.

On the southern side of the square is one of the famous church spires, belonging to the 1855 All Saints Episcopal Church, which now boasts Tiffany and Bavarian stained-glass windows. A local favorite is the cast-iron greyhound put in front of the church rectory by a loving eighteenth-century master. It was rescued from Confederate troops aiming to melt it down for cannonballs and returned to its proper home.

The rest of the city's historic churches can be found within a three-block radius. Stonewall Jackson is said to have fallen asleep during a sermon at the Evangelical Reformed Church, a building whose two towers are modeled after the lanterns of Demosthenes.

Directly across from Court Square is the low, white, double-doored building where two prominent onetime residents, Francis Scott Key, author of the "Star-Spangled Banner," and his brother-in-law, Roger Brooke Taney, chief justice of the U.S. Supreme Court, had law offices. The Taney/Key Museum is maintained in Taney's home on South Bentz Street. It is open by reservation only, so call in advance if you are a law or music buff.

Just around the square on Council Street are two fine adjoining early 1800s mansions. The white house on the right is the family home of former Maryland Senator Charles Mathias. The redbrick Ross House next door was lodging for the Marquis de Lafayette when he visited Frederick after the Revolution. The fine wrought-iron fencing in front of both homes was cast at the old Catoctin Iron Furnace near Thurmont.

Much additional local lore and memorabilia has been gathered by the Historical Society of Frederick County and can be seen in its museum, located in one of the lovely old homes in the historic district.

Some outlying sites are also of interest in Frederick. Rose Hill Manor is the Georgian mansion of Maryland's first governor, Thomas Johnson. Inside the mansion, Rose Hill offers the "Touch and See" children's museum. Also on the grounds are a carriage museum, a collection of farm implements, a 150-year-old log cabin, and a blacksmith shop. Often there are demonstrations of nineteenth-century crafts such as candle dipping and quilting.

The city's oldest dwelling is Schifferstadt, a 1756 steep-roofed German-style stone house near the Hood College campus. Check before you make the trip, however, since the house does not open until April.

Those who are fascinated by old graveyards should hie to the

Francis Scott Key Grave and Monument, where the stars and stripes fly day and night to honor the man who glorified them. Thomas Johnson and Barbara Fritchie rest here, along with many soldiers who fell in the Civil War and several Revolutionary War militiamen.

Many visitors to the Frederick area never get around to seeing the historic sights at all, however, because they have come for a different kind of history—the take-home variety available in a host of antique stores. East Patrick Street has many of the better shops in Frederick, but the most picturesque shopping place is Shab Row, a collection of former shanties transformed into specialty shops.

It's easy to find the shops lined up on Main Street in New Market, a totally charming village that also has been declared a historic district. Drovers on the way to the Baltimore market once led their livestock down the old National Pike, the same street where antiquers now flock to scoop up candlesticks, copper kettles, mahogany dressers, and high-back beds, not to mention wind-up trucks, teddy bears, tin, and tiles. The shops are wall to wall, more than 40 of them in a one-mile stretch, housed in the picturesque period homes on Main Street. A printed guide is available to spell out each shop's specialties. Most of the owners are city dwellers who open for business only on weekends, so be forewarned and don't waste a trip midweek.

For antiquers who want to be in the middle of the action in New Market, there are two appealing inns right on Main Street. The Strawberry Inn is cozy, warm, and welcoming; ask for the downstairs room with its own little porch. The National Pike Inn is a Federal-style beauty with five charming guest rooms.

Frederick has its own list of choice lodgings. Tran Crossing, a spiffy little Victorian home, is right in the heart of Frederick's antique district, and Spring Bank is a stunning brick mansion a couple of miles outside town that is being lovingly restored by its young owners. The Inn at Buckeystown, a haven of Victoriana, is known for its excellent family-style meals. One other attractive choice is the Turning Point Inn, a gracious and spacious home set back from the main road a few miles south of Frederick.

There is one other alternative for nature lovers who want to stay out among the maples. Old Mink Farm Cabins, located just south of Cunningham Falls Park, offers you the chance to live in a cozy log cabin, an oak bungalow, or a cathedral-ceilinged chalet, with your own fireplace or wood stove to warm the March evenings. You'll be secluded in the woods high in the Catoctins with all the comforts of home and all the firewood you can burn. And to add a final sweet taste, you can have maple syrup on your French toast in the morning.

Area Code: 301

DRIVING DIRECTIONS Frederick is at the intersection of routes I-70, I-270, 340, and 15. From D.C., follow Route 270 north. Approximate distance from D.C., 45 miles.

ACCOMMODATIONS *Tran Crossing,* 121 East Patrick Street, Frederick, 21701, 663-8499 (call after 5 P.M.), $$–$$$ CP • *Spring Bank Inn,* 7945 Worman's Mill Road, Frederick, 21701, 694-0440, $$–$$$ CP • *Turning Point Inn,* 3406 Urbana Pike (Route 355), Frederick, 21701, 874-2421, $$–$$$ CP • *The Inn at Buckeystown,* 3521 Buckeystown Pike, Buckeystown, 21717, 874-5755, $$$–$$$$ MAP • *Old Mink Farm Cabins,* 12806 Mink Farm Road, Thurmont, 21788, 271-2204, two-night minimum, $$ • *Sheraton Inn–Frederick,* Francis Scott Key Mall, 21701, 694-7500 or (800) 325-3535, $$–$$$ CP • *Strawberry Inn,* 17 Main Street, New Market, 21774, 865-3318, $$ CP.

DINING *Bushwaller's,* 209 North Market Street, Frederick, 694-5697, old-fashioned ambience, $–$$ • *di Francesco's Italian Restaurant,* 26 North Market Street, Frederick, 695-5499, $–$$ • *The Province, Circa 1767,* 131 North Market Street, Frederick, 663-1441, innovative menu, $$–$$$ • *Court Street Grille,* 30 West Patrick Street, Frederick, 698-9300, regional American specialties $–$$$ • *The Deli,* 57 East Patrick Street, Frederick, 663-8122, for lunch or a take-out picnic, $ • *Cozy Restaurant,* 105 Frederick Road, Thurmont, 271-7373, family-style dinners, lots of important visitors to Camp David have dined in this no-frills cafe, $–$$$ • *Mealey's Inn,* 8 Main Street, New Market, 865-5488, $–$$$ • *Turning Point Inn* (see above).

SIGHTSEEING *Maple Syrup Demonstrations, Cunningham Falls State Park,* Catoctin Hollow Road off US 15 north, Thurmont, 271-7574. Usually held on two successive weekends early to mid-March, 10 A.M. to 4 P.M. Free. Call to check exact dates and times. Park is open daylight hours daily year-round. Free • *Catoctin Mountain Park,* Route 77 west off US 15 north, Thurmont, 663-9388. Daylight hours daily. Free • *Barbara Fritchie House and Museum,* 154 West Patrick Street, Frederick, 663-3833. Hours: Monday, and Wednesday to Saturday 10 A.M. to 4 P.M.; Sunday 1 P.M. to 4 P.M. Adults, $1.75; children, $1 • *Taney/Key Museum,* 123 South Bentz Street, Frederick, 663-8787, by appointment only • *Schifferstadt,* 1110 Rosemont Avenue, Frederick, 663-1611. Hours: April to December 23, daily 10 A.M. to 4 P.M. Donation • *Rose Hill Manor,* 1611 North Market Street, Frederick, 694-1648. Hours: March, November, and December, weekends only April through October, Monday to Saturday 10 A.M. to 4 P.M.; Sunday 1 P.M. to 4 P.M. Closed January and February. Adults, $1; under 18, free ● *Historical Society of Frederick County Museum,* 24 East Church Street, Frederick, 663-1188. Hours: March to December, Monday to Saturday 10 A.M. to 4 P.M. Adults, $2; under 18, $1.

INFORMATION Tourism Council of Frederick County, Inc., 19 East Church Street, Frederick, MD 21701, 663-8687.

First Resorts of the Mid-Atlantic

Go ahead. You deserve it. In a hectic world filled with fast food and Formica, everyone ought to be entitled to splurge once in a while to experience the good life the way it used to be—and still is—at the two great tradition-filled five-star resorts of the mid-Atlantic, the Greenbrier in White Sulphur Springs, West Virginia, and the Homestead, in Hot Springs, Virginia.

Bigger than life and far more serene, each of these splendid dowager queens still offers the kinds of pleasures the privileged enjoyed in a more gracious era. Twenty-two-foot ceilings and crystal chandeliers, high tea to the tune of violins, carriage rides, multicourse meals, fresh linens twice a day, and a staff that outnumbers the guests remain traditions that have been cherished ever since the long-ago days when Southern aristocracy came to take the waters at the mineral springs that inspired the building of both hotels.

That's not to say that these opulent mountain oases have not kept up with today's taste for more vigorous activity—and on a scale befitting their penchant for lavishness. Among the Greenbrier's 6,500 acres, in addition to 12 acres of magnificent formal gardens, you will find 3 18-hole golf courses, 20 tennis courts (five of them indoors), platform tennis, a swimming pool, trap and skeet shooting, horseback riding, bicycling, hiking trails, and fishing streams stocked with trout and bass.

Not to be outdone, the Homestead's 15,000 mountain acres boast their own 3 golf courses, 19 tennis courts, lawn bowling, a children's playground, and more chances to ride, hike, shoot, swim, or fish. In winter, both hotels add ice skating to the list, and the Homestead offers ski slopes as well.

Even at that awkward in-between season, when winter snow has vanished but spring has not yet arrived, you'll find plenty to keep you happy at these indoor-outdoor complexes, from bowling alleys and indoor pools to exercise rooms and saunas. Hot mineral baths and marvelous massages are available at both spas (the Greenbrier recently spent $7 million in spa renovations and improvements), so you can soak away your troubles, or have them kneaded away, just as visitors have done for the past two centuries.

Off-season is a perfect time to come, in fact, if you want to take advantage of lower rates and weekend packages. Each hotel schedules special weekends and theme activities to pick up business when things get slow, such as wine tastings, or a mock murder to be solved by mystery fans. The Greenbrier also has its own highly regarded cooking school in winter.

These two friendly rivals, 45 minutes apart in the Alleghenies, have much in common, yet each has a very distinct flavor and personality, and its own share of history to tell.

Step into the Greenbrier and you are overwhelmed with space, color, and lavish decor. People have been coming to White Sulphur Springs to take the cure ever since the 1770s, when the word got out about a Mrs. Amanda Anderson, a lady crippled with rheumatism, who immersed herself in the odiferous waters and, when she emerged, pronounced herself miraculously cured. The first permanent cottages, Paradise Row and Alabama Row, were built at the springs in the 1800s and are still standing, now housing an art colony where handicrafts are for sale. More cottages continued to go up, and before long aristocratic Southern families began making a ritual of coming to drink the waters three times a day.

The President's Cottage Museum serves as a reminder that some 19 U.S. presidents have visited the Greenbrier from its early days right up to the present. Another illustrious guest was Robert E. Lee, who made the hotel his summer home after the Civil War.

The main hotel is still fondly known to some as the Old White for the original stately building that went up in 1858, with one of the largest ballrooms in America. Many a Southern belle twirled her skirts here, hoping to bewitch a beau on the dance floor. During the Civil War, the hotel changed hands several times and served as a hospital for both sides.

In 1910, the Chesapeake and Ohio Railroad came in and expanded, building the tall-columned Georgian structure that is still the hotel's core and spared no expense to make it the very epitome of lavishness. In those days it was known as the Jewel of the South. For 37 years, guests were met at the train by horse-drawn carriages and driven to the hotel, where a seven-piece orchestra awaited along with long-skirted hostesses offering lemonade. Many others came in their private railroad cars.

After serving as a hospital once again during World War II, the Greenbrier was redecorated on an even grander scale by Dorothy

Draper, whose imprint remains throughout. With a budget of $10.5 million, a more-than-tidy sum in those days, she filled the walls and halls with the floral prints and vivid colors of her own patented designs. Each of the 650 rooms is different from the next, but all are in the oversize patterns Draper felt were necessary to fill such soaring spaces. The pink rhododendrons that abound here in spring are the most common motif, found in the china and the hotel logos, and all through the hallways.

Though each room is redecorated regularly, the fabrics used always are reproductions of Miss Draper's 1948 originals, carefully overseen by her protégé and the present Greenbrier decorator, Carlton Varney. Mr. Varney maintains a store in the shopping gallery of the hotel.

Some things have hardly changed at all here over the years. The rooms are still enormous, the deluxe quarters bigger than some city apartments. Ladies still wear their prettiest dresses, and gentlemen don coats and ties for dinner; waiters, wine stewards, and busboys still hover while musicians play waltzes to aid the digestion. But the economics of hotel keeping have demanded the addition of meeting rooms and a conference center, and nowadays it is likely to be conventioneers rather than plantation owners or dukes and earls and tycoons who come to call. All are still treated royally, however.

The dark redbrick façade, pillared portico, and white cupola of the Homestead bespeak Virginia gentility, and the interior reinforces that impression. This is also a large hotel, boasting 600 rooms and its own maze of corridors and meeting quarters. The 22-foot high, 211-foot-long pillared-and-chandeliered Great Hall is undeniably impressive, yet on the whole the atmosphere at the Homestead is decidedly understated compared with the splash of the Greenbrier. It is almost like the difference between old money and new, which will likely please some guests and disappoint others.

George Washington, Thomas Jefferson, and Alexander Hamilton all were among the early visitors seeking the curative powers of the 108-degree waters at Hot Springs. In 1766, one Thomas Bullitt built the first hotel here, supposedly in self-defense against the spate of uninvited guests at his home. The first Homestead dates from 1846, with the spa building added in 1892. All but the original spa, casino, and cottages were destroyed by a fire in 1901, when the present hotel was begun. The trademark tower went up in 1929. The hotel quickly attracted its own list of the socially elite, Mrs. Cornelius Vanderbilt and the Duke and Duchess of Windsor among them.

If there is less feeling of overwhelming space indoors, there is more sense of the mountains outdoors at the Homestead. They envelop the hotel grounds, beckoning for a brisk walk on wooded paths wending uphill for splendid views. The proximity of the hills inspired the opening of one of the South's first ski areas here in 1959. Golf is another special point of Homestead pride, with the legendary Sam Snead as a resident pro. They boast that the first tee of the Homestead course, laid out in 1892, is the nation's oldest in continuous use, and the Cascades course is ranked by *Golf Digest* as one of the country's 30 best. During the warmer months, golfers may opt to stay at the Cascades Inn, a complex of motel rooms and cottages near the course, and have full Homestead privileges with a somewhat lower tab.

Shoppers will be pleased by the browsing possibilities in a whole new complex of stores called Cottage Row, developed from a former colony of guest cottages. You can also walk into the tiny town of Hot Springs for more shops or a Sam-Wedge at Sam Snead's Tavern.

Around four o'clock at both hotels, everyone gathers indoors for teatime. At the Greenbrier, you help yourself to refreshments and garden views in the opulent upstairs lobby. In the Great Hall at the Homestead, a trio serenades, and as soon as you settle into one of the big wing chairs, a crisply aproned waitress magically appears with your personal tray, set with china teacups, dainty sandwiches, and sweets.

How to choose which hotel to visit? Try both. These tradition-rich resorts are a kind of never-never land in today's world, a return to more genteel times. The Greenbrier calls it "life as it should be." Yes, the tab is steep—but once in a while shouldn't everyone have a taste of gracious living?

Area Codes: West Virginia, 304; Virginia, 703

DRIVING DIRECTIONS White Sulphur Springs is off Route 60, just north of Lewisburg, West Virginia. Hot Springs, Virginia, is about an hour to the northeast. To drive from D.C. to the Greenbrier, take I-66 west to I-81 south. At Lexington, pick up I-64 west to first exit for White Sulpher Springs, and follow US 60 for 2 miles to entrance. Approximate distance from D.C., 250 miles. To the Homestead: Follow directions above to I-81 south. At Mount Crawford exit take Route 257 to Route 42 to Goshen, then Route 39 west to Warm Springs and US 220 south to Hot Springs. Approximate distance from D.C., 220 miles.

PUBLIC TRANSPORTATION Amtrak serves White Sulphur Springs, West Virginia, and Clifton Forge, Virginia, and there is also luxury rail service via the American Zephyr, (301) 951-9672. Commuter air service goes into Ingalls Field, 20 minutes from the Homestead, and U.S. Air serves both Lewisburg, West Virginia (about 15 minutes from Greenbrier), and Roanoke, Virginia (about an hour from either hotel). Connecting limousine service is offered to both hotels from both airports. Check the hotels for current transportation schedules.

ACCOMMODATIONS AND INFORMATION *The Greenbrier,* White Sulphur Springs, WV 24986, 536-1110 or (800) 624-6070, $$$$, MAP, higher April through October ● *The Homestead,* Hot Springs, VA 24445, 839-5500 or (800) 336-5771; in Virginia, (800) 542-5734, $$$$, MAP, higher in season. Ask about special winter weekends and sports package plans at both resorts ● *Cascades Inn,* Route 220, Hot Springs, 839-5355 (closed November to March), $$$$ MAP.

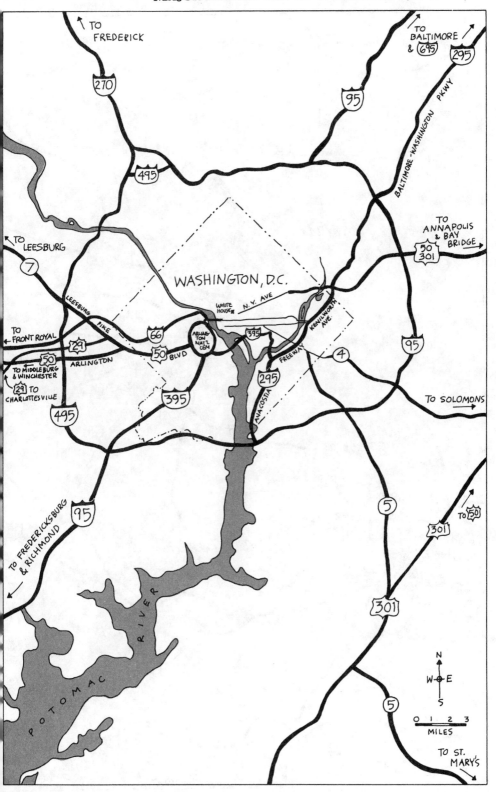

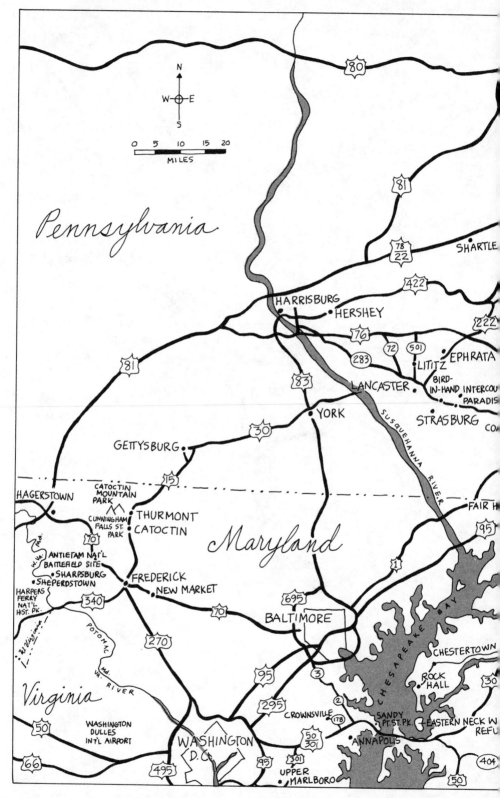

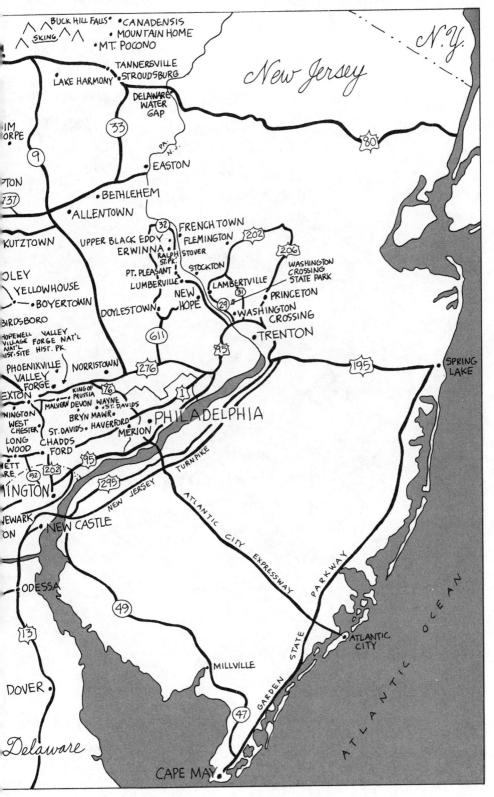

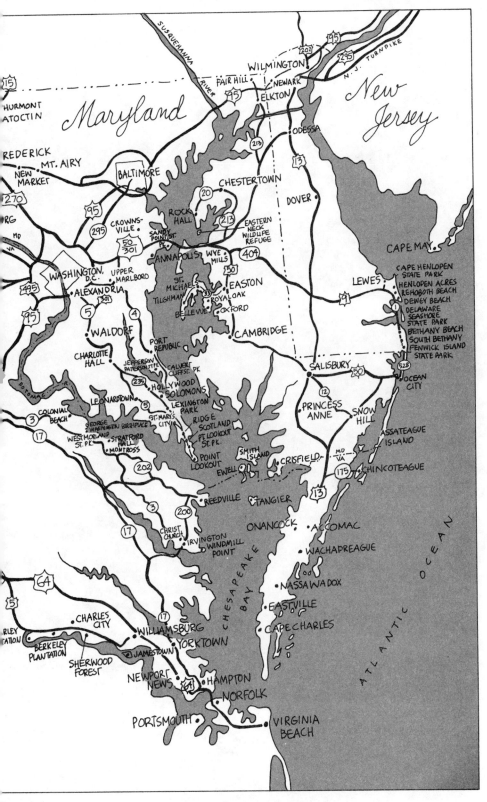

General Index

Category Index

Antiquing

Beaches and Parks

Children's Activities

Crafts and Fairs

Cultural Events

Historic Sites

Museums and Galleries

Nature

Shopping

Sports and Recreation